GALLOWS SPEECHES
FROM EIGHTEENTH-CENTURY IRELAND

Gallows Speeches from Eighteenth-Century Ireland

JAMES KELLY

FOUR COURTS PRESS

Typeset in 9.5 on 14 pt Caslon
and published by
FOUR COURTS PRESS LTD
Fumbally Lane, Dublin 8, Ireland
e-mail: info@four-courts-press.ie
and in North America by
FOUR COURTS PRESS
c/o ISBS, 5824 N.E. Hassalo Street, Portland, OR 97213.

© James Kelly 2001

A catalogue record for this title
is available from the British Library.

ISBN 1–85182–611–4

All rights reserved. No part of this publication may be
reproduced, stored in or introduced into a retrieval system,
or transmitted, in any form or by any means (electronic,
mechanical, photocopying, recording or otherwise),
without the prior written permission of the copyright owner.

Printed in Great Britain
by MPG Books Ltd, Bodmin, Cornwall

Contents

7
PREFACE

11
Introduction
'GOOD CHRISTIANS': THE CONTEXT AND
PURPOSE OF 'LAST SPEECHES'

71
LIST OF SPEECHES

81
LAST SPEECHES: TEXTS

281
SELECT BIBLIOGRAPHY

284
INDEX

Preface

Like the French *placard* which, Roger Chartier has observed, has been 'long neglected by a history interested only in more noble objects', the broadside is the Cinderella publication of early modern Ireland.¹ The most striking testament to this is provided by the fact that, a few only excepted, most exist as unique copies. Moreover, they mainly survive because, being little appreciated at the time and for most of the intervening centuries, they were preserved by private collectors from whose or whose executor's possession they passed into institutional ownership. This is identifiably the case with the Bradshaw, Thorp and Crawford collections in Cambridge University Library, National Library of Ireland and National Library of Scotland respectively. And it may be that a large part of the substantial holdings in Trinity College, Dublin, and the British Library were assembled after a similar fashion.² As a result, broadsides are not just rare, they are frequently difficult to locate, and while the availability of the *Short Title Catalogue* and its predecessor, *The Eighteenth-Century Short Title Catalogue*, is invaluable it does not yet provide a full listing of what is extant. One can also confidently assume that even when complete it will not provide a full record of what was published since there are a number of known 'gallows' or 'last speeches', which are the subject of this collection, that have not survived.³

1 Roger Chartier, 'General introduction: print culture' in Roger Chartier, ed., *The culture of print: power and the uses of print in early modern Europe* (Oxford, 1989), p. 3.
2 *Catalogue of the Bradshaw collection* (3 vols, Cambridge, 1913); catalogue of Thorp pamphlets in National Library of Ireland; James Lindsay, Earl of Crawford, *Bibliotheca Lindesiana: catalogue of English broadsides, 1505–1897* (privately published, Aberdeen, 1898). 3 For example *The last speech of William Paul, clergyman and John Hall, hanged*

The total number of published 'last speeches' is unknown. From what remains, it is apparent that, along with crime and trial reports, they are a valuable and under-utilised source of information on the life histories of those involved in crime, on the society that generated them and, not least, on the criminal justice system that provided the occasion for their publication. They were published in Ireland between 1680 and 1800 and, on the basis of those that can be located, flourished between 1705 and 1740. This coincides with the emergence of the newspaper as a popular print form, with the development of the pamphlet as a vehicle of individual and collective opinion, and with the greater availability of works of religious and personal edification and entertainment. In short, 'last speeches' were a feature of the striking consolidation in print culture that took place during the first half of the eighteenth century that, the work of Pollard, Munter, Fenning and Barnard notwithstanding, remains insufficiently explored.[4]

Though aware of the value of crime broadsides from the work of J.A. Sharpe, Peter Linebaugh, Neal Garnham, Walter Laqeuer, and other students of the social history of crime in Britain and Ireland, and mindful of their usefulness in exploring the issues of duelling and sexual violence,[5] my engagement with 'last speeches' was activated by an invitation by Professor Paul Boucé to participate in a colloquium on '*Crime et Chatiment*/Crime and Punishment' at the Sorbonne in December

---

and quartered at Twyburn on 13 July 1716 for treason (London, 1716, reprinted by Gwyn Needham on Cork Hill, Dublin, 1716). Once in the Crawford Collection, it is no longer present with the main collection in the National Library of Scotland. In addition, a last speech by a 'cook maid' of the bishop of Londonderry, published in Belfast in 1725, eludes identification and location. 4 T.C. Barnard, 'Reading in eighteenth-century Ireland: public and private pleasures' in Bernadette Cunningham and Máire Kennedy, eds, *The experience of reading: Irish historical perspectives* (Dublin, 1999), pp 60–77; Hugh Fenning, 'Dublin imprints of Catholic interest, 1701–39', *Collectanea Hibernica*, 39 & 40 (1987–8), pp 106–54; idem, 'Dublin imprints of Catholic interest, 1740–59' *Collectanea Hibernica*, 41 (1999), pp 65–116; Robert Munter, *The history of the Irish newspaper, 1685–1760* (Cambridge, 1967); Paul Pollard, *Dublin's trade in books, 1500–1800* (Oxford, 1993). 5 J.A. Sharpe, '"Last dying speeches": religion, ideology and public execution in seventeenth-century England', *Past and Present*, 107 (1985), pp 144–68; Peter Linebaugh, 'The Ordinary of Newgate and his *Account*' in J.S. Cockburn, ed., *Crime in England, 1550–1800* (London, 1977), pp 246–69; Neal Garnham, *The courts, crime and the criminal law in Ireland, 1692–1760* (Dublin, 1996); James Kelly, '*That damn'd thing called honour*': duelling in Ireland, 1570–1860 (Cork, 1985); idem, '"A most inhuman and barbarous piece of villainy": an exploration of the crime of rape in eigh-

1997. As part of an inquiry into 'the theater of the scaffold',[6] I consulted the Irish 'last speeches' in Trinity College Library and offered a brief, preliminary commentary upon their import on that occasion.[7] Subsequent investigation of the holdings of major research libraries in Ireland, the United Kingdom and the United States has resulted in the identification of the sixty-two examples presented in this collection. Most conform to the classic definition of a broadside – single sheets of paper of somewhat varying size but generally between 16–17.5 cms (6.5–7 inches) by 25–3 cms (10–12 ins) printed on one side. However, the form was sufficiently flexible that, as well as variation in size, in a significant number of instances 'last speeches' were published on both sides of a single sheet, over two or three single-sided sheets and, in at least one case, on two double-sided sheets extending over four pages. Occasionally during the early eighteenth century, 'last speeches' were published as pamphlets, and one example (that of James Hamilton who was executed at Downpatrick in 1714), though published in Glasgow, is reprinted in this collection.

Locating and securing copies of 'last speeches' has been greatly facilitated by the advice and assistance of librarians and library staff in many institutions. For responding to queries, providing photocopies and other guidance I wish to thank the staffs of the Cregan Library, St Patrick's College Drumcondra; Department of Early Printed Books, Trinity College Dublin, particularly Charles Benson; National Library of Ireland; Royal Irish Academy, particularly Siobhan Raftery; Cambridge University Library; British Library; National Library of Scotland, particularly Brian Hillyard; the Folger Library, Washington; Desmond Law Library, Columbia University; Beinecke Rare Book and Manuscript Library, Yale University, particularly Susan Brady; Harvard Law School Library, particularly Mary

---

teenth-century Ireland', *Eighteenth-Century Ireland*, 10 (1995), pp 78–107. T.W. Laqeuer, 'Crowds, carnival and the state in English executions, 1604-1868 in A.L. Beier, et al., eds, *The first modern society: essays in English history* (Cambridge, 1989), pp 305-55. 6 The phrase is from Pieter Spierenburg, 'The body and the state: early modern Europe' in N. Morris and D.J. Rothinan, eds, *The Oxford history of the prison: the practice of punishment in western society* (Oxford, 1995), p. 55. 7 James Kelly, 'Capital punishment in early eighteenth-century Ireland' in Serge Soupel, ed., *Crime et chatiment/Crime and punishment* (Paris, forthcoming).

PREFACE

L. Person; Library of Congress, Washington DC; University Libraries of Notre Dame; John L. Burns Library, Boston College, particularly John B. Atteberry; Henry Huntington Library, San Marino; and the Russell Library, National University of Ireland, Maynooth, particularly Penny Woods.

Permission to publish the 'last speeches' presented in this collection is gratefully acknowledged to the Board, Trinity College Dublin; the trustees, National Library of Ireland; the Beinecke Rare Book and Manuscript Library, Yale University; the Librarian, National University of Ireland, Maynooth; the Crawford (*Bibliotheca Lindesiana*) Collections, National Library of Scotland; British Library, and the syndics of Cambridge University Library.

I wish, furthermore, to thank Dr Marian Lyons and Dr Raymond Gillespie for their comments on the introduction, and Maria Thornbury for help with transcribing the text of the speeches. I also thank Ray Gillespie for his advice, and my departmental colleagues, Diarmaid Ferriter, Dáire Keogh, Carla King and Marian Lyons, for their fellowship and support. Most of all, I once again express my gratitude and indebtedness to Judith Brady, and Eva and James Kelly for the generous manner in which they continue to allow me the time to pursue subjects in which they have little personal interest.

April 2001

INTRODUCTION

'Good Christians': the context and purpose of 'last speeches'

The early modern western European criminal justice system provided for a varied menu of punishments ascending in severity from terms in the pillory through public whipping, branding and transportation to public execution. Each was possessed of a distinctive ritual, but public execution, in the words of Pieter Spierenburg, 'most clearly embodied contemporary attitudes' because 'it served as a stage on which the drama of justice was enacted in its most visible and conspicuous form before the people'.[1] It is for this reason that Michel Foucault has claimed that 'public execution is to be understood, not only as a judicial, but also as a political ritual. It belongs, even in minor cases, to the ceremonies by which power is manifested'.[2] As a consequence, the practice of public execution was moulded and manipulated by civil and religious authorities to sustain the ends of affirming law and order, of fostering social control and promoting the observance of the law of God. Indeed, Malcolm Gaskill has observed that executions in England 'were stage managed to publicise both divine and secular power'.[3] The situation was comparable in Ireland.

The relationship of the 'divine' and the 'secular' was not fixed, of course, for though their primary standard bearers – the church and the state – were bound inextricably in the conduct and management of public execution, as in so many other communal rituals, it was also contested territory. This is the unmistakable implication of the fact

---

1 Spierenburg, 'The body and the state: early modern Europe', p. 51. 2 Michel Foucault, *Discipline and punish: the birth of the prison* (London, 1979), p. 47. 3 Malcolm Gaskill, 'Reporting murder: fiction in the archives in early modern England', *Social History*, 23 (1998), p. 5.

that the lessons the public was expected to draw, both as audience observing the rituals that attended the occasion and, with the spread of 'cheap print', as readers engaging with such literary productions as these events spawned, varied across time and space. The execution sermon, for example, which was delivered in church as well as at the gallows before offenders in New England between the 1670s and 1740s was unique to that region.[4] It gave way ultimately to the 'last speech' which flourished in North America in the second half of the eighteenth century – a century after it peaked in England and several decades after it peaked in Ireland. Similarly, it was not possible to purchase an account of the crime for which offenders were sent to hang, trial reports or execution ballads in New England in the early eighteenth century, though all were available in Ireland.[5] In other words, literary artefacts such as 'last speeches', execution sermons, conversion narratives, trial reports, and commemorative ballads are not simply the serendipitous or adventitious productions of grasping publishers eager to capitalise on the enduring public enthusiasm for and disposition to participate, however vicariously, in the drama that was public execution. Rather, they are distinctive features of an emblematic cultural and commercial phenomenon that varied over time and place within the Atlantic world in which they flourished in the seventeenth and eighteenth centuries. Furthermore, under appropriate interrogation, together and severally these literary productions cast a sharp light on the society that produced and consumed them since the nature of any polity or community's engagement with the death penalty is equally revealing of its mores, manners and *mentalité*. In the case of early modern New England, Daniel Cohen contends that execution sermons were a product of a phase in the region's history 'when ministers ... dominated the local print culture' and used the press as an instrument 'of religious authority'. Subsequently, with the emergence of a secular *zeitgeist* from the mid-eighteenth century, crime literature 'gradually became an arena of ideological

---

[4] R.A. Bosco, 'Lectures at the pillory: the early American execution sermon', *American Quarterly*, 30 (1978), p. 159; D.A. Cohen, *Pillars of salt, monuments of grace: New England crime literature and the origins of American popular culture, 1674–1860* (Oxford, 1993), part 1 passim. [5] Cohen, *Pillars of salt*, p. vii.

conflict as profit-seeking printers experimented with new forms, clergymen lost their cultural monopoly, and criminals gained a literary voice'.[6] The absence of 'execution sermons' from late seventeenth- and early eighteenth-century Ireland suggests therefore that Irish society differed in important respects from that of contemporary New England, though the fact that in Ireland, no less than in England and the American colonies, 'last speeches' blossomed for a distinct time period cautions against exaggerating the socio-cultural differences between these three polities. Certainly, the publication in Ireland during the first half of the eighteenth century of the 'last speeches' of over a hundred offenders was a development of multifarious import. In the first place, it attests to the technological capability to produce and the commercial capacity to sustain a specialised *genre* of publication. Secondly, it confirms the emergence of a literate audience able to engage directly with printed texts and, given the overlap between print and oral cultures, that mediated both the information and the instruction contained therein to the non and inadequately literate. Thirdly, the form and content of 'last speeches' offer an opportunity to assess the relative societal influence of the religious and the secular and, by extension, of the respective ideologies of church and state since they together exerted a preponderant influence on the ritual that gave public execution meaning. Fourthly, it is revealing attitudinally and legally of contemporary attitudes to crime and punishment, to the human body and, of course, to death. And fifthly, it is revealing linguistically, as the form, content and presentation of 'last speeches' facilitates an assessment (however conjectural it may be in many respects) of popular reading practice and, more generally, of the fast expanding print culture of early eighteenth-century Ireland.

I

Like many features of early modern, particularly urban, popular culture, the idea of printing 'last speeches' for popular consumption was

6 Ibid., p. ix.

transmitted to Ireland from England where it had its genesis in the late sixteenth century. Its emergence in England was a product both of the strong law and order concerns of successive Tudor regimes that prompted a substantial augmentation in the number of capital offences, and of improvements in print technology and popular literacy that generated a new audience for such print artefacts.[7] Printed 'last speeches' certainly appealed to religiously-activated opinion formers who were eager that the contrite final words of capital offenders should be widely disseminated because, in the words of one Elizabethan pamphleteer, it ensured 'that those whose eyes could not behold their deservede ends, might yet by hearing be warned'.[8] This was a weighty consideration with those devoted to the cause of fostering a moral polity since advice given in such circumstances was deemed more than usually influential, as the Ordinary of Newgate prison, London, Henry Goodcole, observed. Writing in 1618, he maintained that

> dying men's wordes are ever remarkable, & their last deeds memorable for succeeding posterities, by them to be instructed, what vertues or vices they followed and imbraced, and by them to learne to imitate that which was good, and to eschew evill.[9]

Guided by such perceptions, the 'last speech' evolved from a set-piece oration, heard once at the scaffold, into a distinctive *genre* of popular didactic literature that interested readers could interact with or mediate as convenient.[10] One consequence of this was the moulding of the recorded utterances of capital offenders to conform to a hermeneutical and literary formula. Central to this was the presentation and interpretation of the biography of the offender and, particularly, of his/her life in crime, within an explicitly providential framework.

---

7 Sharpe, 'Last dying speeches', pp 164–5. 8 *Two notorious murders ...* (London, 1585), p. 3 cited in Gaskill, 'Reporting murder ... ', p. 5. 9 Henry Goodcole, *A true declaration of the happy conversion, contrition and Christian preparation of Francis Robinson ...* (London, 1618) cited in Sharpe, 'Last dying speeches ... ', p. 150. 10 Sharpe, 'Last dying speeches ... ', pp 158–9.

INTRODUCTION

'Every event', Sandra Clark has pointed out, 'could be seen and shown to illustrate some facet of God's relationship to man', and the strongly providential character of 'murder pamphlets' in the late-sixteenth and early-seventeenth centuries not just reflected the contemporary belief system, it affirmed it in a manner designed to promote the observance of human and divine law. As a consequence, though many early seventeenth-century murder 'pamphlets and broadsides were based on first-hand accounts, objectivity was subordinated to embellishment and dramatization'.[11]

As the seventeenth century progressed, the emphasis on the contingent, magical, miraculous, spectral and portentous that was characteristic of the providential world-view of early 'last speeches' diminished. Better-grounded, more realistic 'last speeches' followed mirroring changing sensibilities and the emergence of a more secular world-view.[12] They also reflected changing legal practice as from the later seventeenth century juries were expected to be guided by hard fact, witnesses to be credible, and the truth to be determined according to rules of evidence and procedure that are recognisably modern.[13] At the same time, confessions of guilt and expressions of repentance retained their central place, and since they were central to the objective of affirming the necessity of observing civil as well as divine law, the confessional dimension of 'last speeches' was enhanced.[14]

The main features of a typical seventeenth-century English 'last speech' – the display of penitence and contrition, the exhortation to the young to good behaviour, the acknowledgement of guilt, the resignation to death, the acceptance that justice was being done, and the appeal to God for forgiveness – have been described by J.A. Sharpe.[15] It is his contention also that the penitential 'last speech' became a central feature of the execution ritual because the civil and religious authorities were at one in recognising that it was socially advantageous that public execution should animate emotions other than fear

---

11 Sandra Clark, *The Elizabethan pamphleteers: popular moralistic pamphlets, 1580–1640* (London, 1983), pp 89–90 cited in Gaskill, 'Reporting murder', pp 5–6. 12 See generally C. John Sommerville, *The secularisation of early modern England* (Oxford, 1992); Michael McDonald, *Sleepless souls: suicide in early modern England* (Oxford, 1990). 13 Gaskill, 'Reporting murder', pp 28–9. 14 Sharpe, 'Last dying speeches', pp 164–5. 15 Ibid., pp 144–67 passim.

and revulsion. At the same time, the content and, by implication, the ideological import of 'last speeches' did not always affirm the improving message they favoured. It is noteworthy, for example, that several such publications prepared at the time of 'the Popish Plot' do not conform to the stereotype of a 'penitential' last speech as defined by Sharpe. For instance, when the Roman Catholic Archbishop of Armagh, Oliver Plunkett, was executed at Tyburn on 1 July 1681, his resolve to 'confess the truth without any equivocation' did not cause him to acknowledge his guilt or the fairness of the proceedings that brought him to his inglorious end. Quite the opposite; he condemned his prosecutors as 'men of flagitious and infamous lives', maintained that he did not receive a fair trial and protested his 'innocency'. Significantly, Plunkett's defiant words ensured not just that his speech was published in two separate versions but, unusually, that it was subject to an angry rebuttal.[16]

Clearly, controversy of this kind was not in keeping with the prevailing beneficent and reformative purpose of 'last speeches'. Nonetheless, the *genre* not just survived, it flourished in England in the two decades that followed.[17] A glance at a representative selection of 'last speeches' published in the 1680s reveal that most offenders behaved meekly and contritely at the gallows on the grounds that, as one of their number put it, 'the scandal of dying is to die an evil doer'.[18] Thus Katherine Binks, who was sentenced to death for bur-

---

[16] *The last speech of Mr Oliver Plunket, titular Primate of Ireland who was executed at Tyburn on Friday the 1st of this instant July 1681* (London, 1681); see also *The last speech and confession of Oliver Plunket, titular Primate of Ireland: with an account of his behaviour in Newgate since his condemnation, and also of Edward Fitz-harris, at their execution at Tyburn upon Fryday, July 1, 1681 for high-treason in conspiring the death of the king ...* (London, 1681); Florence Weyer, *The honesty and true zeal of the Kings witnesses justified and vindicated against those unchristian-like equivocations of Dr Oliver Plunkett, asserting in his last speech his own innocency ...* (London, 1681). [17] As well as those discussed below see *The last confession, prayers and meditation of Lieutenant John Stern ...* (London, 1682); *The last dying speeches and confessions of the three notorious malefactors ... executed 4 March* (London, 1681); *The confession of Ed. Fitzharris esq., written with his own hand and delivered to Dr Hawkins, minister of the Tower, July the 1st 1681* [London, 1681]; *The last speech, confession and execution of John Smith alias Ashburnham, a notorious highwayman ... and Ed. Jackson for high treason ... 26th of May, 1684 ...* (London, 1684); *The last speech ... of ... Edward Althann ...* (London, 1688). [18] *The last dying speeches, confessions and execution of Rice Evans, Margaret Corbet, Elizabeth Ford alias Jackson and Katherine Binks who*

glary in 1684, amply fulfilled expectations by employing her time leading up to the implementation of her sentence

> reading the scriptures, and giving heed to such wholesome advice and instructions as was given to her; receiving the sacrament ... expressing herself at the place of execution, like a true penitent, confessing several passages of her ill life, and particularly the fact for which she suffer'd this death, bewailing her great unworthiness to find mercy with God Almighty.[19]

Displays of contrition such as this were encouraged and applauded by the clergy, who maintained a high profile on such occasions. In pointed contrast, the minority of offenders who refused to conduct themselves in an appropriately penitent manner were subject to vehement imprecation though some had good reason for doing so. For instance, when Rice Evans was executed on Kennington Common in 1684 for murdering his wife, he was obliged to rebuff the efforts of no fewer than three clergymen to persuade him to confess his guilt; he maintained that he was innocent, and steadfastly insisted that if he were to state otherwise it would be to 'damn my own soul, [as well as] to deny the truth'.[20] The implication of Evans' action that the ideological hegemony once exercised by religion was no longer unchallenged is affirmed by the essentially secular justification of capital punishment as the equivalent of tree surgery provided in the same 'last speech': it was essential, the narrator pronounced, 'to cut off some rotten branches, that if longer permitted would devour their fellow members, and by infecting the rest, bring all order into confusion, and kingdoms to destruction'.[21]

The fact that by the early eighteenth century, public execution in England was 'becoming more of an embodiment of the secular power' did little in the short term to diminish the appeal of the crim-

---

were executed on Kennington Common in the Co. of Surrey, 19 March 1683/4 ... (London, 1684); *The last dying speeches and confession of the six prisoners who were executed at Tyburn, this 17th of September 1680 with an account of their behaviour in Newgate, and at the place of execution* (London, 1680); *The last dying speeches, confession and execution of John Stokes, Isaac Davis, and Mary Williamson who were executed at Tyburn, the 5th of March 1684 ... also ... Alice Paddon ... who was burnt* (London, 1684). **19** *The last dying speeches, confessions and execution of ... Katherine Binks ...* **20** Ibid. **21** Ibid.

inal confession delivered at the gallows. Indeed, the publication by the Ordinary of Newgate from the beginning of the eighteenth century of an *Account* that included, among other information, the last confessions of some twelve hundred offenders emphasizes its continuing appeal. Parallel with this, separate and distinct 'last speeches' were published regionally. This persisted for over half a century, but by the 1760s the British public's appetite for such works was in rapid decline and the *Account* of the Ordinary of Newgate 'all but disappeared'. The public's enthusiasm for crime reports and criminal biography remained vibrant, but 'last speeches' neither satisfied that need nor convinced the public of the merits of capital punishment. The English reading public sought narratives that were 'more sophisticated and more critical'.[22] A similar pattern can be identified in Ireland, though the *floruit* of the 'last speech' in that jurisdiction was later and shorter than it was in England.

II

If geographical contiguity, institutionalised political links and intensified demographic and cultural interchange suggest that the publication of 'last speeches' in early modern England should have prompted similar publications in Ireland within an equivalent time frame, there are a number of reasons why this was not the case. In the first place, Ireland did not possess the technology to produce such works in proportionate number at any point in the sixteenth and seventeenth centuries. Secondly, and more consequently, the tight control exercised in the seventeenth century over the press through the king's printer patent ensured that the bulk of the print that trickled off Irish printing presses before the 1690s had an official seal of approval and, since the Irish

---

22 Sharpe, 'Last dying speeches ... ', pp 165–6; Linebaugh, 'The Ordinary of Newgate and his *Account*', pp 246–8; Michael Harris, 'Trials and criminal biographies: a case study in distribution' in Robin Myers and Michael Harris, eds, *Sale and distribution of books from 1700* (Oxford, 1972), pp 16–26; Philip Rawlings, *Drunks, whores and idle apprentices: criminal biographies of the eighteenth century* (London, 1992), passim, but especially pp 4–7, 24–5; Gaskell, op cit., pp 28–9; *Account ... dying words ... S. Goodere, M. Mahony, C. White ...* (Bristol, 1741).

administration had good reason to apprehend that the dissemination in print of 'last speeches' might prove counter-productive, it discouraged their publication.[23] As a consequence, the defiant 'last speeches' made by Darby O'Hurley, the Catholic archbishop of Cashel, prior to his execution in 1583 and by Conor O'Devany, bishop of Down and Connor in 1612, were not published in Ireland.[24]

The political and religious considerations that prompted the authorities in Ireland to discourage the publication of the last words of Catholic martyrs did not apply in the case of John Atherton, the Church of Ireland bishop of Waterford, who was sentenced to death in 1640 for homosexual acts. Disturbed by the prurience of much contemporary speculation, Atherton's spiritual advisor and one time chaplain, Nicholas Bernard, prepared a detailed statement of his last days entitled *The penitent death of a woeful sinner* ... for publication in Dublin in 1641. The author was, as his title suggests, eager to present his subject in the best light, and to this end he drew heavily on Atherton's last words though the bishop was far from abjectly contrite. He confessed to 'reading of naughty books, viewing of immodest pictures, frequenting of plays and drunkenness'; he conceded that he had pushed church reform with 'too much zeal and forwardness', and admitted that he had neglected 'public preaching and catechising in the church and private prayers in his family'. However, his acknowledgement of 'the moral' justice of the verdict delivered in his case, notwithstanding, he refused to accept 'the legal justice of his condemnation' and denied 'the main thing in the indictment which the law laid hold of'. Clearly, Bernard's narrative was not an orthodox 'last speech', but it was the closest early seventeenth-century Ireland came to producing one. It was certainly more proximate than

---

23 M. Pollard, 'Control of the press in Ireland through the King's printer patent, 1600–1800', *Irish Booklore*, 4 (1980), pp 79–95; Pollard, *Dublin's trade in books, 1500–1800*, pp 14–15; Munter, *The Irish newspaper*, chapter 1. 24 'Rawlinson Class B', in *Analecta Hibernica*, 1 (1930), pp 125–8; P.J. Corish, ed., 'A contemporary account of the martyrdom of Conor O'Devany, OFM, bishop of Down and Connor and Patrick O'Loughran', *Collectanea Hibernica*, 26 (1984), pp 13–19. An account in Latin of O'Devany's execution, published in Cologne in 1614, survives unlike others published in Spain and at Bordeaux. There are also a number of manuscript accounts, see Corish, op. cit., pp 14–15.

the lurid 'rhyming pamphlet', *The life and death of John Atherton*, published in London at the same time. However, any anticipation, arising out of the fact that Barnard's pamphlet bore the colophon of the Society of Stationers, that its publication paved the way for a stream of orthodox 'last speeches' was destined not to be realised. No such works were published in Ireland in the following four decades.[25]

The disposition of the authorities in Ireland to continue to resist the publication of 'last speeches' was highlighted by the neglect of the final utterances of the Catholic bishops of Clogher – Heber McMahon – and of Emly – Terence O'Brien – who were executed in 1650 and 1651 respectively. As a military commander of some stature, McMahon was a controversial figure, and his pronouncement at the gallows that he died 'contrary to the law of nations' ensured that, like Bishops O'Hurley and O'Devany before him, his final words were not recorded in print in Ireland.[26] O'Brien's experience was different. His carefully crafted and scripturally learned 'last speech' was published, but in London rather than in Dublin. Its publication can be accounted for by his preparedness to defend the 'just Rights and Priviledges' of the House of Stuart rather than his assertive reference to 'the truth ... of the ancient Catholique Religion' and the necessity of 'the settlement of this distracted and distressed people ... in their Native Liberties'. None the less, O'Brien's is the *first* identifiable printed 'last speech' of Irish origination. The manner of its publication, as the second item in a pamphlet whose first was a petition from a royalist highwayman, was not typical of later Irish (or contemporary English) 'last speeches'; neither was O'Brien's extended theological discourse; nor his failure to discuss openly the offence for which he was sentenced to die. However, it conformed otherwise to the standard format, as exemplified by the recourse to 'Good People' as an opening salutation and a concluding appeal for divine mercy.[27]

In common with Bishop Atherton's confession a decade earlier,

---

25 Aidan Clarke, 'The Atherton file', *Decies*, 11 (1979), pp 45–54; Robert Winnett, 'The strange case of Bishop John Atherton', *Decies*, 39 (1988), pp 5–17 especially pp 8–9; Nicholas Bernard, *The penitent death of a woefull sinner ...* (Dublin, 1641). 26 Benignus Millett, 'Heber MacMahon, bishop of Clogher, d. 1650', *Clogher Record*, 16 (1997), p. 143. 27 *The humble petition of James Hind ... together with the speech and confession of the Bishop of Clonwel at the place of execution at Limerick in Ireland on the 9 instant November,*

INTRODUCTION

the uniqueness of Terence O'Brien's situation no less than his commentary ensured that the publication of his last words was a one-off and no identifiable 'last speeches' of Irish origin were published in England or in Ireland during the 1660s or early 1670s. The restrictive impact of the king's printer patent remained the primary reason, for though the 'last speeches' of the conspirators executed for their involvement in Blood's plot in 1663 survive in manuscript, they were never published.[28] However, even the sedulous Duke of Ormonde, who was viceroy for most of the restoration era, could not close Ireland off completely, and there were clear signs by the late 1670s that it was just a matter of time before 'last speeches' were permitted. The reverberations of the Popish Plot provide the most salient indicator.

The Popish Plot excited enormous interest in Ireland as well as England, not least because of the implication of a number of Irishmen in the supposed conspiracy. Conscious of the need to satisfy public curiosity, some carefully selected London editions were reprinted in Dublin. The first of these was *The last speeches of the five notorious traitors and Jesuits ... who were justly executed at Tyburn, June 20, 1679*, which was published with a Dublin imprint the same year.[29] Four years later, the fall-out from the Rye House Plot prompted a Dublin reprinting 'at His Majesty's Printing House' of *The last speech and behaviour of William late Lord Russel* for his supposed complicity in a scheme to kill Charles II and of *The last speeche, behaviour and prayers of Capt Thomas Walcot, John Rouse Gent., and William Hone* ...[30] It is not apparent how widely these broadsides were distributed or the

---

1651 ... (London, 1651). The text is introduced by Hugh Fenning, 'The last speech and prayer of Blessed Terence Albert O'Brien, Bishop of Emly, 1651', *Collectanea Hibernica*, 38 (1996), pp 52–8. **28** James McGuire, 'Ormond and Presbyterian non-conformity, 1660–3' in Kevin Herlihy, ed., *The politics of Irish dissent, 1650–1800* (Dublin, 1997), p. 49; Worcester College Library, Oxford University, William Clarke Letterbook, Ms 33 ff 174, 176, 179; Bodleian Library, Carte 68 ff 576-8. I wish to thank Raymond Gillespie for the latter references, and James McGuire for his guidance on this point. **29** *The last speeches of the five notorious traitors and Jesuits ... who were justly executed at Tyburn, June 20, 1679 for conspiring the death of His Sacred Majesty, and the subversion of the government of the Protestant religion* (London, later reprinted Dublin, 1679). **30** *The last speech and behaviour of William late Lord Russel upon the scaffold in Lincoln's inn's-field, a little before his execution, on Saturday July 21, being condemned for High Treason in conspiring the death of the*

response they generated, but the manner and timing of their publication suggest that by the 1680s, with the Protestant interest apparently in secure control, the authorities in Ireland, no less than those in England, were conscious of the positive propaganda value of 'last speeches'.

The impact of the Popish Plot notwithstanding, the publication of Irish 'last speeches' cannot be said to have commenced for another decade when the political and social environment was very different to that of the Restoration era. A key factor was the abandonment of censorship in the aftermath of the Glorious Revolution (1688) because it liberated printers from politically motivated control, but the growing public interest was equally critical. 'News' was in constant demand, and the public's desire for the same, as well as for the status possession of 'news' conveyed, can be demonstrated by the payment of subscriptions to Dublin stationers and printers for named journals of English as well as Irish origin.[31] At the same time, the publication of 'last speeches' in Ireland from the mid-1690s cannot be accounted for solely by these factors because 'last speeches' did not simply relay news. They were also possessed of a reforming purpose, and their production both dovetailed with and expanded the existing tradition of religious improving literature, the publication of which also increased in the 1690s. Furthermore, and for the first time, the kingdom possessed the technological capacity, illustrated by the identifiably larger number of individuals in Dublin with access to, as well as the skills necessary to use, print machinery to produce such works in substantial numbers.[32] This would have been pointless, of course, without a parallel improvement in literacy that has caused Toby Barnard to conclude that by the 1690s 'high literacy' was common

---

King and subversion of the Government (Dublin, 1683); *The last speeche, behaviour and prayers of Capt Thomas Walcot, John Rouse Gent., and William Hone, Joyner ... published by Authority ... and to be sold by Joseph Wilde, bookseller in Castle St.* (Dublin, 1683). I have not located a copy of the second of these, but its reprinting is indicated on the Royal Irish Academy's copy of *The last speech and behaviour of ... Lord Russel* (RIA, 3.B.55). 31 Pollard, *Dublin's trade in books*, pp 14–15; Barnard, 'Reading in eighteenth-century Ireland', pp 70–71. 32 Raymond Gillespie, 'The circulation of print in seventeenth-century Ireland', *Studia Hibernica*, 29 (1995–7), pp 46–56; Munter, *Dictionary of Irish printers, passim*; idem., *The Irish newspaper*, pp 11, 18. According to Munter the number of printers in Ireland rose from 3 in 1690 to 14 in 1710 to 33 in 1760.

INTRODUCTION

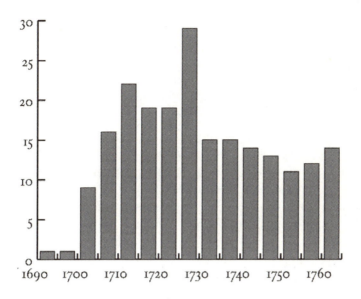

FIGURE 1: SERIAL PUBLICATIONS, 1690–1765

'among the middling sort – petty functionaries, skilled craft-workers and modest traders and their sons'.[33]

The precise trajectory of this complex of technological, attitudinal and intellectual developments cannot easily be applotted, but a statistical analysis of newspaper publication between 1690 and 1765 suggests that after a slow and rather faltering start, a critical level of public interest and technological capacity had been achieved by 1705 to sustain a large number of new publishing initiatives (Fig. 1). It is significant in this context that the short-lived *Dublin Intelligence* (1690–3) and the irregular *Flying Post* (1699–1713) were followed by more substantial and reliable organs such as Pue's *Impartial Occurrences* (1703–71) and the *Dublin Gazette* (1706–1921).[34] More consequently, the number of newspapers that were published measured across five-year spans grew

[33] Barnard, 'Reading in eighteenth-century Ireland', p. 61; idem, 'Learning, the learned and literacy in Ireland, c.1660–1760' in T.C. Barnard, et al., eds., '*A miracle of learning*': *studies in manuscripts and Irish learning* (Aldershot, 1998), pp 219–21. [34] R.L. Munter, *A hand-list of Irish newspapers, 1685–1750* (Cambridge, 1960), pp 3, 5; James O'Toole, *Newsplan Ireland* (Dublin, 1998).

INTRODUCTION

impressively from 9 in 1701–5 to 22 in 1711–15 to 29 in the quinquennium 1726–30. Most of these titles were very short-lived and, it can safely be assumed, commercially unsuccessful, due as much to organisational deficiencies as to problems associated with securing good copy and reliable advertising. It took a quarter of a century for a degree of equilibrium to be achieved, for it was not until the 1730s that the production of serial publications stabilised in the low-teens at which level it remained for a number of decades (Fig. 1).[35]

Given the fragile and transient character of so many publishing and printing enterprises in the early eighteenth century, broadsides were attractive print artefacts because they were among the easiest and cheapest to produce. Moreover, since, like the newspaper, they were produced for immediate consumption, they brought an immediate financial return. It is a measure of their attractiveness that no less than twenty-two different enterprises were responsible for the publication of the fifty-three 'last speeches' produced between 1694 and 1740 that can definitely be attributed.[36] These included prominent and important figures like Cornelius Carter, 'the most energetic and enterprising printer of his time', who was responsible for an impressive twenty-three per cent of that total; John Whalley, the so-called 'father of yellow journalism in Ireland', who published *Whalley's Flying Post* (1704–8) and *Whalley's Newsletter* (1714–28); Edward Waters who published some of Jonathan Swift's early Irish pamphlets as well as the *Flying Post: or, the Post-Master* (1708–29); Gwyn Needham who joined in partnership with the Dicksons following his marriage into that busy print family; John Harding, who published Swift's *Drapier's letters* as well as a number of newspapers; and George Faulkner who had just embarked on a publishing career that was to result in his becoming the 'dominant Irish stationer of the eighteenth century'.[37] Other participants included spe-

---

35 Munter, *The Irish newspaper*, pp 131–2. 36 The word 'enterprise' is used deliberately since in a number of cases the names of different family members were placed on speeches produced by family businesses. Thus the pairings of Sarah Sadleir and Elizabeth Sadleir, John Harding and Sarah Harding, and Francis and Richard Dickson are deemed to represent one enterprise. Similarly, where it is known that someone succeeded to an existing enterprise, as instanced by Nicholas Hussey and Sarah Harding, and Catherine Hicks and Charles Goulding, it is counted once. Information on these points is taken from Munter, *Print trade, passim*. 37 Munter, *Print trade*, pp 292–3,

cialised publishers and printers like Elizabeth Sadlier, who published well-known authors such as Puffendorff and Burnet; and Catherine Hicks, who concentrated on producing material 'for the country trade and ballad hawkers', who published at least six 'last speeches' between 1723 and 1731.[38]

Since most of those listed already were or became established publishers, 'last speeches' were only a part, and in most instances, a very modest part of their output. Significantly, but understandably given the facility with which they could be produced, 'last speeches' also attracted a less successful and a less honourable element. This inclusive category embraces John Brocas, John Gowan and Nicholas Hussey who attempted unsuccessfully to succeed as newspaper publishers.[39] It also embraces evanescent individuals such as Edward Jones, J. Neil, Thomas Dudlow, William Taylor, W. Robinson and Samuel Lee whose involvement is known only by a single imprint and who receive little mention in most standard works of reference.[40] The best known of these, Samuel Lee, epitomised the shady and disreputable end of contemporary publishing. Described by the English bookseller and author, John Dunton, as 'a pirate' whose rapacity and disregard for the interest of others made him so unpopular he was obliged to flee London for Dublin in 1693, he persisted in the same business practices at his new place of residence.[41]

Disreputable or not, Lee is of more than passing interest because he was responsible for the first surviving 'last speech' of Irish origin with a Dublin imprint (1).* Dating from 1694, it presents 'the last speech and confession' of James Geoghegan, a Catholic priest, who was sentenced to death for theft. On first consideration, Geoghegan's homilistic narrative seems more directly comparable with the religiously inspired examples of seventeenth-century England than with

---

283–4, 50–1, 195, 77–8, 76, 127–8, 96–8; idem, *The Irish newspaper*, pp 111, 112. 38 Munter, *Print trade*, pp 240, 132–3. 39 Ibid., pp 36, 117, 141. 40 Ibid., pp 149, 195, 166. Munter does not include any entries on Dudlow, Robinson and Taylor. 41 Munter, *Print trade*, p. 166. The recent publication of M. Pollard's *A dictionary of members of the Dublin book trade, 1550–1800* (London, 2000) adds substantially to our knowledge of those engaged in the profession. Unfortunately, its publication came too late to be of use to the preparation of this introduction. * Reference numbers in the text in bold brackets are to the number given the 'last speeches' printed below.

the more secular approach of a majority of the texts produced in eighteenth-century Ireland. The fact that it *ante* dated by twelve years its nearest surviving equivalent (2), published by John Brocas who was an established printer of crime broadsides, suggests further that it stands outside the main tradition of Irish 'last speeches'. However, one must not underestimate the continuing influence exerted by religion as well as the essential continuity of the *genre*. Geoghegan's pronouncement that 'obedience is the golden basis and foundation of all laws, humane and divine' certainly indicated that the authorities no longer had good reason to apprehend publications of this ilk, and if this suggests that more should have followed in short order, Lee's death in October 1694 ensured that it was over a decade before their publication commenced in earnest.

If (and it seems reasonable to suggest there was a connection), Samuel Lee was encouraged to embark on the publication of 'last speeches' in Ireland in 1694 by the extant tradition of improving religious literature as well as by the emergence of religious societies for the reform of manners, one cannot attribute their accelerated production from the early eighteenth century to the impact of the reforming societies since these bodies were already in decline by the time the publication of 'last speeches' was an established feature of the Irish literary landscape.[42] A more prosaic explanation, and one not accorded sufficient weight in most studies (other than that of Laqeuer) of the phenomenon in Britain or America, is to be found in the strong public interest in crime narratives deriving from the timeless human curiosity in criminality that contemporary newspapers were ill-circumstanced to satisfy. It is not merely coincidental therefore that broadsides of 'last speeches' flourished at the same time as broadsides relaying crime and trial reports. One of the earliest examples of the latter, published in 1700 by John Brocas, describes how William Sherloge and his paramour murdered his wife and children.[43] Within twenty years broadsides carrying lengthy accounts of cel-

---

[42] T.C. Barnard, 'Reforming Irish manners: the religious societies in Dublin during the 1690s', *Historical Journal*, 35 (1992), pp 805–38. [43] Laqeuer, 'Crowds, carnival and the state', passim; *An account of a most inhumane and barbarous murder committed by one William Sherloge and his whore, upon the bodies of his own wife & child, and how he sett his house on fire, was apprehended ...* (Dublin, [1700]).

ebrated trials, brutal crimes and riotous behaviour were commonplace.[44] Such publications, which overlooked the quotidian in favour of the sensational may have appealed primarily to those with an interest in the salacious, but it is salient that their emergence in Ireland coincided with that of the 'last speech'. It is salient also that their rise and *floruit* corresponds with the emergence of the newspaper (compare Figs. 1 and 2), and that they went into decline as the newspaper consolidated its place in Irish print culture during the mid-eighteenth century. Because of this, it is preferable to see such print artefacts as the 'last speech', trial and crime reports, newspapers, even addresses to parliament or by parliament as features of an expanding popular print culture rather than as discrete or disassociated items targeted at and accessed by particular niche audiences. In this context, it is hardly a coincidence that many early eighteenth-century newspapers compare closely with broadsides in size and in tone.[45] What news-sheets did not possess, and what gave

---

[44] Examples include *Tryal and examination of Nathaniel Gunning before her majesty's Judges of the King's Benches the 29th of January 1703/4* (Dublin, 1704); *A true account of the riot committed at the Tholsel on Friday the 6th of November, 1713* [Dublin, 1713]; *An account of the tryal of John O'Bryan, and Bryan O Donnell, who were try'd yesterday, at the King's-Bench for Robbing of John Molloy and Catherine his wife and a carman ...* (Dublin, 1716); *Tryal and examinations of John Lester, Anthony Dwyre, and George Frazier, the said Lester and Dwyre for killing James Byrne, and Frazier for killing Mr Desborough: as also the whole and open confession of Owen Brady, for the inhumane and Barbarous and Bloody Murder of Elinor and Mary Brady, his own natural children* (Dublin, 1717); *An account of the tryal and examination of Mr Brown who was tried for a rape committed on the body of one Mrs King of the city of Dublin* (Dublin, 1717); *A full and true account of the surprizing and apprehending of Capt. Fitz Garrald and four of his rapperies near Tallow-Hill, in the House of one Mr Ransford on the fifth of this instant December in the morning 1717* (Dublin, 1717); *A strange and wonderful account of a most horrid, barbarous and bloody murder, committed by Thomas Doyle, a stone-cutter, living at Loughlins-Bridge, in the County of Carlo, on Saturday the eight day of November, 1718. On the body of his wife and mother ...* (Dublin, 1718); *A full and true account of the barbarous and bloody murther of one John Lee Gent; who was kill'd at the Tholsel, by one Henery Smith of Smithfield Gent. On the 28th of this Inst. Jan. 1718-19* (Dublin, 1718-19); *The whole tryal and examination of Henry Smith, Gent. Who was try'd at the King's Bench, this 10th of February, 1718 for killing one William Lee, Gent. ...* (Dublin, [1719]); *The whole tryal and examination of James Johnson, alias Macshane, who was tried at the King's Bench the 26th of this Instant November 1719 for Coyneing and counterfeiting sixty moyders* (Dublin, 1719). [45] *Flying Post*, 1709 and Francis Dickson's *Dublin Intelligence* (1705-09) are examples of newspapers that are printed, albeit on two sides, as a broadside. This point is reinforced by fact that some papers published postscripts of urgent news (e.g. *Dublin Gazette*, 21 Apr. 1708) in broadside form; Munter, *The Irish newspaper*, p. 75.

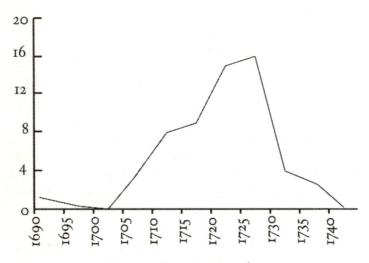

FIGURE 2: LAST SPEECHES, 1690–1740

the broadside its distinctive quality and appeal, was the space to satisfy the public's appetite for an extended and frequently personalised account of a particular crime.

With a growing market for the categories of news and information that were conveyed through these print media, the way was clear for the acceleration in the output of print that commenced in the second half of the first decade of the eighteenth century, and the 'take–off' that followed in the 1710s and 1720s (see Figs. 1 and 2). Though neither sales figures nor other dependable evidence exist to demonstrate how many or how widely broadsides circulated at any given time, there is considerable circumstantial evidence to indicate that the progressively augmenting number that survive from the 1710s and 1720s accurately reflect a growing audience. This conforms to the trend Philip Rawlings has identified in England, and is substantiated further by the warnings against 'sham speeches' published with increasing frequency in the 1720s (12, 30, 31, 35).[46] This conclusion is

---

46 Rawlings, *Drunks, whores and idle apprentices*, pp 1–2; Niall Ó Ciosáin, *Print and popular culture in Ireland, 1750–1850* (Basingstoke, 1997), pp 87–8.

reinforced by the emergence during the acrimonious public debate in 1720–21 on the utility of establishing a Bank of Ireland of 'last speech' parodies criticising political initiatives deemed contrary to the public interest. Individuals were also the targets of such works.[47]

The re-publication in Ireland of select English 'last speeches' serves as a further illustration of the expanding public appetite for such narratives that developed from the mid-1710s.[48] Among their number were two appertaining to Irishmen – Robert Malone who was convicted of highway robbery in 1723 and Captain Collins who acknowledged his guilt for an unspecified crime – both of whom were publicly executed in England (23, 24). Though of English origin, these speeches were republished in Dublin because Irish readers could identify with their authors. The appeal of other English reports reflected a more voyeuristic interest that the young George Faulkner sought particularly to cultivate. He was responsible in the mid-1720s for the republication of, among others, the dying speeches of three men executed for sodomy at Tyburn on 9 May 1726 and of Catherine Hayes who was burned alive on the same day for murdering her husband. The reprinting of the final words of Jonathan Wilde, Captain John Jayne and two clergymen sentenced to death for treason was sustained by less prurient motives, but there is no evading the con-

---

47 [Jonathan Swift?], *Last speech and dying words of the Bank of Ireland, which was executed at College Green on Saturday the 9th instant* (Dublin, 1721); *The Bank's ghost appearing to the people of Ireland, or an answer to the last speech and dying words of the Bank* (Dublin, 1721); *An elegy made on the last speech and dying words of the ever to be forgotten Bank of Ireland* (Dublin, 1721); [Jonathan Swift], *The last speech and dying words of Ebenezor Ellison who is to be executed this second day of May 1722. Published at his desire for the common good* (Dublin, [1722]); *The last speech and dying words of William Wood, who was executed at St. Stephen's Green, etc. Dublin* (Dublin, 1724); *An express from Elisium to the once Revd. Dr M-gee, couple beggar shewing the only wasy for H. Wood to gain the hearts of the unjustly irritated Hibernians* (Dublin, 1724); *The last speech of wisdom's defeat. etc a scandalous libel, burnt this second day of October, 1725 by the Common hangman* (Dublin, 1725); *A letter from Hans Hue- and-Cry, Van Hang-and-draw, executioner in Holland, to his trusty friend, Sir John, St Stephen's-green-proof, in the City of Dublin …* (Dublin, 1730); *The last speech and dying words of D –n A—b—kle, author of the Weekly journal* [Dublin, 1733]. 48 *The last speech of William Paul, clergyman and John Hall, hanged and quartered at Twyburn on 13 July 1716 for treason* (reprinted Dublin, 1716); *A true copy of the speech of Captain John Bruce who was executed at Lancaster on Tuesday the second of this instant October 1716 for high treason against his majesty, King George* (Dublin, 1716).

clusion that the primary purpose of their publication was profit rather than edification.[49] It was tempting for publishers to reproduce such narratives because the market for the sensational was very strong as emphasized by the parallel publication during the mid-1720s of the proceedings of controversial trials and 'true accounts' of 'horrid, barbarous and bloody murders'.[50]

For reasons that can only be guessed at, only a small percentage of those offenders whose crime or trial was reported in a broadside were the authors of published 'last speeches'. In keeping with what has already been observed of the pattern of the publication of broadsides on crime, most date from the mid-1720s. Equally significantly, all appertain to crimes that caused a sensation at the time. Six stand

---

49 *The last speech, confession and dying words of Jonathan Wilde, the notorious thief taker and keeper of Newgate in London, who was executed at Tyburn on Monday the twenty fourth of May 1725* (Dublin, 1725); *The last speech of Mr Gabriel Lawrence, who was executed a Tyburn, with William Griffen and Thomas Wright, for Sodomy, the 9th of this Inst. May 1726* (Dublin, 1726); *The last speech, confession and dying words of Mrs Catherine Hayes, who was burn'd alive at Tyburn, for the murder of her husband, on Monday the 9th, of this instant May 1726* (Dublin, 1726); *The last speech of Capt. John Jayne, late commander of the Ship Burnet of Bristol, deliver'd to a friend, the night before his execution, in the Press-Yard of Newgate* (reprinted Dublin, 1726); *The whole life and character, birth, parentage and conversation, last dying speech and confession of James Cluff, who was executed at Tyburn on Friday 25th of July 1729* ... (reprinted Dublin, 1729); *The last office, performed by the Reverend Mr Robert Lyon A.M., minister in Perth, for himself and unhappy brethren, 28 of October 1746. Being the festival of St Simon and St Jude, the day he suffered, with his last speech. With the genuine 1st speech of Mr David Hume, and James Nicolson, both gentlemen well known etc.* (Belfast, [1746]). 50 *The whole tryal, and condemnation of Mrs Jane Wade, who was try'd at Mullingar the 13th of this Inst. July 1724; for the barbarous murder committed on the body of Mr Wedgworth at Zerill's Pass, in the County of Westmeath* (Dublin, 1724); *The whole tryal and examination of Venisent-Fitzgerald, John Jackman who were try'd this present Tuesday being the 14th of this instant June 1726. for Blaspheming also the tryal of Mathew Jnkinson, for the ravishing of Sarah Harris, the third of May, last* (Dublin, 1726); *The tryal and examination of Capt. Dunbar, who was yesterday, being the 12th of Oct. 1725. try'd upon three endictments of robbery; the first, for taking a diamond ring; second, a purse of gold; and the third, as spying-glass, from Mr Albert Angle, a Norway Captain* [Dublin, 1725]; *A full account of a horrid barbarous and bloody murder committed on the body'd of three children the eldest not exceeding four years of age, who was found this morning being the 31st of this Instant March 1726 under one of the arches of Bloody Bridge, with their little bodies cut and mangled in a most barbarous manner; and is to be seen by any that is so curious as to misdoubt the credibility of this* (Dublin, [1726]); *The whole tryal and examination of Captain Spranger and Lieutenant Southwell and Lieutenant Jolly; who was tryed at the King's Bench Bar, this present Tuesday being the 7 of this instant Feb 1726–7 for the murder of William Carry, Watchman, at Essex Bridge* (Dublin, 1727); *A full and true*

out.[51] The first chronologically is that of John Comber, who was sentenced to be 'hang'd and quarter'd' on 30 April 1725 for the murder of Councellor Hoar in a botched street robbery in Dublin. Eager to capitalise on the high level of public interest in the case, Elizabeth Needham produced an account of Comber's trial that cut across Cornelius Carter's plans to publish Comber's 'last speech'. Carter also had to contend with a rival 'last speech', presented to the public at the time of Comber's execution, which he sought to discredit by claiming that his was personally 'deliver'd to the printer' (30, 31).[52] Carter's pronouncement is immediately comprehensible since competition between publishers to acquire trial reports and 'last speeches' was intense during the mid-1720s. This was highlighted later the same year when four men were tried for mugging George Scrivener, the 'gentleman' of the recently appointed lord chancellor, Richard West, on Grafton Street in Dublin in September 1725. This was not a particularly heinous offence, but because of the eminence of the victim's employer, public interest was high, and the city's leading publishers of 'last speeches', Cornelius Carter and Catherine Hicks, each pre-

---

account of a horrid, barbarous and bloody murder committed on the body of James Gibson who was barbarously murder'd this morning being the 21st of this instant December 1727, by one call'd Owin Mc'antee, suppos'd to be a highway man ... (Dublin, 1727); *The tryal and examination of William Todd, attorney for the murder of Pierce Rice the 20 of February last at the Golden Bottle in St Nicholas Street Dublin* ... (Dublin, 1730); *The tryal and examination of Mrs Catherine Tully for the murder of Margery Eagan, her own servant-maid, who was with child; (on Friday the 8th of January last) this present Monday being the 8th of this Instant March 1731* ... (Dublin, 1731). Further examples are listed in Paul Higgins, *A bibliography of Irish trials and other legal proceedings* (Abingdon, 1986). 51 As well as those discussed in the following paragraph, there is also *The whole and true trryal of Cornet Joseph Poe who was try'd and condemn'd at Kilmainham this 8th of October 1725 for the assault and robbery of Michael Hall and Anthony Costelow on 25 September last in the High Road near Tallow Hill* (Dublin, [1725]) and 36 below. 52 *The tryal and examination of John Comber, who was try'd and found guilty, this present Friday being the 30th. of this instant April 1725. For the murder of Councellor Hoar on the 19th of January last about the Hour of 9 at night* (Dublin, 1725). There is also *The whole tryal and examination of James Hand and John Pitts who were try'd last night at the King's Bench for the Barbarous murder of Councellor Hoar, the 10th of January last 1724-5* [Dublin, 1725]; *The whole tryal and examination of Oonagh Dun, Patrick Dun, Loughlin Brady and Margaret Carney, the four informers who were try'd and found guilty this day, being the 9th instant May 1725, ... for willful perjury and unlawfully conspiring to take away the lives of Mr John Pitts and John Hand who were try'd last term for the murder of Councellor Hoar. Also the sentence pronounced against Eleanor Sills* [Dublin, 1725].

sented versions (34, 35). Carter, with some reason, claimed that his alone was authentic, but the fact that the public also had a choice of reports of the trial in which four of those responsible were sentenced to death suggests that public demand could sustain this volume of publication in individual instances.[53]

In sharp contrast to the acute commercial rivalry manifest in these cases, George Faulkner had no competition, other than tantalising and inadequate newspaper reports, when Moses Nowland was 'condemn'd for enlisting men with a traitorous design for the service of the Pretender' in June 1726. Despite his admission of guilt, he produced an account of the trial and a detailed 'last speech' (42) of questionable authenticity.[54] A familiar battle for the public's pennies was enjoined in 1726 when John Audouin was tried for the murder of his servant maid, Margaret Keef. Because of the exceptional interest in this case arising out of the fact that Audouin, who was a surgeon by profession, protested his innocence until the end, no fewer than five publishers sought to cash in. As a result, not only were the public provided with a much abbreviated 'last speech' by Sarah Harding (47), they could choose between three accounts of his trial from the presses of Elizabeth Needham, Thomas Walsh and John Overton, or engage with the short biography published by Catherine Hicks. And if they sought still more information, they could appeal to the popular press where the case was afforded exceptional coverage.[55] Indeed, only one

---

53 *The whole and true tryal of John M'Coy, Tho. Barnet, J. Smith and Owen Gahagan who were try'd and condemn'd at the Tholsel this 9th of October, 1725 for assaulting and robbing of Mr. Geo Scrivener the Chancellors Gentleman, and taking from him 4l. sterl. The 8th of September last* (Dublin, [1725]); *The tryal and examinations of John MaCoy, John Smith, Thomas Barret and Owen Goghagan who were this day try'd for robbing my Lord Chancelour's Gentleman and are to die for the same* [Dublin, 1725]). 54 *The whole tryal and examination of Capt. Moses Nowland, who was try'd and condemn'd at the King's Bench Bar, this day, being the 28th of this instant June, 1726, for listing men for the Pretender's service* (Dublin, 1726); *Dublin Intelligence*, 3, 9 July 1726; John Brady, *Catholics in the eighteenth-century press* (Maynooth, 1966), p. 312; below p. 45. 55 *The whole life actions, birth, parentage, and education of Doctor John Audouin. Who was Drawn Hang'd and Quarter'd, on Wednesday the 5th of this instant June, 1728* (Dublin, 1728); *A full and impartial account of the Tryal of Mr John Audouin, Surgeon, with the depositions of witnesses for and against the prisoner ...* (Dublin, [1728]); *An account of the tryal and examinations of Mr John Audowin, Try'd this day at the King's Bench for the barbarous murder of his servant Margaret Kief, on Saturday the 20th of April, 1728 ...* [Dublin, 1728]; *The whole sentence of*

other offender garnered nearly so much notice. This was the London attorney Daniel Kimberly, who was executed in May 1730 for breaching the 1707 abduction act by organising the marriage of a twelve years old heiress, Bridget Reading, to an impoverished graduate of Trinity College without the permission of her parents. Kimberly maintained steadfastly that he acted in Reading's best interests and the exceptionally long 'last speech' he delivered at the gallows represented his final effort to demonstrate his *bona fides* (51). Its acquisition was a coup for Richard Dickson, given that the prior publication of a trial report and a long exculpatory series of letters by the offender had animated a high degree of public interest.[56] The exceptional public interest in the misfortunes of Kimberly was replicated later the same year in the case of Richard Johnson and John Porter. Charged and found guilty of murder for their involvement in a bar-room affray in which Patrick Murphy was stabbed to death, both men protested their innocence; their plight struck a chord since, as well as a last speech (53), a 'funeral elegy, an ode and a 'paraphrase on the 139th Psalm', purportedly written by Johnson, were printed for public sale.[57]

Though elegies upon the death of notables were commonplace in the early eighteenth century, their composition or publication for capital offenders was unusual.[58] Indeed, from 1730, paralleling the decline in the publication of 'last speeches', trial and crime reports in

---

death pronounced this present Wednesday being the 29th of this instant May, 1728. Against Doctor John Audouim, for the barbarous and bloody murder of Margaret Kief, the 20th of April last (Dublin, [1728]); *Dublin Intelligence*, 1, 4, 8, 15 June; *Dublin Weekly Journal*, 1, 8 June 1728. 56 *Original letters of Daniel Kimberly, Gent. Written some time before his execution* (Dublin, 1730); *The tryal of Daniel Kimberly and Parson Ambrose a degraded clergyman of the Church of England ...* [Dublin, 1730]; James Kelly, 'The abduction of women of fortune in eighteenth-century Ireland', *Eighteenth-Century Ireland*, 9 (1994), pp 20–21; *Dublin Weekly Journal*, 30 May 1730. 57 *A Funeral elegy on the ever to be lamented deaths of Mr Richard Johnson and Mr John Porter; who were both unfortunately hang'd and Quartered on Saturday the 12th of this instant December 1730. For the murder of Patrick Murphy, the 21st of October last* (Dublin 1730); *A new ode on the last speech, confession and dying words of Mr John Porter, and Mr Richard Johnston Gentleman, who were executed near St Stephen's Green, this present Saturday being the 12st of this instant December 1730 ...* (Dublin 1730); *A Paraphrase on the CXXXIX Psalm found in the pocket of Mr Richard Johnston lately executed at Steven's Green* (Dublin, [1730]); *Dublin Weekly Journal*, 19 Dec. 1730. 58 Examples are to be found in the library of Trinity College, Press A.7.3–5.

broadside format, few offenders were the subject of more than one such publication. The most notable was Edward Sewell, 'a degraded clergyman of the Church of Ireland' whose execution in Dublin in 1740 for celebrating a clandestine marriage prompted both Catherine Hicks' successor, Charles Goulding, and the little known Edward Jones to produce speeches that each claimed were 'true' and 'genuine' (59, 60). Both could not be correct, of course, and their mutually incompatible claims symbolised the declining public interest in such works. Few were published thereafter, though the metaphorical import of a 'last speech' endured. During the 1750s, when Irish politics were adrift in a sea of factionalism and ill-feeling, several satirical pamphlets in the style of 'last speeches' were published for propaganda purposes.[59]

The publication of such ostensible 'last speeches' in pamphlet form reflected the evolution of Irish printing in the eighteenth century. The broadside as a form survived the shift in public taste and printing style to which this attested, but it was now confined to a narrower range of publications. Proclamations continued to be produced in large broadside format; occasional political pronouncements, lords lieutenants' speeches, parliamentary division lists and a gamut of notices and announcements were produced in the familiar smaller format; but whole categories of print, such as 'last speeches' and trial

---

[59] *The last speech and conference of Jack L—— e with Cutty Mamy, on Wednesday the 18th September, 1751* (Corke, [1751]); *The last speech, confession and dying words of E[ato]n S[tannar]d, Esq. Who was executed at St Stephen's Green, Tuesday, Jan. the 15th, 1754, for a most barbarous, inhuman and wicked attempt on the liberty, property and (even) life of his lawful and tender mother* ... (Dublin, 1754); *The last speech, confession and dying words of B-w-n S-h-l, representative in parliament for the borough of D—n who was executed the 8th of January, 1756, for violating his faith and honour* ... (Downpatrick , 1756); *Ireland's deliverance from invasion, by the confession, last speech and dying words of Road money presentment, Esq. Who with many of his relations were tried, condemn'd and executed for levying money extorted above and contrary to limitations of law for his high roads, and sundry high crimes and misdemeanours at the prosecution of Mr Statute labour* (Dublin, 1756) *The last speech, confession and dying words of the old traytor ... who was executed on ... 17th ... March 1756 ...* (Dublin, 1756). Significantly, these were published as pamphlets not broadsides. At the time of the agitation of the Act of Union (1800) a broadside was published bearing the title: *The last speech and dying words with the birth, parentage ... of that notorious and flagitious British imposter, known by the nickname of the Sun who was burnt ... in College Green, Dublin, on Monday the 11th of February, 1799* (Dublin, 1799).

reports, that were previously available virtually exclusively as broadsides, were now published only as pamphlets if at all.[60] Indeed, the 'last speech' effectively disappeared as trial reports emerged gradually as the primary form of crime literature. Moreover, as in England, they became increasingly clinical and formalised until, by the early nineteenth century, they provided a full and extensive record of what transpired.[61] Parallel with this, the task of persuading the public to observe the law was assumed by the judiciary; as a result, 'judges' charge to the jury', hitherto unreported, were afforded increasing notice and were widely circulated by the early nineteenth century.[62]

Publications of this ilk, by definition, possessed little of the character or implicit moral ambiguity that made 'last speeches' popular reading. This was a matter of satisfaction to officials and middle class opinion formers whose object was to foster a more law abiding, Godly and mannered society. Unwilling to sustain the 'last speech' and other familiar forms such as the crime report, the extensive distribution of trial reports achieved by the early nineteenth century may be seen, at least in part, to reflect their preference, but the public's appetite for accurate, clinical reports of proceedings in the court room was not satisfied exclusively from that quarter. Parallel with the rise of these specialised narratives, newspaper coverage improved. The evolution from the essentially telegrammatic reports carried by the press in the early eighteenth century when the broadside flourished to the extended court report commonly found in the 1790s was incremental, but in the case of serious crimes this frequently resulted in the publication of a large amount of pertinent information. Significantly, though there is rarely evidence as to their content, reference continued to be made in newspaper reports to the 'last speeches' delivered by those sentenced to death.[63] As was the case

---

60 See, for example, *The defence of Richard Cox* (Dublin, 1749); *Rules and orders to be observed in the Lying In Hospital in Great Briain Street* (Dublin, 1764); *Tryal of Saml Goodere and others* (Dublin, 1740); *Tryall of Mrs and Miss Branch for Murder* (Dublin, 1740). 61 Harris, 'Trials and criminal biographies', pp 26–7; Rawlings, *Drunks, whores and idle apprentices*, pp 24–5; Higgins, *Bibliography of Irish trials, passim*. 62 For examples see Higgins, *Bibliography of Irish trials, passim*; *Freeman's Journal*, 27 Jan., 5, 9 Nov. 1799. 63 An exception is that of Thomas Longeran whose 'authentic written declaration' was published in the *Freeman's Journal*, 27 Nov. 1781.

when 'last speeches' were published earlier in the century, the primary requirement was that offenders conducted themselves with 'contrition and resignation'. To this end, they were expected to 'behave ... in a penitential manner'; to make 'ample confession' of the crimes for which they were to die and any others they might have committed; to 'acknowledge the justice of their sentence'; to appeal to onlookers not to emulate their misconduct; and to be seen to wish to make 'peace with God' by praying publicly for mercy.[64] A sufficiently large number of offenders are recorded as having done so to vindicate the system. This obviously helped sustain capital punishment as a credible penalty, and it had few critics for most of the eighteenth century.[65] A minority of offenders did decline, generally to a chorus of public disapproval, to offer any 'final remarks'; while others, displaying no evidence of contrition, 'indecently averred [their] innocence' or 'died with a lie in their mouths'.[66] To 'die hard', as it was termed, was regarded with stern disapproval by most commentators, who were divided in their analysis of such incidents between suggesting that the frequency with which capital sentences were resorted to encouraged this response and concluding that such offenders were irredeemably recalcitrant.[67]

The frequent mention of 'last speeches' in news reports of executions in the second half of the eighteenth century demonstrates that they continued to arouse interest despite the fact that the virtual disappearance of the published 'last speech' from 1740 meant the public rarely had access to the text. There is no obvious explanation for this.

---

64 There are many examples; see *Dublin Daily Post*, 12 Apr. 1740; *Faulkner's Dublin Journal*, 10 Apr. 1759; *Dublin Gazette*, 26 Mar. 1765; *Hibernian Journal*, 28 Oct. 1771, 20 Mar., 10, 17 May 1775, 24 Apr. 1782; *Finn's Leinster Journal*, 24 Oct. 1770, 10 Apr., 25 Sept. 1773, 3, 27 Apr. 1776; *Dublin Chronicle*, 9 Sept. 1788, 14 May, 3 Nov. 1791, 24 Dec. 1792; *Freeman's Journal*, 11 Feb., 19 May, 14 June, 12 July, 4 Oct. 1798, 9 Oct. 1787, 3, 19 June 1800; *Dublin Evening Post*, 19 Apr. 1787, 13 Oct. 1798, 25 May, 20 June 1799; *Anthologia Hibernica*, 1 (1793), 240–1, 2 (July 1793), 74. **65** King to Fitzgerald, 24 Dec. 1696 (Trinity College Dublin, King Papers, Ms 750/1 f. 52); Nicolson to Wake, 9 Aug. 1720 (Gilbert Library, Wake Papers, Ms 27 ff 266–7). **66** For examples, see *Hibernian Journal*, 20 Mar. 1780; *Dublin Chronicle*, 3 Nov. 1787, 13 Dec. 1788; *Walker's Hibernian Magazine*, Sept. 1797, p. 14; *Dublin Evening Post*, 6 Nov. 1798; *Freeman's Journal*, 1 Nov. 1798, 3 Sept. 1799, 4 Jan. 1800. **67** *Dublin Evening Post*, 1 July 1786; *Dublin Chronicle*, 13 Dec, 1788, 4 Aug. 1789; *Freeman's Journal*, 20 Aug. 1799.

Simply to observe that the reading public found the newspaper and pamphlet more informative, appealing or fashionable is to beg the question since 'last speeches' continued to be made and to be the subject of comment. To suggest that it was an incidental outcome of the decline in public belief in the merits and efficacy of capital punishment is equally unconvincing since the identifiable strand of anti-capital punishment sentiment that emerged from mid-century did not strike a public register until the 1770s. A more likely explanation is to be found in the fragmentation and evolution of the audience that had once sustained the 'last speech' as a commercial print artefact.

At its peak, the broadside attracted an audience spanning a range of what Chartier has denominated 'interpretive communities'.[68] This reading audience expanded and developed as the eighteenth century progressed, but as an increased number of more complex print artefacts were produced to satisfy public demand, the market that sustained the broadside contracted. Categories of readers, previously content, opted for other elements of an augmented print menu that included a more vigorous newspaper sector, a substantially larger choice of better produced, longer and more accessible pamphlets and an emerging popular literature.[69] Reliable reader profiles of those who engaged with the main categories of print do not exist, but there are grounds for concluding that by the mid-eighteenth century newspapers and pamphlets attracted the competently literate, politicised, middle class end of the reading spectrum that had once read 'last speeches' for the moral lessons they offered. This left the more popular end of the reading spectrum that was drawn to the broadside for criminal drama to be provided for, and they were catered for through popular collections of criminal autobiography whose emergence coincides, significantly, with the decline of the crime broadside. These collections were, Niall Ó Ciosáin has argued, within 'official culture',

---

68 Roger Chartier, 'Texts, printings, readings' in Lynn Hunt, ed., *The new cultural history* (Berkeley, 1989), p. 158; James Raven, 'New reading histories, print culture and the identification of change: the case of eighteenth-century England', *Social History*, 23 (1998), p. 270. 69 Munter, *The Irish newspaper*, passim; R. Cargill Cole, *English books and Irish readers, 1700–1800* (London, 1986), passim.

but they took as their subjects figures who were very emphatically 'outside ... or marginal to it'. Works such as *The lives and actions of the most notorious Irish highwaymen, tories and rapparees*, four editions of which were published between 1747 and 1795, were not without moral import, but that dimension was largely implicit and subordinate to the demands of the larger narrative.[70]

The implication, that there was a section of Irish society which consumed 'last speeches' for their stories rather than their moral lessons and which, in their absence, was catered for by popular accounts of criminal derring-do is reinforced by the contrasting fortunes of the *Life of Nicholas Mooney, alias Jackson* and the *Life and adventures of James Freney*. Mooney's life is essentially a moral tale, but in contrast to the more neutral narrative of Freney's life and deeds, his experiences generated little public or commercial interest. Paradoxically, Freney's *Life and adventures*, first published in 1754, takes the ostensible form of a last confession, and given the obvious similarities between his conduct and that of tories who had forfeited their lives to little public cheer, his heroisation is remarkable. It is all the more noteworthy since Freney confessed that he was not averse to informing on his accomplices. However, the episodic character of his *Life and adventures* appealed to less skilled readers whose reading habits encouraged them 'to extract (or emphasise) those sections or stories which best fit the folk image of the bandit hero' and thereby to appropriate him as a hero of the dispossessed at a time when the public showed less deference to the gallows and to the public hangman.[71]

This latter observation deserves fuller consideration than it can be afforded here, but a preliminary examination of the accounts of public executions and of the crowd's deportment and demeanour on such occasions, suggests that the mid-eighteenth century witnessed a decisive shift in public attitude. Certainly, the absence during the

---

70 J. Cosgrave, *A genuine history of the lives and actions of the most notorious Irish highwaymen, Tories and Rapparees: from Redmond O'Hanlon, the famous gentleman-robber, to Cahier na Gappul, the great horse-catcher, who was executed at Maryborough, in August 1735* ... (Dublin, 1747, 1776, 1782, 1795). 71 Ó Ciosáin, *Print and popular culture*, pp 94–6.

early eighteenth century of popular opposition implies that execution was accepted by the public, as well as by most offenders, as a just sentence in cases of serious transgression.[72] It cannot be shown that the publication of 'last speeches' was related directly to this, but it is surely significant that their popularity was at its greatest when the public consensus on capital sentencing was at its strongest. For this reason also, it is more than mere coincidence that the demise of the 'last speech' as a popular print artefact in the 1740s coincides with a palpable hardening in public dissatisfaction with the administration of justice and an increased disposition to demonstrate discontent. One symptom of this is displayed in the greater readiness of local officials to request the presence of parties of military at executions 'under some apprehension of the mob'.[73] That response, it might be countered, was nothing more than a manifestation of the reflexive alarmism of local officials, but this conclusion is invalidated by the sheer number of news reports dating from the 1740s that bear witness to the public's propensity to express their disapproval of capital punishment in certain circumstances. For example, one encounters frequent accounts of mobs taking the bodies of condemned men who protested their innocence from the gallows to the door of their prosecutors' house, a ceremony known as 'laying the deceased persons death at the man's door'.[74] Likewise, bodies left on gibbets or hung in chains were taken for reviving, or waking and burial; informers were sometimes assaulted and ill-treated, hangmen were occasionally stoned; gibbets were pulled down; and attempts were made to rescue condemned men.[75]

---

72 In the 1730s, the public hangman was applauded for wearing Irish made clothes (see Garnham, *The courts ...*, pp 269–70 for a related occurrence). 73 Waite to Weston, 11 Aug. 1750 (Public Record Office of Northern Ireland (henceforth PRONI), Wilmot Papers, T3019/1613); *Universal Advertizer*, 24 Apr. 1759; *Freeman's Journal*, 29 Apr. 1766; *Finn's Leinster Journal*, 13 Apr. 1774, 30 Aug. 1775, 18 Sept. 1776; *Hibernian Journal*, 30 Oct. 1780. 74 *Dublin Courant*, 26 Dec. 1747, 2 Jan, 1748; *Public Gazetteer*, 10 Jan. 1761; F.H. Tucky's *The count and city of Cork Remembrancer* (Cork, 1837), pp 148–9; *Hibernian Journal*, 10 Jan. 1776, 30 Oct. 1780. 75 Colles to Bindon, 13 Aug. 1749 (National Archives, Prim Collection, No 87/40); Tucky's *Cork Remembrancer*, p. 134; *Pue's Occurrences*, 30 Apr. 1743, 23 May 1752, 10 Apr., 27 July 1756, 18 Apr. 1769; *Finn's Leinster Journal*, 15 Sept. 1770, 17 Sept. 1774, 11 Feb. 1778; *Hibernian Journal*, 4 Dec. 1771; *Freeman's Jn.*, 22 Apr. 1769, 10 Feb. 1778.

INTRODUCTION

In an environment characterised so strikingly by diminishing consensus, it was inevitable that changes should occur in the manner by which capital punishment was reported and perceived by society at large. The decline of the 'last speech' as a print artefact can thus be seen to reflect changes in society as well as in technology, in *mentalité* as well as in conduct. At the same time, the fact that 'last speeches' continued to be made ensured that while the broadside version withered as a feature of the country's print culture it did not disappear as a phenomenon though reports of their content suggest they seldom displayed the ideological vigour of their predecessors. This is not apparent from the 'last speeches' of Gerald Byrne and James and Patrick Strange, who were hanged for their involvement in the abduction of Catherine and Ann Kennedy in County Kilkenny in 1780, but then this is best regarded as a provincial hangover from an earlier era **(61)**. This conclusion is reinforced by the fact that the spate of 'last speeches' produced in the late 1790s when the authorities were busy wreaking vengeance on those who embraced republicanism were quite different in form, approach and content. One example, that of Thomas Neil who was executed in 1798 and which was printed as a broadside, is presented to illustrate how different in style and mood they were to the classic versions published more than half a century earlier **(62)**. The same point could be made in respect of the 'last speeches', notably that of William Orr, published abroad or as pamphlets, prepared by sympathisers or friends, for propaganda purposes.[76] As this suggests, public interest in crime, in punishment and in the 'last speeches' of those sentenced to death remained strong.[77] However, the public engaged with each in a different way than had

---

[76] *The last speech and dying declaration of William Orr, who was executed on Saturday the 15th instant, near Carrickfergus, for the crime of treason, and delivered by himself at the place of execution* (London?, 1797); *The trial of William Orr, at Carrickfergus Assizes, for being an United Irishman: with his dying declaration ...* (Philadelphia, 1798); *The last speech and dying words of Martin M'Loughlin, who was taken prisoner after the defeat of the French and rebels, at the Battle of Ballinamuck ... and ordered for execution, ... on Monday 10th Sept. 1798* (Cork and Dublin, [1798]), another edition, with a *true account of the battles of Castlebar, Coloony and Ballinamuck, and the merry adventure of Captain Tom Pakenham* (Cork, 1798). [77] Interestingly, the first fourteen parts of *The Newgate Calendar*, which provided 'genuine and circumstantial narratives of the lives and transactions ... and dying speeches of the most notorious criminals of both sexes ... from the year 1700' was

been the case in the early eighteenth century; the traditional broadside 'last speech' no longer met their needs and because of this it did not re-emerge as a strong feature of popular print culture.

III

Frank McLynn has argued in his study of 'crime and punishment' in eighteenth-century England that 'the death penalty was not regarded by the élite as *primarily* a deterrent to crime. The deterrent effect of laws against crime rests on the certainty of prosecution ... Their principal aim was social control.'[78] This conclusion may not secure general endorsement, given the variety of means by which capital sentences were effected and the emphasis placed on inflicting physical punishment when compared with the rehabilitative potential of mooted alternatives such as imprisonment with hard labour or incarceration. However, despite the multiplicity of offences that elicited the death penalty and the vicious manner in which it was sometimes inflicted, as the execution of Charles Carragher at Dundalk in February 1719 vividly attests (20), public execution was not 'a simple display of brutality intended to cow or entertain' the populace.[79] Public execution involved a ceremony possessed of distinctive rituals whose purpose and function was to emphasise the gravity of what was at stake and to impress upon the public the serious consequences should they emulate the misbehaviour of the offender. There were occasions when the rituals surrounding the implementation of capital sentences were cut short, but they were exceptional and normally only occurred in cases of especially reprehensible crimes when the guilty were sent for immediate execution without the opportunity to prepare to make a 'good death'. This happened very rarely during the era of 'last speeches'. However, following the direction in 1740 that John Leadwell, who had wielded the knife when Lieutenant John Hume

advertised for sale in Dublin in 1773 (*Freeman's Jn.*, 9 Mar. 1773). 78 Frank McLynn, *Crime and punishment in eighteenth-century England* (London, 1989), p. 258. 79 Nicolson to Wake, 9 Aug. 1720 (Gilbert Library, Wake Papers, Ms 27 ff 266–7); Sharpe, 'Last dying speeches', p. 146.

was slashed to death in a fracas in a tavern at Roscrea, County Tipperary, two years earlier, should be hanged immediately after sentencing, the authorities sought to demonstrate their stern disapproval of particularly odious crimes by denying offenders the chance of a 'good death'.[80] Such occasions were comparatively uncommon.[81] Paradoxically, the fact that they occurred at all emphasises the importance of the execution ritual in the large majority of cases in which the offender was executed on 'the appointed day', usually a week or more after the passing of sentence.

The expectation was that the capital offender would, as Judge Alexander Crookshank advised in 1799, 'pass the short interval between his sentence and execution, in effecting every reparation in his power, and making peace with God'.[82] This admonition was taken seriously by a majority of convicts since, however disinclined they were in life to observe the law of the state, all but a handful demonstrated no disposition to defy that of God in the face of death. Contrition was, of course, urged strongly from many quarters on capital offenders. Indeed, its redemptive capacity was deemed to be greater in such cases because of the suggestion implicit in the process that the prospect of an after life, provided a 'soul saving conversion' took place, was not precluded those who forfeited their lives for heinous offences. This fact alone gave the 'last speeches' of seventeenth-century England and eighteenth-century Ireland and conversion sermons of eighteenth-century New England greater consequence than other associated narratives. The emphasis placed on 'soul saving conversion' was stronger in New England than elsewhere in the Atlantic world. But the fact that it was acknowledged theologically throughout, not alone justified clerical involvement, it ensured that the execution ritual would continue to possess a religious dimension as long as religion remained a core part of the public belief system.[83]

---

80 Kelly, 'Capital punishment in early eighteenth-century Ireland'; *Dublin Newsletter*, 25 Mar. 1740; S.J. Connolly, *Religion, law and power: the making of Protestant Ireland, 1660–1760* (Oxford, 1992), pp 69–71; Kelly, *'That damn'd thing call'd honour'*, pp 61–2. 81 For examples, see Kelly, 'Capital punishment'; *Anthologia Hibernica*, 1 (1793), p. 240; *Dublin Mercury*, 18 Apr. 1767; *Finn's Leinster Journal*, 20 Jan. 1776; *Dublin Chronicle*, 14 May 1791. 82 *Freeman's Journal*, 27 Jan. 1799. 83 The situation in New England is

INTRODUCTION

Reflecting their shared Christian conviction in the redemptive potential of contrition and their attendant role in ushering people towards a just death, clergymen of all denominations engaged actively in the process whereby capital sentences were implemented. In England, and probably in Ireland also, clergy made themselves available to minister to the condemned, to preach on the eve of execution day and to accompany offenders to the gallows.[84] Clergymen embraced this role assuredly because they, and by extension society at large, acceded to the convention that a 'good death' was, if not a demonstration of the redemptive power of Christianity, a manifestation of its likelihood. It is a measure of the strength of this conviction that John Gother's *Instructions and devotions for the afflicted and sick with some help for prisoners, such especially as are to be tried for life*, published in London in 1725, was reprinted in Dublin five years later.[85] In this work, prisoners were enjoined to 'make an advantage of their misfortune, and improve it to the good of their souls' by denying the temptations of 'ill company' and alcohol and by making peace with God. They were encouraged to accept that their fate was the 'Will' of God, to identify their suffering with that of Jesus Christ, to perceive themselves as 'lost sheep that now returns to [the] Shepherd' and to devote their time remaining to 'contrition and repentance'. To help with this, Gother presented offenders with a selection of prayers they could relate both on the way to and at the place of execution.[86] They were also encouraged to prepare a 'last speech' for delivery at the scaffold.

The civil and religious authorities in eighteenth-century Ireland, no less than those of seventeenth-century England, facilitated the delivery of appropriately tuned 'last speeches' because they 'legit-

---

explored in Cohen, *Pillars of salt*, passim but on the point at issue pp 62–3. **84** John Beattie, *Crime and the courts*, p. 455. **85** [John Gother], *Instructions and devotions for the afflicted and sick, with some help for prisoners, such especially as are to be tried for life* (London, 1725) reprint [Dublin], 1730. The copy in the collection of the Irish Dominicans, Tallaght, County Dublin, does not contain a place of imprint, but Hugh Fenning ('Dublin imprints of Catholic interest, 1701–39' in *Collectanea Hibernica*, 39 and 40 (1987–8), p. 144) believes it is Dublin. My assertion that there was no Dublin edition of this tract therefore needs modification (Kelly, 'Capital punishment'). **86** Gother's *Instructions and devotions* ... ; the quotations are from the London edition.

imized not only the punishment being suffered by the individual felon, but also the whole structure of secular and religious authority'.⁸⁷ Some clergy may have preferred to have had exclusive control of the occasion to promote religious conviction. They were certainly heartened by victims like John Auduoin, who prayed and sung psalms at the gallows and who died with the ejaculation 'Lord Jesus receive my soul' on his lips, and others whose last action was publicly to read from scriptures, to say the rosary or simply to spend 'some time at devotion'.⁸⁸ However, only a minority (1, 11, 32, 47, 53, 59) behaved after such a fashion. Moreover, in Ireland even death was not exempt from denominational tension as some Protestants, congenitally suspicious of the role played by Roman Catholic priests, alleged that the assurances 'of salvation' offered by the latter enabled offenders face the gallows 'with great composure' and thereby to negate the terror of the scaffold. Influenced by such suspicions, a number of agrarian protestors 'were immediately hanged pursuant to their sentence without being allowed a clergyman or any religious ceremonies' at Clonmel in 1776.⁸⁹ This was exceptional, but the fact that it happened at all bears vivid witness to the fact that whilst the clergy of the main Christian denominations were granted preferential access to offenders and a prominent place at the scaffold, the rules were determined increasingly by the state.

The main religious denominations were content to go along with this because most offenders, well-schooled in the punitive precepts of Christianity and in the image of a vengeful God, were more than willing to request divine mercy at the gallows, and thereby to affirm the redemptive power of Christianity. The fact that such requests were made towards the end of the 'speech' and normally constituted the closing apostrophe served to underline their import and to affirm the value of 'dying well'.⁹⁰ This may reflect the influence of publishers as well as clergy, since it was in their interest to ensure that Irish

---

87 Sharpe, 'Last dying speeches', p. 163. 88 *Dublin Intelligence*, 8 June 1728; *Dublin Evening Post*, 25 May 1799; *Freeman's Journal*, 25 May 1799, 19 Dec. 1801. 89 *Freeman's Journal*, 18 Apr. 1767, 1 Dec. 1781; *Finn's Leinster Journal*, 20 Jan. 1776. 90 The phrase 'dying well' is taken from Sharpe, 'Last dying speeches', pp 160–1.

'last speeches' conformed to the formula made familiar over several generations in England. This has led to their characterisation as 'highly stylised productions', and generated speculation that they were not the composition of the offender in whose name they were issued.[91] It is improbable that many 'last speeches' were prepared without some input from clerics or printers; but even a cursory reading of those assembled for this collection offers the strong impression that genuine, if not necessarily complete, life histories are being related. This, of course, left plenty of scope for embellishment and for forgery since it did not demand particularly intense scrutiny of a malefactor's background to establish sufficient information to prepare a 'last speech'. One such work is *The last speech of Moses Nowland* (42), a wordy and not uninformative homily that (according to a newspaper report) the subject himself maintained was an invention as he 'made no speech' because he did not believe he had committed any crime.[92] In the absence of independent corroboration, there are no clear-cut grounds for accepting the newspaper over the broadside, but the fact that the unscrupulous George Faulkner was the publisher and that the text reads like a forgery is suggestive. If so, it was not, as shall be seen below, the only case in which a publisher intervened to provide the public with what s/he believed they wanted. But it is immediately comprehensible in this instance because the crime at issue – enlisting men in the service of the Pretender – was regarded with such alarm by the Protestant population that the 'last speeches' of several offenders implicated in this offence were published (23, 29, 43). In the normal course of events, within the parameters of the *genre* and the expectation that 'the repentant criminal denounced his (or her) past life as immoral and told the crowd (or the reader) to benefit by his example', offenders had considerable freedom both over what was related and the manner of its narration.[93]

As this suggests, Irish 'last speeches' varied considerably in length, content and approach. This is not surprising given the range in denomination, gender, age and life experience of those whose pro-

---

91 Ó Ciosáin, *Print and popular culture*, p. 88. 92 *Dublin Intelligence*, 9 July 1726. 93 Ó Ciosáin, *Print and popular culture*, p. 88.

nouncements reached print. From a sample of one hundred and ten cases where the denomination of the offender can be established, slightly less than 73 per cent were Roman Catholic, slightly more than a quarter were Church of Ireland or Church of England and a modest 1.8 per cent was Presbyterian (Table 1). The gender of the offenders was even more strikingly skewed as an overwhelming 94 per cent of the 117 capital offenders whose 'last speeches' survive were male (Table 2). These ranged in age from fourteen to eighty, but it is difficult to establish the age profile of offenders with precision because many described themselves as 'about' rather than a specific age. Operating on the problematic assumption that those who defined themselves as 'about thirty' belong to the cohort 21–30, nearly 44 per cent were between the ages of 21 and 'about thirty'; slightly less than a quarter were twenty years or less; a further quarter were in their thirties; less than 7 per cent were in their forties and a modest 2.24 per cent were fifty years or over (Table 3).

TABLE 1:

DENOMINATION OF LAST SPEECHMAKERS

Denomination	Church of Ireland/England	Roman Catholic	Presbyterian
Number	28	80	2
Percentage	25.5	72.7	1.8

TABLE 2:

GENDER OF LAST SPEECHMAKERS

Gender	Male	Female
Number	110	7
Percentage	94.02	5.98

INTRODUCTION

TABLE 3:
AGE PROFILE OF LAST SPEECHMAKERS

Age (years)	1–20	21–30	31–40	51–50	51–60
Number	21	39	21	6	2
Percentage	23.59	43.82	23.59	6.74	2.24

Given these variations in age, religion and gender, it is only to be expected that the literary capacities of last speechmakers should vary greatly. It may be that literacy was one of the main factors in determining who prepared speeches for publication since few make reference to the engagement of an amanuensis to record their final words. The fact that many speeches are replete with syntactical, grammatical and orthographical infractions may seem to support the conclusion that the texts were written by those in whose names they were issued and printed as delivered, but this is to assume that printers received texts that followed the 'last speech' pattern, that they were loathe to rewrite what they received and that they were well-schooled in and attentive to the rules of English grammar. This is improbable. Indeed, it is particularly clear from the four instances – John Comber in May 1725 (30, 31), John McCoy, Thomas Barnet, John Smith and Owen Geoghegan in October 1725 (34, 35), James Stevens and Patrick Barnwell in 1726 (40, 41) and Edward Sewell in 1740 (59, 60) – documented in this collection in which rival versions of the 'last speeches' of offenders were published that some printers were manifestly more concerned with releasing a marketable commodity than with accurately capturing and conveying their last words. To be sure, questions of authenticity were not regarded as an irrelevancy, and printers who acquired 'last speeches' they knew to be genuine had no hesitation in advertising the fact. Thus, Francis Dickson included authenticating declarations from the attending clergyman in 1712 (7, 8); while John Brocas in 1706, Edward Waters in 1707, Cornelius Carter in 1714, 1720 and 1725, Richard Dickson in 1726, George Faulkner in 1726 and Charles Goulding in 1740 (2, 3, 4, 12, 22, 31, 35, 37, 39, 40, 41, 59) among others pronounced boldly, or cited offenders as pronouncing, that they alone presented the true and correct version of particular 'last words'.

If the fact that four 'last speeches' are known to be forgeries posits a large question mark against the reliability of the remainder, it is reassuring to note that those that were forged are just less, rather then erroneously informed when compared with those that are genuine. Significantly, these cases and a number of others (41) indicate that printers were pro-active in eliciting texts from offenders. Unfortunately, they do not indicate their involvement in the preparation of texts, but given their similar structure, the presence in most of basic biographical facts, of an account of the offenders' descent into criminality, other transgressions and other standard data it is reasonable to assume that, at the very least, offenders were coached as to what to include. Alternatively, some, such as Daniel Ross and Alexander Graham who were executed for robbery in Dublin in 1729 (49, 50), may have provided the printer with the requisite information to structure and to organise.[94] It is equally reasonable to assume that in those cases where the offender was educated or insistent s/he was innocent, that the 'speech' that ensued was primarily his or her own work. What is certain is that the concept of 'author' employed today to define an individual who composes a text is inappropriate since it is likely that the composition of many 'last speeches' involved the combined input of offenders, clergy, printers, publishers and, possibly, family members, gaolers and other prisoners. If this is seen to stretch the concept of authorship to breaking point, it should be noted that recent work, highlighting the collective character of contemporary poetry writing, indicates that the concept was applied more elastically in the early eighteenth century than it is now.[95]

However precisely each 'last speech' was composed, it is manifest that offenders had different stories to tell and a variable readiness to articulate them. The most basic measure of this is the number of words each offender used to convey his or her experience. The aver-

---

[94] This can be shown to have happened in the English case of *The last speech, confession and dying words of John Reid* (Rawlings, *Drunks, whores and idle apprentices*, p. 6).
[95] A.C. Elias, '*Senatus Consultum:* revising verse in Swift's Dublin circle, 1729–1735' in H.J. Real, *Reading Swift* (Munich, 1998), pp 249–67.

age word count of the sixty-two broadsides presented here is eight hundred and ninety-five words. The shortest – that of Thomas Neil (62) who was executed in 1798 – amounts to a modest three hundred words. Another six (24, 26, 48, 49, 52, 61) range between four hundred and five hundred while, at the other extreme, three examples (11, 32, 51) are over two thousand words and in the case of the longest (51), fall just short of four thousand. Of the remainder, fifteen (4, 8, 9, 13, 16, 22, 28, 35, 40, 42, 53, 54, 56, 58, 60) range from a thousand to one thousand seven hundred and fifty words, but by far the largest number (thirty-seven) fall within a standard five hundred to a thousand words. If, on first consideration, this may be seen to have provided offenders with sufficient space to provide a full and candid account of their life and experiences, the reality, because many broadsides presented the statements of a number of offenders, was that a large number of individuals were allotted no more than a few hundred words. At the opposite end of the spectrum, Daniel Kimberly's extended essay in self-exculpation reached an exceptional three thousand nine hundred.

While space obviously exerted a critical influence on the content of 'last speeches', it is impossible to ascertain if this was made known to offenders in Ireland prior to their composition. It is also unclear if printers exercised an interdiction on what was included or omitted, and, if so, if they were guided in their use of this power by reasons of space. Whatever the determining influence, five hundred words was generally ample to allow the typical offender not just to provide an account of his background but to indicate how his refusal to follow the guidance and example of his poor but honest parents prompted him along the path to perfidy. This journey began typically with the abandonment of an apprenticeship, loss of employment or dismissal from service (3, 9, 10, 15, 33, 35, 54), demobilisation (3, 4, 5, 6, 8, 12, 34, 38) or a change in environment (moving to Dublin featured prominently (3, 9, 10, 15, 33, 35, 54)). It was frequently foreshadowed by the neglect of religion (5, 11, 15), the embrace of swearing, profanity, bad company and an enthusiasm for drinking, gambling, consorting with 'lewd women' and other morally dubious practices. The dangers inherent in succumbing to the wiles of 'lewd women' is a recurrent theme of 'last speeches' (2, 3, 4,11, 15, 27, 31, 40), and the negative impression conveyed of women's sexuality as well as of sexuality *per se* is reinforced by the fact that most of the women whose last words are recorded in print were, by their own admission, promiscuous (16, 22, 33, 37, 52). Sexual continence was, as this suggests, extolled no less than adherence to the civil law arising out of the conviction that to live a good life meant observing the law of God no less than the law of man in all its aspects (53). To this end, the conviction that the 'choice of company is one of ye most essential things for youth' and that a man had led a good life if, on his death-bed, he could boast 'that he never had, either when a bachelor or a married man, criminal conversation with a woman; never was drunk; never broke his word; nor never us'd tobacco' was embraced across the Atlantic world. Indeed, so pervasive were the assumptions that sustained such proscriptive utterances that ready parallels can be identified in English 'last speeches' and in New England execution sermons.[96] Arising out of this, there are grounds for concluding with R.A. Bosco that one of the primary targets of 'gallows literature' was children. It is possible of course that children were shielded from the experience of hearing last speeches *in situ* and that they were only introduced to their parabolic content via the printed word, but there is no evidence to sustain this. Quite the contrary; given that the youngest author of a 'last speech' in this collection was only 14 years old (52) and that their tone and content was less 'terror inducing' than a typical New England gallows sermon, it is likely that, in common with adults, children were introduced to 'last speeches' at first hand.[97]

Once the author of a last speech had described his or her slide into bad company and immorality, the next task was to account for his or her embarkation on a life of crime. This varied from case to

---

[96] M.J. O'Connell, *The last colonel of the Irish Brigade* (2 vols, London, 1892), I, 17; A.C. Elias, *Memoirs of Laetitia Pilkington* (2 vols, Athens, Georgia, 1997), I, 10. The idea of a descent into crime through loose living is echoed in the Sunday Observance Act, 1695 and many acts against gaming. For the situation in New England, see Bosco, 'Lectures at the pillory', pp 157–8; Cohen, *Pillars of salt*, pp 85–9, 129–30; Rawlings, *Drunks, whores and idle apprentices*, pp 19–20. [97] Bosco, 'Lectures at the pillory', pp 169–72; Cohen, *Pillars of salt*, p. 55.

case, but common themes included succumbing to the temptation to make an easy financial killing, moral weakness, being led astray by an experienced malefactor, and desperation. Typically, the story of the crime for which the narrator forfeited his or her life is described in detail, usually in an appropriately remorseful tone, though the amount of information provided does not conform to any discernible pattern. There are cases, such as that of Sarah Grew (16), who was sentenced to death in 1717, in which the details provided exceed what is necessary to relate the experience adequately, and others in which the barest outline is offered (22). This can hardly have been to the satisfaction of many readers since longer narratives generally provide the fullest insights into the state of mind of offenders, into the specifics of the crime for which they were sentenced to die and, in many instances, into the contingent and fortuitous events that culminated either in their committing a crime or in their being caught.

Most such expositions are presented in a tone of what seems sincere regret. This was usually inspired by the realisation that death was imminent and by the calculation that this might prove advantageous in the hereafter (54). In a substantial number of cases, offenders declared themselves reconciled to their 'wretched end' or 'shameful and ignominious death' (5, 6, 25, 42, 47, 60) by hanging on the grounds that they were 'justly' tried and found guilty according to law (1, 3, 5, 6, 12, 13, 17, 20, 22, 23, 37, 39, 44, 48, 49, 54, 55, 56, 57, 58, 62). In some instances, experienced criminals avowed that they were not guilty of the offence for which they were to die, but acknowledged responsibility for other crimes (1, 4, 23, 25, 31, 39, 41, 58). Capital offenders were both encouraged and disposed to make a clean breast of past offences on the grounds that it represented a visible testament to the fact that they were making a 'good death'. This obviously took on a particularly vivid hue in those instances in which offenders confessed that they allowed innocent men go to the gallows (1, 17, 18, 20, 23, 31, 36, 49) for crimes they, or others, had committed; in the significant number of cases in which offenders accepted their fate because they had committed crimes other than those for which they were sentenced (1, 4, 13, 15, 22) and in the disturbing number of cases in which offenders sentenced to death protested their innocence (7, 15, 17, 18, 22, 25, 26, 27, 40, 43, 46, 47, 50, 51) or highlighted mitigating circumstances that an indulgent court might legitimately have used to commute their capital sentence (7, 8, 9, 12, 13, 28, 29, 30, 36, 46, 53). All are not equally convincing, and it is noteworthy that while the narrator indicated his readiness to die in a number of cases, it was not an invariable practice. In general, the tone of contrition and penitence that pervade most 'last speeches' reached its acme as the narrative moved to a conclusion. Most conform to a simple and straightforward formula. The narrator advises his audience to shun bad company and the temptation to do ill, begs forgiveness of those, such as his parents, he has injured (2, 11, 14, 35); forgives those, such as his accusers, who have injured him (1, 22, 33, 61); appeals that his example should serve as a warning to all to observe the laws of God and man (2, 3, 5, 19, 27, 28, 29, 31, 50, 54), indicates his religion, appeals to God for mercy and begs the prayers of all 'good people' (4, 29, 30, 33, 37, 38, 42, 47) thereby echoing the preferred opening salutations of 'Good people' or 'Good Christians'. However, there are a number of examples in which the homiletic quality of what is provided is both qualitatively and quantitatively more accomplished. In the main these were the handiwork of individuals with an educated or advanced religious sensibility. This is the case, for instance, of James Geoghegan, the Franciscan priest executed in 1694, who presented his pithy injunction to his audience to obey the laws of God and man in an intellectually sophisticated fashion (1). It is the case also of the 'last and true speech' attributed to Edward Sewell in which he specifically exculpated the Church of Ireland for his misconduct and presented a hymn encapsulating the moral of his 'wretched plight' (60). But the two speeches that offer the most sustained homilies are those penned by the Presbyterian offenders – James Hamilton and James Dunbar (11, 32). Both are of above average length, and both used the additional space they were allowed to proffer unusually detailed confessions and admonitions. Of the two, Dunbar's is the more impressive scholastically because he cites Scripture accurately and appositely in his extended appeal to his children to live Godly lives and to reinforce his contrite prayers that he might be the beneficiary of divine mercy.

Because 'last speeches' were usually prepared in prison, offenders travelled to the gallows with them at the ready. For this as well as for other reasons, the procession from the place of incarceration to the place of execution (in Dublin it was from Newgate prison to the site near Stephen's Green where the city gallows was located) should be seen as part of the execution ritual. Offenders, such as Richard Johnson and John Porter, who travelled to the gallows 'in a mourning coach' or Edward Sewell, who sang a hymn of his own composing in the coach *en route* (60), gave the procession added piquancy, though these were exceptional.[98] However, no matter what their demeanour, all were transported to the scaffold, usually in a cart, sometimes accompanied by a clergyman and, occasionally, by a coffin (52), until the relocation of the city gallows at the New Gaol in 1783. In the ordinary course of events, diurnal traffic was stopped to enable the cart and its passengers complete their journey without interruption.[99] The sense of occasion this generated was reinforced by the fact that execution days, which normally fell on a Wednesday or a Saturday in Dublin, generated a holiday atmosphere.[100] They were not public holidays, but both the contrived and real drama of the occasion, allied to the wish of the authorities to impress upon the public what lay in store for wrongdoers, generally ensured most public executions a large audience.[101] Precise figures do not exist, but suggestions in the 1780s, when the authorities first began to discourage large gatherings at such events, that executions commonly occupied several thousand people for several hours are reinforced by other references to the presence of 'a great concourse', 'a large crowd' and so on. Some executions certainly attracted exceptional audiences, amounting to an estimated ten thousand to observe the employment of a 'drop gallows' in Dublin for the first time in 1783, and to double that figure to witness the execution of three Rightboys near Fethard in County Tipperary

---

98 *A funeral elegy on the ever to be lamented deaths of Mr Richard Johnson and Mr John Porter ...* [Dublin, 1730]; *Dublin Weekly Journal*, 19 Dec. 1730. 99 Chetwode to Marlay, 1734 (Chetwode Papers, see NLI, Reports on private collections, no. 97 p. 959); Brian Henry, *Dublin hanged: crime, law enforcement and punishment in late eighteenth-century Dublin* (Dublin, 1994), pp 23–6. 100 *Hibernian Journal*, 25 Feb. 1775. 101 *Volunteer Evening Post*, 8 Nov. 1785.

in April 1787.¹⁰² At the other extreme, on the rare occasions that there was a rival spectacle, attendances could drop precipitously as happened in November 1787 when the funeral procession of the Lord Lieutenant, the Duke of Rutland, ensured a modest six people were present at Newgate Gaol to witness the execution of a female offender.¹⁰³

Once the gallows was reached, the offender was 'the central participant in a theatre of punishment'.¹⁰⁴ Most were attended by a clergyman of their own denomination, generally the person who had ministered to them since they had received sentence.¹⁰⁵ Some were so eager to bring events to their inevitable *dénouement* they had to be reminded that they were expected to address the assembled throng.¹⁰⁶ A proportion simply delivered a paper containing their last thoughts to a nearby official for later dissemination but the majority played the part expected of them. The length and quality of the 'last speeches' that were made varied greatly as the recorded examples presented in this collection attest. Many, consisting of little more than a profession of identity, an admission of guilt and an expression of contrition, were short and to the point (12, 13, 17, 21, 22, 43, 44, 48, 54), and the attenuated reference to such pronouncements in the press once the era of the 'last speech' was over suggests this became the norm. Others were fuller, while in exceptional instances, such as that of Daniel Kimberly (51) who protested his innocence to the end and called on God 'for heavy vengeance on him if he died guilty', the crowd was treated to a prolonged oration, in this case extending 'above two hours and a half'.¹⁰⁷ A minority declined to speak. A significant number of these involved offenders who refused to co-operate with the cleric deputed to minister to them; others refused to acknowledge guilt for the offence for which they were to die, while a small number simply showed no fear.¹⁰⁸ Such recalcitrants were often the target of hostile

---

102 Ibid.; *Dublin Mercury*, 18 Apr. 1767; *Hibernian Journal*, 18 May 1772; *Finn's Leinster Journal*, 17 Apr. 1776; *Dublin Evening Post*, 5 Aug. 1783; *Anthologia Hibernica*, ii (1793), p. 75. 103 *Dublin Evening Post*, 20 Nov. 1787. 104 Sharpe, 'Last dying speeches', p. 156. 105 *Hibernian Journal*, 20 Mar. 1775; *Dublin Chronicle*, 22 June 1790; *Freeman's Journal*, 12, 21 July 1798, 6 Dec. 1802. 106 *Volunteer Evening Post*, 13 Sept. 1785. 107 *Dublin Intelligence*, 8 June 1728. 108 *Hibernian Journal*, 20 Mar. 1780; *Dublin Chronicle*, 3 Nov. 1787, 13 Dec. 1788, 4 Aug. 1789; *Dublin Evening Post*, 1 July 1786.

comment because, it was averred, 'the populace ... like to see the victim's eyes and hear his final words'. The general expectation was that the offender should be contrite; what is not clear is how the public regarded those who chose to 'die hard'. The civil and religious authorities certainly disapproved, but it may be that the crowd was less censorious.[109] Indulgence was certainly extended by officialdom to offenders who spent periods as long as forty minutes to two hours in prayer, which was less than exciting for the watching public.[110] Whether the crowd was as forgiving of those who refused to manifest any evidence of contrition or to address them is less clear.

Other than gleaning from the substantial corpus of reports of capital punishments that the public *generally* fulfilled the role assigned them of providing an attentive audience, it is singularly difficult to assess how those present at an execution responded to the last speeches made largely for their benefit. On the basis of newspaper reports, it is tempting to assume that they welcomed the contrite and disparaged the defiant, as the civil and religious authorities desired, but the response was almost certainly more complex. It is probable that the defiant manner in which some met their end in the 1790s aroused more than a tincture of sympathy, and it may be that this was extended during the early eighteenth century to Jacobite recruiting agents like Moses Nowland (42) or Captain MacDermott (29), and to those who insisted they were innocent of the crime for which they gave their life.

IV

How the public engaged with printed 'last speeches' is problematic since, in most instances, the interaction took place in an environment and at a time quite different to that in which 'last speeches' were delivered. This raises a large number of complex questions for which the information necessary to offer even tentative answers is not read-

[109] *Dublin Chronicle*, 3 Nov. 1787; *Freeman's Journal*, 20 Aug. 1799. [110] *Freeman's Journal*, 27 July 1779, 19 June, 12 July, 1 Nov. 1798; *Dublin Evening Post*, 25 May 1799.

ily available. One cannot, for example, even establish with confidence for how much they sold. Nor can one say with any certainty that the printed version corresponds with that delivered at the gallows though the difference between the time that Daniel Kimberly is recorded as having spoke and the length of the published 'last speech' suggests that in this instance at least, the published text did not correspond to what was delivered orally.[111] It may be that the published version was subject to editorial tightening, but it is equally plausible that there may have been more consequential changes; what is absolutely clear is that the printed versions of 'last speeches' required an engagement different to that accorded the oral.

From the testimony of a number of 'last speeches' that were 'deliver'd to the printer' in the presence of witnesses by their authors (52, 53, 59, 60), and the specific information that Daniel Kimberly completed his 'declaration' five days in advance, it can be established for certain that some 'last speeches' were ready in time to be printed and available for sale by the date of his execution. This seldom happened in the early eighteenth century. But the presence of the anticipatory formulations 'are to be' 'is to be' in the titles of speeches from 1717 onwards indicates that it soon caught on, and it became common practice in the mid-1720s (17, 22, 25, 27, 30, 31 etc.). Thereafter, a majority of the 'last speeches' published in Dublin were ready for sale by the day of execution. Indeed, English criminals cited the fact that it was 'very common in Dublin' in their dealings with the Newgate Ordinary when they wished to see their final words in print on the day of their execution. This appealed to prisoners in London and Northumberland because it was the best security against misrepresentation, and there is good reason to believe Irish offenders thought likewise (38, 40, 41).[112] It was welcomed by printers and publishers too because it meant that they could depute hawkers to circulate among the crowds that gathered to witness public executions and to cry them

---

[111] Kimberly supposedly spoke for two and a half hours; if true, this meant he uttered substantially more than the 3900 words in the printed version. [112] Linebaugh, 'The Ordinary of Newgate', pp 258–9; G. Morgan and Peter Rushton, *Rogues, thieves and the rule of law: the problem of law enforcement in north-east England, 1718–1800* (London, 1998), p. 147.

about the streets later the same and during the following days. Of course, last speeches were also available for purchase direct from publishers, some of whom had bookshops and others of whom worked from taverns, in Dublin as well as from the extant 'commercial networks of booksellers and their agents'.[113]

Such references to 'agents' emphasise that early eighteenth-century Dublin printers catered for an audience beyond the capital. This mirrored the situation elsewhere in Europe because, as Chartier has observed, broadsides, being among 'the most elementary products of the printing press', enjoyed the widest distribution. The Dublin book trade included among its ranks a number of printers who specialised in supplying the 'chapmen' and 'pedlars' that carried songbooks and other 'little books', ballads and broadsides 'about and dispose of them to the country people'.[114] As this suggests, in contrast to proclamations that came bearing a warning or the possibility of financial gain, 'last speeches' were commercial products. It is unlikely therefore that they were posted for general scrutiny. Like the newspaper, they were bearers of news, and they were purchased by individuals for private consumption, by taverns and coffee houses for use by their customers and, perhaps, but I have no evidence of this, by interests committed to social and moral improvement who were hopeful that their reforming message would promote enhanced conduct and behaviour.[115]

It is important for this reason to make some attempt to understand how 'last speeches' were read. Certainly, one must not assume

---

113 *The last speech and behaviour of William late Lord Russel upon the scaffold in Lincoln's inn's-field ... being condemned for High Treason in conspiring the death of the King and subversion of the Government* (Reprinted at His Majesty's Printing House on Ormonde's Quay, where are also reprinted *The last speeche, behaviour and prayers of Capt Thomas Walcot, John Rouse Gent., and William Hone, Joyner ... published by Authority ... and to be sold by Joseph Wilde, bookseller in Castle St.* (Dublin, 1683); *The whole life and character, birth, parentage and conversation, last dying speech and confession of James Cluff, who was executed at Tyburn on Friday 25th of July 1729 ...* (London printed and Dublin reprinted and sold opposite the Tholsel in Skinner Row, 1729); G.W. Painter, 'Eighteenth-century Dublin street cries', *Journal of the Royal Society of Antiquaries of Ireland*, 54 (1924), pp 69, 73, 75; Gillespie, 'The circulation of print', pp 37–8; Munter, *The Irish newspaper*, pp 79–80. 114 King to Canterbury, 1 Aug. 1719 (Trinity College Dublin, King Papers, Ms 750/5 f 189); Munter, *Print trade*, p. 133; Chartier, 'The culture of print', p. 3; Munter, *The Irish newspaper*, pp 79–80. 115 Raven, 'New reading histories', p. 277; Munter, *The Irish newspaper*, pp 50, 81.

that all were read in the same manner or that they were read primarily as reforming tracts, which is how they are largely perceived today. This raises two related but distinct questions. Who read 'last speeches' and what did they read in them? In this context, Daniel Cohen's argument that the conversion narrative of seventeenth-century New England was shaped by the religious origins, orientation and intellectual primacy of ministers in New England is pertinent because it draws attention to the fact that such print artefacts were produced with an audience in mind. However, compared with conversion sermons, Irish 'last speeches' are both more secular in tone and personal in their narration. This suggests that 'flesh-and-blood examples' had greater appeal in contemporary Ireland than 'theological argument' though the strongly scriptural content of those by Geoghegan, Hamilton and Dunbar (1, 11, 32) indicate that there was an audience for such works as well.[116] At the same time, the social role accorded the clergyman in Irish society was less central than was the case in New England, though both the conversion sermon and the 'last speech' each advanced distinctly redemptive messages.[117] Significantly, in the case of Irish 'last speeches' this is presented in a context that is more obviously punitive. There is no obvious explanation for this, but it was undoubtedly influenced by the fact that 'last speeches' arose out of a 'print culture' that attached more emphasis to news and was more attracted to sensationalism than was the case in New England.

This 'print culture' embraced a readership that consisted largely of those sometimes described as the 'middling classes'. Because this encompassed the audience – the 'social strata below the gentry' – Sharpe has identified as the readers of 'last speeches' in seventeenth-century England who (according to Rawlings) were accepting of a very stereotyped view of crime, and who may have found 'last speeches' particularly appealing, it is tempting to conclude that the situation was similar in Ireland.[118] However, Toby Barnard's detection,

---

116 Cohen, *Pillars of salt* ... , pp 57–8. 117 Ibid., chapter 1 passim; Bosco, 'Lectures at the pillory'. 118 Rawlings, *Drunks, whores and idle apprentices*, pp 3–4; Sharpe, 'Last dying speeches', p. 161.

albeit 'from dangerously small samples' from Dublin and Waterford, of 'high literacy among the middling sort – petty functionaries, skilled craft workers and modest traders and their sons'– indicates that there was a larger potential audience in early eighteenth-century Ireland.[119] This was, as Barnard notes, predominantly an urban phenomenon.[120] But the fact that chapbook men peddled their wares outside the capital suggests that there was a non-metropolitan audience as well. This is certainly compatible with the fact that the target audiences for the moral message of 'last speeches', as indicated by those whose sentiments reached print, embraced children, apprentices, servants, casual workers, tradesmen and demobilised soldiers who were not only to be found in the capital. It also suggests that literacy levels among these social groups may also have been sufficiently advanced to allow many to engage personally with such publications. One must, at the same time, take notice of Chartier's warning,

> that it is no longer tenable to try to establish strict correspondences between cultural cleavages and social hierarchies, creating simplistic relationships between particular cultural objects or forms and specific social groups. On the contrary, it is necessary to recognize the fluid circulation and shared practices that crossed social boundaries.[121]

In this context, Lord Chesterfield's frequently cited observation that 'solid folios are the people of business with whom I converse in the morning. Quartos are the easier mixed company with whom I sit after dinner; and I pass my evenings in the light, and often frivolous chitchat of small octavos and duodecimos' is cautionary, not because there is no mention of broadsides but because it reveals the variety of texts that an individual could embrace and elides the social distinctions traditionally drawn between the consumers of what continue to be denominated 'high' and 'popular' culture.[122] Based on the fact that

---

[119] Barnard, 'Reading in eighteenth-century Ireland', p. 61; idem, 'Learning, the learned and literacy', pp 220–1. [120] Barnard, 'Reading in eighteenth-century Ireland', p. 62. [121] Chartier, 'Texts, printing, readings', p. 169. [122] Ibid., pp 166, 168 (the Chesterfield quote is taken from p. 168); Rawling, *Drunks, whores and idle apprentices*, p. 14.

'last speeches' were part of a larger broadside phenomenon that specialised in sensational crimes, it may be tempting to assume that the audience was lower class because this is what appealed to persons of this socio-economic cohort rather than to the educated elite. However, it cannot be sustained evidentially, and the fact that 'last speeches' were commercial products meant they were available to anyone who could afford to buy them. Moreover, there is no conclusive evidence to suggest that the elite were any less interested than the *hoi polloi* in such publications. It is simplistic for this reason to present the 'last speech' in Gramscian terms as a quintessential hegemonic product that sought to foster a conformist ideology among the populace because, while it is indisputable that a majority promoted the merits of living a moral, law-abiding and Godly life, it is not clear that these were the messages that were received. In this respect, the fact that they were not all equally accessible and therefore, by implication, neither targeted at a uniform audience nor received in the same manner by those who engaged with them is significant.

This is hardly a contentious conclusion since it is now recognised that in the past as much as in the present, printed texts 'crossed social boundaries and drew readers from very different social and economic levels'.[123] This is not empirically demonstrable for early eighteenth-century Ireland because of the lack of evidence on the reading habits of substantial numbers of individuals across a range of social groups, but there is no *a priori* reason why 'last speeches' could not sustain a number of 'interpretive communities'. Taking Chartier's definition of a 'community' as a group of 'readers whose members share the same reading styles and the same strategies of interpretation', it can be suggested that gallows's speeches were read and interpreted differently by individuals within as well as across a variety of socio-economic categories.[124] It is improbable, certainly, that the experience was the same for the *canaille* who provided a majority of those who were executed, and who were the primary target of their didactic and homiletic messages; for those of a 'middling sort', eager to promote adherence to

---

123 Chartier, 'Print culture', p. 4. 124 Chartier, 'Texts, printing, readings', p. 158; Raven, 'New reading histories', p. 270.

the laws of God and man; and for members of the ruling elite who facilitated and favoured their production. Moreover, within and across these socio-economic categories, the response generated differed depending on whether individuals or groups engaged with the speeches as reformist tracts, as works of religious edification, as news items or as sensationalist literature. In short, while the predominant ideological message of 'last speeches' may have conveyed accurately the political, legal, religious and social aspirations of the hegemonic elite, it is equally likely that each 'interpretive community' engaged with certain texts more closely than others and that each drew different lessons from the experience. Thus middle and upper class readers were drawn to the speeches of Edmund Budd (7), Charles Donnell (8), Joseph Poe (36), John Audouin (47), Daniel Kimberly (51), Edward Sewell (59, 60), Gerald Byrne, and James and Patrick Strange (61) because these alerted them to the fact that even members of the elite could end up on the gallows, while readers of a lower socio-economic station were reassured to learn that their 'betters' could be brought to heel. Obviously, the length and complexity of narratives also had a bearing on who bought and, by extension, on how individual 'last speeches' were read. It is improbable, for example, that the long 'speeches' uttered by middle class offenders (47, 51) or those with a strongly didactic Scriptural content (11, 32) were read by the same audience or were interpreted in the same way as the shorter, less varnished narratives of habitual criminals. Similarly, it is unlikely that avowed Jacobites read the last words of those involved in recruiting for the Pretender such as Robert Malone (23), Captain MacDermott (27) and Moses Nowland (42) or those of Tories such as Charles Carragher (20) or Daniel Crossagh O'Mullan (56) in the same manner as strong Williamites, or that either were more attracted by moral didacticism than they were by the details of the acts for which the offenders were sent to die.

To conclude that people read 'last speeches' and interpreted them differently depending on their social interests, political orientation, attitudinal disposition, life experience is not a modern insight. The sixteenth-century Spanish playwright Fernando de Rojas said of one of his plays that it was subject to three different 'readings'. The first category of readers was that which focussed on 'certain detached episodes' rather than on the play in its entirety. Others recalled only 'easily memorized' phrases and terms that they introduced as 'clichés and ready-made expressions' into daily conversation; while the third reading involved embracing 'the text in its complex totality'.[125] Such a schema may not be applicable to simpler publications such as a 'last speech' but, no less than de Rojas' play, it was not possessed of 'a single fixed meaning', though 'the construction of meaning by which readers diversely appropriated the object of their reading' in this instance is especially elusive.[126] A potential way forward, identified by Chartier and endorsed by Raven, McGann and others, is to combine 'for each sort of material considered, a description of formal elements (print format, page layout, the nature and placement of pictorial material) with an identification of the uses, implicit or explicit, that relied on those formal elements'.[127] This is beyond the scope of this introduction, but a number of points can be made.

One of the most striking features of Irish, and indeed of English, 'last speeches' is the austerity of their presentation. This was a result in the first instance of the fact that they were simple print artefacts. The typical broadside restricted text to one side of a single leaf of paper. Further, the text was generally printed in black in roman type of a standard size,[128] relieved only by capitalisation and italicisation, with little or no ornamentation. Indeed, compared with the French *placard*, many of which were profusely illustrated, or contemporary funeral odes which highlighted their doleful purpose by presenting text, complete with symbolic wood cuts, within a black outline, they can seem dull and uninteresting.[129] This conclusion is not invalidated

---

125 De Rojas conclusions are outlined by Chartier, 'Texts, printing, reading', pp 154–5. 126 Chartier, 'Texts, printing, reading', passim. 127 Chartier, 'The culture of print, pp 4–5. This approach has received wide endorsement; James Raven cites D.F. McKenzie and Jerome J McGann in support of 're-examining evidence relating to the physical text, from its composition, typographical presentation and material form, to the social, economic and political circumstances of its publication' (Raven, 'New reading histories', p. 269). 128 It is significant, in this context, that collections of statutes and proclamations frequently used Gothic text. See the collection of proclamations in the National Archives of Ireland, and the printed acts of parliament. 129 See, for example, *England's sorrow and the soldiers in tears for the loss of their king and General, William III*

even by the case of the 'last speech' of Catherine McCanna (52) since the unsophisticated woodcut of an execution procession in which a female offender, accompanied by a clergyman and a coffin, was being ferried to a gallows was not optimally located beneath the title.[130] The comparative crudeness of the imagery presented in this 'speech' and its complete absence elsewhere ensured that the interaction between the consumer and the 'last speech' was with words rather than with images. This meant literacy was essential if an individual was to gain full access. Moreover, given that as many as a thousand words could be crowded onto a single page, and that a significant proportion of speeches extending to two or more pages were longer, this must have posed a challenge to those whose literacy skills were but passing fair.

To be sure, the layout of 'last speeches', like that of crime and trial reports, was not utterly unaccommodating. Most, though not all, came equipped with generously large titles that amply advertised the fact that what followed presented the 'last speech', 'dying words', 'particular confession' or 'genuine declaration' of a capital offender. The size of the font used in the title ranged greatly from standard 12 point to 24 to 36 point, and it was not unusual for as much as 20 per cent of the page to be allocated to the title. Furthermore, most commenced with the inviting apostrophe 'Good Christians' or 'Good People', and concluded, equally consistently with a direct invitation to readers to forgive and to pray for the author. The text was written in almost all cases (that of Sarah Grew (16) is an exception) in the first person and in an autobiographical form, which facilitated the reader's engagement with the narrative. Obviously, the sense of authenticity thereby generated was negated in those instances in which two 'last speeches' were each described as genuine.[131] This was, as already shown, uncom-

---

... (Dublin, 1701); *An elegy on the death of the French King* ... (Dublin, 1709); *An elegy on the much lamented death of Joseph, Emperor of Germany* ... (Dublin, 1711); *An elegy on the much lamented death of the Rt hon R. Freeman, one of the Lords Justices* ... (Dublin, 1711); Christian Jouhaud, 'Readability and persuasion: political handbills' in Chartier, ed., *The culture of print*, pp 235–60. 130 In *A funeral elegy on the ever to be lamented deaths of Mr Richard Johnson and Mr John Porter* [Dublin, 1730] there is a woodcut of a mourning coach drawn by eight horses featured at the bottom of the broadside. 131 See above, pp 47-8.

mon, but in order to deflect suspicion some publishers offered an invitation to readers to inspect the original at their offices, and while it may be significant that this happened rarely, it is striking that even those that can clearly be identified as forgeries (41, 60, for example) were not misleading.[132] Furthermore, the existence of a number of unpublished autobiographical memoirs written by offenders while awaiting their date with the gallows tends to reinforce the conclusion that most 'last speeches' provide an honest account of their subject's life and deeds.[133]

Engagement with the content of 'last speeches' was eased further by the fact that they were written in straightforward, accessible language unencumbered with the recondite learning derived from history or classical mythology that characterised the *placard*.[134] Such learning as was manifested was Scriptural, and was to be found particularly in those 'last speeches' prepared by offenders with a developed religious sensibility (1, 11, 32). The length of the 'speech' or 'confession' varied according to the disposition, profile and notoriety of the offender. The shortest were invariably presented in broadsides that related the final words of multiple offenders and they were invariably conveniently sign-posted by 'visible landmarks' that indicated clearly whose speech followed.[135] Short speeches of this ilk could be read and absorbed by those with appropriate reading skills in the space of a few moments. Wordier examples took longer, but since slightly above 50 per cent were less than 750 words and nearly 75 per cent less than a thousand, most could be read comfortably within a short time by those with an adequate reading ability. Indeed, even *The declaration and dying words of Daniel Kimberly* (51) was not so demanding that an individual, silent reading, could not take it in at a single sitting. Moreover, in this, as in other instances, the extensive use of italics and different fonts was an effective if unsophisticated device to guide readers through extended slabs of text and to highlight key points (2, 10, 14, 17, 20, 23, 26, 32, 40, 51, 59). In those examples in which the speeches of multiple offenders

---

132 In this context, Philip Rawling's discussion of the case of John Reid is pertinent (*Drunks, whores and idle apprentices*, pp 6, 7). 133 See, for example, 'The birth, life, education and transactions of Capt. William Owen, the noted smuggler' (National Library of Wales, Ms 21834). 134 Jouhaud, 'Political handbills', pp 235–60 passim.

were provided, the judicious use of italics served a similar purpose (4, 5, 12, 17, 18, 22, 25, 43, 50).

A familiarity with the formula according to which 'last speeches' were constructed obviously helped readers. So too did the language employed when what originated as essentially oral testimony was presented in a manner that was sensitive to speech patterns, colloquialisms and vernacular usage. This may not always seem obvious to the modern reader who can find the erratic or grammatically erroneous punctuation this encouraged obstructive, but it is palpably less so if the modern reader engages with the text as oral testimony rather than as writing that is grammatically deficient. In should be noted in this context that modern readers find deviations from orthographic and syntactical norms more challenging than contemporaries who had less exacting expectations. An instructive comparison can be made with the '*bibliotheque bleue*' of eighteenth-century France. It appealed to 'the rudimentary reader' who 'was comfortable ... with brief, self-contained, often disjointed sequences, and apparently was satisfied with minimal global coherence ...' Indeed, in direct contrast to the sophisticated reader, 'the rudimentary reader could tolerate the dross left in the text by hasty and cheap manufacturing processes (for example, the countless misprints ... confusions of names and words, multiple errors).'[136] There was certainly plenty of 'dross' in evidence in some poorly written and hastily composed 'last speeches' of Irish origin to appeal to the aforesaid 'rudimentary reader'. Moreover, because their reading style was predisposed to engage in an episodic way with the text, this was not especially discouraging. The fact that over time readers became familiar with the structure and approach of the 'last speech' more than compensated for syntactical inconsistencies and typographical errors. It also facilitated them to make sense of the text because they approached it with a significant measure of 'preknowledge' that could be mobilised to facilitate comprehension.

If this empowered 'rudimentary' readers, they and others were helped also by the fact that the layout of most was generous compared with early eighteenth-century newspapers, where the print size

---

135 Chartier, 'Texts, printing, reading', p. 164. 136 Ibid., pp 164–5.

was uniformly smaller, and where stories, reports and advertisements were packed tightly into printed columns that employed fewer and smaller headlines. Pamphlets too made few concessions to their readers. Most were tightly printed, loosely sown and, unless bound to order, were contained within limp covers that were neither aesthetically pleasing nor especially functional. To be sure, pamphlets and newspapers were well suited to personalised, private reading, because of their size and the layout of print on their pages, but the broadside had the advantage when it was a matter of shared or public readings, both of which were commonplace in Ireland. For, as Gillespie has noted, it was expected that those who were literate would read to those who were not, and given that public reading was a central feature of civil, religious and private life – town criers read proclamations, clerics read Scripture, individuals read to each other in the tavern, the coach and at home – the public reading of 'last speeches' was neither unusual nor unanticipated.[137] But it was not only the reading aloud by the literate to the illiterate that the broadside facilitated; by reason of its form and manner of printing, the broadside was particularly suited to shared reading, and to 'decipherment in common' when those who knew how to read guided those who did not. Such occasions invested the reading of the 'last speech' with qualities quite different to those generated by 'solitary book reading'.[138]

The oral, vernacular and autobiographical approach of 'last speeches' meant they were particularly suited to reading aloud. Oral narratives, as Chartier has argued, tend to be less disciplined, more circumlocutory than literary narratives. However, in the case of 'last speeches' the oral character of the printed narrative facilitated understanding when read aloud because it meant that the audience was listening to what was essentially an oral narrative in print. This was quite different to the experience of reading or hearing a purely written text. It was also a different experience to individual silent reading.[139] What this emphasises is that the distinction traditionally drawn between oral and written culture cannot be sustained for the early

---

137 Gillespie, 'The spread of print', p. 33; Chartier, 'Texts, printing, readings', p. 159.
138 Chartier, 'Print culture', pp 1–2. 139 Ibid., p. 7; idem, 'Texts, printings, readings', pp 159–60.

eighteenth century when mass literacy did not exist. This conclusion is reinforced by the popularity of ballads as a medium of communication and commentary on current events and by the overlap that existed between them and the 'last speech'. A ready example is provided by the ballads generated by the Johnson/Porter case in 1730. In this instance the experience of Richard Johnson and John Porter was publicly recorded in a 'last speech', a ballad and an elegy as well as in newspapers, thereby reinforcing Robert Darnton's observation, based on his exploration of the *chansonniers* of eighteenth-century Paris, that it makes 'no sense ... to separate printed from oral and written modes of communication, as we casually do when we speak of 'print culture' because they were all bound together in a multi-media system'.[140] It is hoped that this collection will contribute to the recognition that 'a multi-media system' existed also in eighteenth-century Ireland.

V

The sixty-one broadsides and one pamphlet presented in this collection are reproduced from extant original copies. The guiding editorial principle that has informed the preparation of this edition has been to provide an accurate transcription of the original printed text inclusive of the eccentric punctuation, erratic capitalisation and inconsistent spelling that are a feature of many originals. There are a number of exceptions; the layout of the title, which conforms in the originals to no precise pattern, has been systematised; the sibilant 'f' is silently altered to 's'; in the small number of occasions that the printer inverted a 'u' or an 'n', these have been silently corrected in the belief that they were unintentional and that their retention would be confusing. Similarly, in the even smaller number of cases where two 'V's were aligned to create a capital 'W' this practice has not been repeated. These apart, every effort has been made to present an accurate text of the 'speeches' as they were published, complete with pub-

---

[140] Robert Darnton, 'An early information society: news and media in eighteenth-century Paris', *American Historical Review*, 105 (2000), pp 28–30; Chartier, 'Texts, printing, readings', p. 170.

lishers' imprint and date and place of publication where available. Since, as already observed, the rules of grammar were adhered to less rigidly in the early eighteenth century than is the case today, this makes demands on the reader above the ordinary, as authors and printers took considerable liberties with orthography, typography, punctuation and good printing practice. The problem is compounded in the case of those 'last speeches' that have not survived complete. In the largest number of cases, cropping at binding has resulted in the loss of the publisher's imprint. In a number of other instances dampness or decay have achieved the same result. In all, ten broadsides have experienced this loss (13, 17, 18, 27, 32, 33, 35, 36, 46, 56). More consequently, there are a smaller number of examples in which defective or deficient copies of the original are all that have survived. The most seriously affected is *The last speech, confession and dying words of James Dunbar* (32), which has experienced a significant loss of text to one column recto and verso. A close reading of the text has allowed a suggested reading to be offered at a number, but not all points. These readings are presented in square brackets, but their tentative character must be stressed. A tear at the bottom right hand corner to the *Last speech and dying words of Richard Lawler, Jeremiah Fitzpatrick, James Quin and Alexander MacCann* (13) has also resulted in a loss of text but it is confined to a small number of words in the speeches of James Quin and Alexander McCann. Once again, and with somewhat more success, a conjectural reading of the original is offered, and it is possible to read the text with minimal inconvenience. This is true also of *The last speech and dying words of Valentine Kealy and Cornelius Svlevan* (27), which has also experienced a small tear, and the loss of a number of words, that are conjecturally reconstructed and indicated in square brackets.

 The narratives printed below are not individually annotated for the simple reason that they are, in most instances, the primary source of information on the individuals and incidents they describe. It is possible, of course, to expand on the cases that brought a number of individuals to the gallows,[141] but since this would serve to highlight

---

141 For example, John Audouin (for whom see Kelly, 'A most inhuman and barbarous

INTRODUCTION

the absence of information in most other instances it has not been attempted. Each of the narratives relayed in this collection provides a life history that the reader can engage with on a number of levels without the need for guidance from what, in any event, could only be an inadequate attempt to gloss most of the individuals and incidents that populate the collection. Its presentation will, I hope, help to rescue a *genre* of early publication from obscurity. More consequently, it should facilitate further and deeper exploration of the *demimonde* of the early eighteenth century as the colourful parade of characters revealed illuminate a world filled by the marginalized as well as the criminal, the unlucky as well as the opportunistic, the incorrigible as well as the innocent. As a result, it should facilitate further reconstruction of the *milieu* as well as the *mentalité* that generated crime and the response thereto in eighteenth-century Ireland.

piece of villainy', p. 85); Gerald Byrne and the Strange brothers (see Margery Weiner, *Matters of felony: a reconstruction* (London, 1967); Kelly, 'The abduction of women of fortune', pp 31–2); Charles Carragher and Shane Crossagh (see Stephen Dunford, *The Irish highwayman* (Dublin, 2000), pp 115–24, 163–70).

List of speeches

1. The Last Speech and Confession of Mr. James Geoghegan, Priest of the Order of St Francis, who was Executed at the Common Place of Execution near Dublin, on Saturday the Tenth of this Instant February, 1693. As it was delivered by his own Hand to be Printed, before he went to Execution (Dublin, 1694).

2. The Last Speech and Dying-Words of John Balfe, Who was Executed at St. Stephens-Green, for Robbery, On Saturday the Fifteenth of June, 1706 (Dublin, 1706).

3. The Last Speech and Dying-Words of Edward English, Butcher. Who was Executed at St. Stephens Green, for Robbing of one Mr. Beasley at the Green-Hills, On Friday the 5th of December, 1707 (Dublin, 1707).

4. The Last Speeches and Dying Words of Edward Flood and Hugh Caffrey. Who was Executed at St. Stephens Green, On Friday the 5th of December, 1707 for Robbing of Mr. Casey, at Cabbra [Dublin, 1707].

5. The True Speech and Last Dying Words Of Patrick Illan, Lawrence Halpeny, James Quin, and Patrick Mc.Shane, who were Executed at Killmainham, on Thursday the 25th day of March, 1708 (Dublin 1708).

6. The Last Speeches and Dying Words of Thomas Renals, and Richard Perry Alias Barry, who were Executed at Kilmainham, on Wednesday the 7th of May 1712 (Dublin, 1712).

7. Ensign Edmund Budd's Speech Who Suffered near St Stephen's Green, on Saturday the 8th of November, 1712 (Dublin, 1712).

LIST OF SPEECHES

8   The Last Speech and Dying Words of Charles Donnell of the City of Dublin Gent, who was Executed near St Stephen's Green, on Saturday the 8th of November, 1712 (Dublin, 1712).

9   The Last Speech and Dying Words of Peter Dalton, Who was Executed near St. Stephen's Green, on Saturday the 23d of August 1712 (Dublin, 1712).

10   The Last Speeches and Dying Words of John Davis, James Demsye, and William Ledwidge, Who were Executed near St Stephens-Green, on Saturday the 27th of June, 1713 (Dublin, 1713).

11   The Last Speech and Dying Words of James Hamilton in the Parish of Kilmore in the County of Down; who was executed at Downpatrick for the Bloody and Hainous Murder of William Lammon, the 17 of April, 1714 (Glasgow, 1714).

12   The Last Speeches And Dying Words Of John Riley, Alexander Bourk, Martin Carrol, James Commins, Thomas Neal, Neal Lacy, Michael Cleary, alias Mc. Daniel, Who were Executed on the 26th of June, 1714 (Dublin, 1714).

13   Last Speech and Dying Words, Of Richard Lawler, Jeremiah Farrel, James Quin, and Alexander Mac Cann, who were Executed at St Stephen's-Green, on Saturday the 10th of December, 1715 [Dublin, 1715].

14   The Last Speech And Dying Words of Garrett Landergan who was Executed at St. Stephens-Green on Saturday the 19th of this Inst. January 1716-17 (Dublin, 1717).

15   Speeches and Dying Words of James Nowlan, and John Fitz-Symmons, who were Executed near St Stephens-Green, on Saturday the 23d of February, 1716-17 (Dublin 1716-17).

16   A Particular Confession of Sarah Grew just now going to Execution at St. Stephens-Green, being the 13th day of July 1717 With particular Accounts of Thefts and Correspondents, and Receivers of the Goods, for which she was Convicted and Condemn'd (Dublin, [1717]).

LIST OF SPEECHES

17   The Speeches of Captain Maurice Fitzgerald, Charles Burn and Francis Burn, who are to be executed at Blessing-town, on Friday the 27th of this Instant December, 1717 [Dublin, 1717].

18   The Last Speech And Dying Words of Daniel O Neal, Edmond Mc.Guire, and Henery Graham, who was Executed near St. Stevens Green, on Wednesday June the 4th 1718 [Dublin, 1718].

19   The Last Speech And Dying Words of John Magee who was Executed near St. Stephens Green this 18th, Day of February 1718-19 for stealing a Bay Gelding from Mr. Robinet the Attorney (Dublin, [1719]).

20   The Last Speech and Dying Words of Charles Calahar alias Collmore who was Try'd on Tuesday the 17th Inst. Feb. 1718/19 at the Sessions of Dundalk, for being a Proclaim'd Tory, and was the next Day Hang'd, Quarter'd and his Intrals burn'd (Dublin, 1719).

21   The Last Speeches Of Patrick Carraghar, Nephew of the great Collmore, and Two Arthur Quinns, who were Executed on Saturday the 21st of this Instant February, 1718/19 at Dundalk, Together with the Tryal of Capt. Collmore (Dublin, 1719).

22   The Last Speeches And Dying Words of Darby McCormock, James McManus; Hugh Ferloy, Edward McMahan, Anne Buttler alias Morris; Rose Gorman and Sisly Burke, who are to be Executed near St.Stephens-Green on Saturday the 12th Instant. 1720 [Dublin, 1720].

23   The Last Speech And Dying Words of Robert Malone, late Informer of the City of Dublin who was Executed at Tyburn the 30th of April 1723: For the Robbery of a Clergyman, near London (Dublin, 1723).

24   The Last Speech And Dying Words of Captain Collins Who was Executed at Kingston in Surry, the 4th, of October Inst. (Dublin, [1723]).

25   The Last Speech, Confession and Dying Words of Henery Watts, Philip Reily, and Edward Fox a Boy, who are all to be Executed near St. Stephen's Green, this present Saturday being the second of this Instant November 1723 (Dublin, 1723).

LIST OF SPEECHES

26 The Last Speech, and Dying Words of James Casady, Beggar Man who was Executed this Day, being the 27th of this Instant January, 1724-5, at Kilmainham, for robbing on the High-Road (Dublin, 1725).

27 The Last Speech And Dying Words of Valintine Kealy, and Cornealus Svlavan, who is both to be Executed near St. Stephen's-Green, this present Saturday being the 13th, Inst. March 1724-5. For Robberys Committed by them [Dublin, 1724-5].

28 The Last Speech, Confession and Dying Words of William Dickson, who was Try'd and Condemned, for High Treason against his Majesty King George, for Counterfeiting the current Coin of Great Britain, at the General Assizes holden at Ardmagh, the 23d of March, 1725, and was Executed, Tuesday the 13th of April, for the same; with an Account of the Coller he had to save himself, as it was taken from his own Mouth in the Goal, &c. (Dublin, 1725).

29 The Last Speech and Dying Words of Cap. Mc.Dermot who was formerly concern'd in Listing men for the Pretender; and was Hang'd and Quarter'd at Cavan, on Tuesday the 30th of March 1725, for most barbarously Murdering of one J. Dalley on the High-Road (Dublin [1725]).

30 The Last Speech, Confession and Dying Words of John Comber; who is to be Hang'd and Quarter'd this present Wednesday, being the 5th, of this Inst. May 1725. Near St. Stephen's Green; for Murdering Councellor Hoar, in January last (Dublin, 1725).

31 The Last Speech, Confession, and Dying Words of John Coamber, who is to be Hang'd, Drawn and Quarter'd this Day, being the 5th of this Instant May 1725, for the Murder of Councellor HOAR in Henry Street the 19th of Jan. last (Dublin, 1725).

32 The Last Speech, Confession And Dying Words of Mr. J. Dunbar, who was Try'd and Condemn'd, for High Treason against his Majesty King George; at the Assizes, of Oyer, Terminer, or Goal Delivery, holden, at Carrickfergus, for and in the County of Antrim, the 17th Day of Ma. 1725. And was Executed Saturday, April 10th for the same together with his last Advice to his Children prov'd by Scripture Texts, &c. As it was

LIST OF SPEECHES

taken from his own Mouth in the Goal, and desir'd to be Printed [Dublin, 1725].

33 The Last Speech And Dying Words of Ellinor Sils, who is to be Burn't alive this present Wednesday being the 19th of this Instant May 1725. For Murdering her own Child [Dublin, 1725].

34 The Last Speech, Confession and Dying Words of John Mc Coy, Thomas Barnet, John Smith, and Owen Geoghegan; who are to be Executed near St. Stephen's-Green, this present Wednesday being the 13th Inst. October 1725. For Robbing Mr. George Scrivener, the 25th of September last, of a Silk Purse vallued one Shilling; with Sixteen Moydors in Gold [Dublin, 1725].

35 The Last Speeches and Dying Words of John Mc.Coy, Tho. Barnet, Owen Geohegan, and John Smith, who are to be Executed this Day being the 13th of this Inst. Octob. 1725, for Robbing the Lord Chancellors Gentleman in Grafton-street [Dublin, 1725].

36 The Last Speech And Dying Words of Cornet Joseph Poe, and Nicholas Cox, who are to be Executed near Kilmainham on Wednesday the 20th, of this Instant October 1725, Cor. Poe for the Robbing of Michael Hall and Anthony Costelow, two Frizemongers, on the 25th of September last, on the High Road near Tallow-Hill. And Nicholas Cox for Cow Stealing [Dublin, 1725].

37 The Last Speech And Dying Words Of Anne Pepper, who is to be Executed at St. Stevens-Green on Saturday the 22d of this Inst January 1725 (Dublin, 1725).

38 The Last Speech And Dyeing Words of Thomas Craven and William Anderson, who is to be Executed this present Saturday being the 29th of this Instant January 1725-6. near Killmainham (Dublin, 1726).

39 The Last Speech, Confession and Dying Words of Francis Mc.Cabe, William Cunneen, and Edward Fox, who are to be Hang'd this present Saturday being the 14th, Inst. May, 1726 near St. Stephens Green; the two Former for Robbing Mr. Delamin, the Latter for picking Mr. Smith's Pocket in Newgate (Dublin, 1726).

LIST OF SPEECHES

40   The True Last Speech, Confession, and Dying Words of Mr. James Stevens and Account of Patrick Barnwell, who are to be executed at St. Stephens Green, on Wednesday the 25th Inst. May, 1726, being condemn'd for feloniously taking from Mr. Philip Kennersly of Dame-street, a Glass-case, Value 50l (Dublin, [1726]).

41   The Last Speech, Confession and dying Words of Patrick Barnel, and James Stephens, who are to be executed at St. Stephens Green, this present Wednesday, the 25th of this Inst. May 1726. For the Robbery of Mr. Kennersly in Dames-Street (Dublin, [1726]).

42   The Last Speech, Confession and dying Words of Moses Nowland who is to be hang'd at St Stephen's Green, for inlisting Men for the Service of the Pretender, on Wednesday being the 6th of July 1726 (Dublin, [1726]).

43   Speech, Confession and Dying Words of James Dealy Constable, John Dobin Butcher, and Edward Dunn; who are to be Executed near St. Stephens Green, this present Saturday being the 21st. of this Instant January 1726-7 (Dublin, [1727]).

44   The Last Speeches And Dying Words of Tully Slevin, John Dempsy, and Patrick Murphy, who is to be hanged Drawn and Quartred at St. Stephens Green for Coyning Gold this present Wednesday being the 3d of May 1727 (Dublin, 1727).

45   The Last and True Speech, Confession and Dyeing Words of John Mac-Gurran, alias Cockels, and Michael Tankard, who are both to be Executed this present Wednesday being the 27th of this instant September, 1727. For feloniously breaking open and Robbing the Dwelling House of Squire Winfield in Caple-street, the beginning of this Instant [Dublin, 1727].

46   The Last and True Speech, Confession and Dyeing Words of Martin Mackanally and Bryan Lacy, who are to be Executed near Kilmainham, this present Wednesday being the 18th of this Instant October 1727. Martin Mackanally for Ravishment, and Bryan Lacy for Robery [Dublin, 1727].

LIST OF SPEECHES

47 The Last Speech, Confession and Dying Words of Surgeon John Odwin, who is to be Executed near St Stephen's-Green: On Wednesday being the 5th of June, 1728. For the Murder of his Servant Maid Margaret Keef (Dublin, 1728).

48 The last and True Speech, Confession and Dying Words of Alexander Mac Daniell, and Philip A-Thoush (alias Malone,) who is to be Executed near St. Stephen's-Green, this present Saturday being the 24th day of January 1728-9 (Dublin, [1729]).

49 The Last and True Speech, Confession and Dying Words of Daniel Ross, who is to Executed near St. Stephen's-Green this present Saturday, being the 15th of this Instant February 1728-9 (Dublin, [1729]).

50 The Last Speech, Confession and dying words, of Alexander Graham, and Michael Kearone, who is to be Executed near St. Stephen's Green, this present Saturday, being the 6th of this Inst. Sept. 1729, for several Robberies committed by them (Dublin, 1729).

51 The Declaration, And Dying Words of Daniel Kimberly, Gentleman, Who was Executed at St. Stephen's Green, on Wednesday, May 27th, 1730 at 38 Minutes past three o' Clock in the Afternoon (Dublin, [1730]).

52 The Last Speech, Confession and Dyeing Words of Cathrine M'Canna, who is to be Executed near St. Stephens Green, this present Wednesday being the 23d of this Instant September 1730. She being Guilty of several Robberies, in and about the City of Dublin (Dublin, [1730]).

53 The True and Genuine Declarations of Mr. Richard Johnston and John Porter, Who were Executed near Stevens-Green, on Saturday the 12th day of Dec. 1730. for the Murder of Patrick Murphy, a Salter of Beef and Herrings, at the Union on Temple-Bar, early on Wednesday Morning, the 21st of October last (Dublin, [1730]).

54 The Last Speech, Confession and Dying Words of Edward Keating, Charles Neil, Terence Riely, James Graham, and Will. Henry, who are to be Executed this present Saturday being the 27th of this Instant February 1730-31. near St. Stephens Green (Dublin, [1731]).

LIST OF SPEECHES

55   The whole Declaration and last Speech, Confession and Dying Words of Capt. Daniel M'Guire, who is to be Executed near St. Stephens Green, this present Wednesday being the 28th of this Inst. July 1731. For Robbing of Thomas Bryan in Fingal, and puting him on a hot Griddle to make him Confess his Money, the 18th of November last (Dublin, [1731]).

56   The Last Speech and Dying Words of Daniel Crossagh O-Mullan, Shaen Crossagh O-Mullan and Rory, alias Roger Roe O-Haran, who were Executed at London-Derry, April the 18th, 1733 [Dublin, 1733]

57   The Genuin Declaration, and last Dying Speech Of Pierce Tobin and Walter Kelly Sailors, who are to be Hang'd and Quarter'd near St. Stephen's Green, for the Murder of Vastin Tunburgh a Dutch Skipper, this present Saturday being the 27th of this Instant July 1734 (Dublin, [1734]).

58   The true Declaration, and last Speech, Confession and Dying Words of Denis Watch alias Watson and John Dougherty, who are both to be Executed near St Stephen's Green this present Saturday being the 31st of this Instant July 1736. For several Robberies committed by them (Dublin, [1736]).

59   The Genuine Declaration Of Edward Shuel a degraded Clergyman of the Church of Ireland, who is to be Executed near St. Stephens Green, this present Saturday being the 29th of this Instant November 1740. For celebrating the Clandestine Marriage of one Mr. Walker a Protestant, to Margaret Talbot a suppos'd Catholick, on Sunday the 16th of August last, at the World's End near Dublin (Dublin, [1740]).

60   The Last and True Speech of Mr. Sewell, a degraded Clergyman, who was executed last Saturday the 29th of November 1740, at St. Stephen's-Green, for a clandestine Marriage delivered by him at the Place of Execution [Dublin, 1740].

61   The Last Speech, Confession, and dying declaration of Gerald Byrne and James and Patrick Strange, who were executed at Gallows-green, Kilkenny, on Saturday the 2d of December, 1780, for carrying away

LIST OF SPEECHES

Catherine and Ann Kennedy, from Graigenamana, in the County of Kilkenny (Enniscorthy [1780]).

62 The Final Confession of Thomas Neil [Dublin, 1798].

LAST SPEECHES: TEXTS

I

THE LAST SPEECH AND CONFESSION OF

Mr. James Geoghegan

Priest of the Order of St. Francis, who was Executed at the Common Place of Execution near Dublin, on Saturday the Tenth of this Instant February, 1693. As it was delivered by his own Hand to be Printed, before he went to Execution.

Being lately called to an Account for my manifold Misdemeanors, and my Crimes having justly render'd me undeserving the Society of Men, I am now to end a Scandalous Life, by a deserved Ignominious Death. My Capital Crime, (out of which all my Iniquities have Sprung) is Disobedience: For as Obedience is the Golden Basis and Foundation of all Laws, Humane and Divine, and as 1 *Pet.22. Ex side nascitur, & sacrificiis praestantior;* Disobedience being directly opposite, is the Source of all *Evil*, and renders a Man incapable, whilst in that State, of the Protection of the *Eternal Being* (on which all things depend, and which can Annihilate as well as Create this World, and all things therein) as likewise of the Temporal Laws which rules us here. Into this great Gulf I have (*dear Christians*) unfortunately plunged my self; and when once I relished of the *Evils* of a Voluptuous Life, one Mischief ushered in another, *Abyssus abyssum invocat*; and I no longer acted like a Loyal Subject to my Redeemer, but became an Apostate and perfect Child of *Belial*. In this State and condition I continued for several years, falsely accusing the Innocent, Violating by my untrue Testimony both the Liberties and Properties of honest Men, and abusing the Sacred Order of which I was an unworthy Member, and Several other Sacred Religious Orders, by pretending to be of their Confraternities, whilst an Apostate, the better to attain to my wicked ends. Most dear Christians, there is nothing now left principally, but the Sacred Name of Christ, *Christus satisfactio est sine qua nemo videbit faciem Dei:* it is by Him, and through the Merits of his Passion I expect Salvation; He is the Balsam that Cures and Removes the Iniquities of this frail Life: *Sicut ligat Diabolus qui peccata connectit, ita solvit Christo qui debita demittit.*

I do, dear Christians, to the World acknowledge my self guilty of several grievous Crimes, as well as of that whereof I have been by the Law *Convicted*, tho' not in the same manner as I have been Accused; the things alledged to be Stolen by me being Lent me, and not Stolen; yet now I freely forgive my Accuser. To repeat my manifold *Errors* might require more time than the present Circumstances of a Penitent Criminal can well afford: But in particular I humbly beg Pardon of Mr. *Peaton*, my Lord *Bussine,* one Mr. *Broughil*, and *Garret Nugent*, being severally most Unjustly Accused by me of Crimes they never committed. For all which I am truly penitent and sorrowful; and do humbly implore all others which I have offended to forgive me; Acknowledging that I never knew any Mans Crime either against State or Government, of which I did accuse them. And wishing that the Infamous Death which justly I am to undergo, may be acceptable in the presence of the Lord and his People, as a Satisfaction for the Crimes I committed. And I do in the sight of God declare my self Innocent of the Blood of my Lord Primate *Plunket*, tho' I have been Charged to have accused him wrongfully. Now trusting to Him whose Mercy is infinite, I humbly beg the Prayers of all Faithful Christians, and especially of that Order of which I was (tho' most unworthy) a Member. Now confiding in the Mercy of God, I conclude with the Saying of St. *Paul, Cupio dissolvi, & esse cum Christo.*

JAMEES GEOGHEGAN.

DUBLIN, Printed by Samuel Lee in Skinner-Row, near the Tholsel. 1694.

(Location: National Library of Ireland, Thorp Pamphlet, No. 710)

2

THE LAST SPEECH AND DYING-WORDS OF

John Balfe

Who was Executed at St Stephens-Green, for Robbery, On Saturday the Fifteenth of June, 1706.

I Was born in *Ballinestocken*, in the County of *Wicklow*, and Barony of *Talbotstown*, being tenderly brought Up, and Educated as became a Gentleman, until I was Seventeen Years of Age; and then was by Lewd Women deluded from my Study. One *Art Byrne* was the Man that persuaded me first to Take or Steal any of my Neighbours Goods: And soon afterwards I took to the Roads and so continu'd 'till my Brother came to the Country. But I do declare that it was always contrary to my Inclination, that my Brother should follow the course of Life that I did; and therefore I often desir'd him to go Home, follow his Trade and live Honest; but cou'd not persuade him thereto, until he came to his untimely End.

There was one *John Carny* Hang'd at the Assizes of *Wicklow*, about *April* or *March* last was a Twelve Month, for the robbing of Mr. Piercy. Now as I am a Dying Man, the said *Carny* was not any way concern'd in the said Robbery, nor in any respect privy to it, for it was I and my Comrades that committed the Robbery. And soon after my Brother was Executed I went to *Scotland* hoping to be safe there, as Living truly, justly, and honestly there; but unfortunately I came to the house of one *John Mac-Donnald*, Laird of *Largy* where I was civily Entertained for some time, until he seemingly grew Jealouse of his Wife, upon my account; and thereupon had me Imprisoned for Two Months, most of which time he kept me Confined in a pair of Stocks, and then he took away from me my Cloaths, Arms and

Money, to the value of Forty Pounds, which I hope (if recoverable) the Government will take and Distribute among the Poor. And finding that I wou'd not Comply with him, nor Accuse his Wife, to confirm his Jealousie of her, he then offer'd me Forty Pounds, if I wou'd but Swear that I had Debauched his Wife, that so he might be Divorced from her, they having no Children: And finding that I wou'd not Comply, he then, under colour of Friendship, brought me out of Prison and pretended, together with Captain *Mac-Neal*, to bring me to the Earl of *Argile's* House, in order to go with the Recruits for *Flanders*, where I intended to follow my Study, and like a true Penitent, reform my self to a Vertuous and Christian Life, but contrary to my Expectation, my private enemy, *John Mac-Donnald*, and Captain *Mac-Neal*, brought me to the Seaside, and immediately Bound me, set me on Board, and Convey'd me to this Kingdom, (where according to the Just Laws of this Land, I have received the Rewards justly due to my CRIMES:) But I sincerely Declare, that tho' I have Robbed many, yet I never committed any Murther, nor used any Gentleman barbarously, nor to my Knowledge, ever Robber a Poor-man.

And as for the Robbery of Mr. *Haris*, my Brother and I were actually there: And my Brother was Accus'd for taking the Rings off the Gentlewomans Fingers, and threatening to Cut them. Now as I am a Dying Man, neither my Brother nor I ever took the said Rings off her Fingers, but one of the Company did.

And now as I am a Dying Man, and shall Answer before ALMIGHTY GOD, I never did Carnally know *Grisell Mac-Donnald*, Wife of the said *John Mac-Donnald*, nor any other Woman, from the first Hour of my going into *Scotland*, unto the last Minute of my coming away from thence. And I do really believe, that the said *Grisell Mac Donnald*, is a true, honest, and faithful Wife to her Husband: And I hope this will Convince all Charitable Christians of the Wrong, Injury, and Defamation which she Undeservedly suffer'd on my account; and for which I am sensibly afflicted.

And as for my Father and Brothers, that are now living, I do Declare, that they nor any of them were ever privy to any of my ill and unhappy Actions: And that they nor either of 'em ever had the value of a Shilling of any of my ill gotten Gettings.

And as to the fact of cutting *Art Byrne's* Tongue, it was thus occasioned. I had left Fifty Nine pieces of Gold in his Hands, (after often dividing our Robberies in his House) and he never returned me but Ten or Eleven pieces of the said Gold: And when he appointed me to come for the Rest, he Betray'd me, and brought the Country to Take me; so that the next time I met him, I wou'd not Kill him, but cut his Tongue.

And, now Dear Christians, *I beg that all Men may take Warning by this my Ignominious End; and Carefully avoid all such Occasions, as have brought me to it. So, most heartily begging Pardon of Almighty God, for all my Sins and manifold Offences, And desiring the Prayers of all Good Christians, I conclude.*

John Balfe

This is my True Speech, and none other, *John Balfe.*

Printed by *John Brocas* in *School House-Lane,* 1706

(Location: Trinity College Library, Press A.7.3. No 53)

3

THE LAST SPEECH AND DYING WORDS OF

Edward English, Butcher

Who was Executed at St. Stephen's-Green, for Robbing of one Mr. Beasley at the Green Hills, On Friday the 5th of December, 1707.

Good Christians,

NOW that I am brought to this place of Execution, it behoves me to let the World know, (and am Resolv'd to give 'em full satisfaction, of) all the Transactions of my sinful Life; which I hope may be a warning to all poor Young Men.

I was Born at *South-Gate* in Cork, and lived there for the space of Fourteen Years; during which time my poor Parents endeavour'd to keep me to School; soon after I left *Cork*, and came for *Dublin*; to which place my tender Father had a recourse, upon my account only; where he did endeavour like an honest Man to get his Bread and did keep me at School full Two Years more, and then bound me Apprentice to one *William Carter*, Butcher in *New-street*, and did continu'd there for Five Years and a Half, performing my Duty as it behov'd a just Servant, having the good Will of all my Neighbours. One Serjeant *Hamlin* was the only Person that brought me to this untimely End. When I left my Master, I Listed my self Soldier; and do Confess, to be Guilty of this Fact for which I now am to suffer for; but of any other Robbery or Thievery I never had any hand in it (it being now too soon.) I do Confess I was viciously prone to Cursing, Swearing, and Lewd Women, which is grievous to my poor Soul. This said *Hamlin, William Collin, Nicholas Elrington* and my self, was Sworn along time before this Robbery was, to be true to one another, and 'twas agreed between us, that *Elrington, Hamlin*, and my self were the Three Persons that was to commit this Robbery, Collin being appointed to meet us the Morning after the Robbery was committed in *Cavan's-Fields*, and there was to receive his share of the Money; but we did not agree to go for that time; so that it was a Month after it was done, in which time it was quite out of my Mind. Then *Hamlin, Elrington* and *Collin* was the Persons that was to commit this Robbery; but the Night that it was to be Executed, this *Collin* got drunk, and bid them go and get another Man; for he was not able to go along with 'em: Then *Hamlin* and *Elrington* came to me about a Eleven a Clock at Night; where they found me in Bed in my Dear Father's-House. *Hamlin* alone enter'd in, and Commanded me out of my Bed saying, That I was Commanded by my Captain to go along with 'em in search for Disarters: To which, I made Answer, that it was too late. Then he said, if I wou'd not Obey my Captain's Order, he wou'd have me Confin'd in Captain *Tooly's* Marshalls; at which I rise up, and went along with him; but when I came out, I saw *Elrington*; then *Elrington* and *Hamlin* brought me to an Ale-House in *Swifts-Alley*, where they disclos'd their doleful Subject. Then we went down to this *Collin*, and we ask'd him, was he able to undertake the Project; who told us he was not. So parting with *Collin*, we made the best of our way to the *Green-Hills*, and lay there all Night. Next Morning, about 8 or 9 a Clock we espy'd the Man that was Robb'd and another coming up the Rode; then we stept out and laid hands upon them; I took hold of the Man that was Robb'd, and *Hamlin* hold of the other, which Person struck him on the Hand and caused him to let his hold go, so made his Escape and rais'd the Country presently on us, who soon Apprehended us, and fetch'd us where now we are to receive the just recompence for our Crime. Which I pray God may be a Warning to all. So Fare well.

Edward English

This is the true copy of, the Dying Person, as deliver'd by him.
Printed by *E. Waters* in *School-House Lane*.

(Location: Trinity College Library, Press A.7.3 No 151)

4

THE LAST SPEECHES AND DYING WORDS OF

Edward Flood and Hugh Caffery

Who was Executed at St. Stephen's-Green, On Friday the 5th of December, 1707 for Robbing of Mr. Casey, at Cabbra.

Good Christians,

NOW that I am brought to so scandalous and End, and within a few Minuts of my last Breathing; I here declare before God and the World, that I was not Guilty of this Fact for which I am now to Dye for; neither was I privy thereto, nor to any other Robbery all my Life-time. One of the same Company that I belong'd to being Confined in the Castle Guard, and transmitted to New-Gate for stealing Cloaths, was in a starving Condition; and that Mr. *Casey*, who was Robbed, hearing there was some of the Regiment in New Gate, and being Robb'd by some of the same Regiment, as they suppos'd, came to New Gate, to see if he cou'd hear any thing of this Robbery among them. Then this Man who belong'd to the same Company that I was in, by name *Bryan Mac Couly*, being in a starving Condition, and *Casey* making him Drink, and Bribed him, Swore against Four of the same Company; for which we were Apprehended. In a considerable time after, his Conscience prick'd him; and sent for the Reverend Mr. *Jones*, who examin'd *Mac Couley*, who Declared he Wrong'd us Four. Mr *Jones* Advis'd us to send for a Justice of Peace: So we sent for Alderman *Page*; who Examined the said *Mac Couley*, and Writ his Examination, Declaring that he Wrong'd us. That *Elizabeth Price*, Mother-in-law to the said *Casey*, hearing that *Bryan Mac Couly* had made the second Examination, came to him, and said; If he would not Swear against us, she would swear against *Caffery* and I; so she desired him to Swear, and that he shou'd have for his Reward two Guineas, but he wou'd not. Then Mrs. *Price* Swore against *Caffery* and I, and said she knew us Both well enough. The Regiment was drawn out for Them before we were Apprehended, and we among the Battallion, yet had nothing to say to us: But Mrs. *Price* pitch'd upon one Man of the Battallion, and said, that was one of the Men, and would have had him confined only he had good proof to the contrary; and made out where he was that Night. Likewise I declare once more before God and the World, I know nothing of this Robbery that I am to Die for; altho' I deserved Death before now, but I thank my God not for Robbing or Stealing, but for keeping Company with Women, and I was much given to that Crime, and do trust that God of his great Mercy will forgive me. Some time ago I was forc'd upon the account of Debt to break up House-keeping, and went to the County West Meath, and there came Aquainted with one *Anne Fitz Gerrald*, insomuch, that we kept together for the space of Fifteen Months and more, by which time my Married Wife came down to the place where we were; but when she that kep with me saw my Lawful Wife, she then urg'd me to deny my Wife, but cou'd not; but my wife soon finding the greatness that was between us two, was for returning Home, and accordingly did, and left me behind; then I being uneasy in my Mind followed her up last Easter, but could not shew my Face in Town, so I was forced to List as a Soldier unhappily. I was Born in the Barony of Fore, and County Westmeath; and kept House in St. Michan's Parish a considerable time; and do hope none of my Neighbours can give me an ill Character, more that that of Women, and that they can; which I hope the Lord Jesus, through the Infinite washing away on our mortal Sins, will Seal up my Pardon e'er I go hence, and be no more see. And heartily beg the Prayers of every good *Christian*. So Lord Jesus receive my poor sinful Soul. Amen.

Edward Flood

The Last SPEECH and Dying Words of *Hugh Caffery*, &c.

Christians,

Since it has pleased Almighty God, that I should Dye this most unfortunate Death; these few minutes that I have to live, shall be to satisfy the World of what was laid to my Charge. And now that I am to dye, I hope all Good Christians do believe that I have a tender regard for my poor soul, (which I hope God will be Merciful to,) and not think that I will dissemble with the World so as to deprive my self of Eternal happiness. Dear Christians, these being my last Words, I do declare I never was Guilty of this Crime that I now suffer for, nor was I ever Guilty of so hainous a Crime as Stealing or Robbing; but all other small Vices I have been Guilty of, (and hope my Heavenly Father will pardon the same) Cursing, Swearing, and Women was the only Vice I was Guilty of; And that I do heartily forgive the Persons that hath occasion'd this my untimely End. And do further declare, that I never before knew any that was privy to the fact I suffer for; nor did I see Mrs Price for 3 Years to my knowledge, 'till she came to New Gate. I lived with one Ignatius Taffe, at the sign of the Black Swan *in* Smite-Field; *during which service, I have been often in her House, yet never did her any wrong. I Confess I deserv'd Death long ago for the matter of keeping Company with Lewd Women, and I was as much given to that, which is all that troubles my Conscience. I never wrong'd any living Soul, except I did my Master when I was sent to Buy small Conveniencies for the House, then some small thing or other I often kept for my own use: Which is all I shall answer at the Tribunal. And pray God that all Christians may eschew those Vices of Lewd Women, Cursing and Swearing; God will one time or other revenged on 'em that Practice 'em. I desire the prayers of all that sees my untimely End. So fare well.*

Hugh Caffery

These are the true Copies of the Dying Persons as delivered by 'em. Printed by E. *Waters* in *School-House-Lane.*

(Location: Trinity College Library, Press A.7.3 No 150)

5

THE LAST SPEECHES AND DYING WORDS OF

Patrick Illan, Lawrence Halpeny, James Quin and Patrick Mc.Shane

who were Executed at Killmainham, on Thursday the 25th day of March, 1708.

Since it has been our ever to be Lamented Fate, to come to so untimely and shameful an end, we thought it a Duty incumbent upon us before God and Man, to make this last sincere and unfeigned Confession to the open World, of the innumerable Enormities and heinous Wickedness we have been guilty of during the whole course of our wicked Lives, as well for the good of our own Souls, as to precaution all our fellow Christians to avoid with all possible Diligence and Care, Devotion and prayer all Temptations of evil Conversation, breaking of the Lords-day, by turning it rather to a day of idle Pleasure, and unlawful Pastimes, than spending it in Devotion, and glorifying the great God of Sabbath, who ordain'd that day to be set apart for his peculiar Service, to have a vigilent care of Swearing, Cursing, Gaming, Lying, Stealing, Robbing, and Whoring, all which Sins are the Sources and Originals of this our unhappy and untimely departure out of this World, so soon, and in so reproachful a manner.

I Was born in *Lurgan Clanbrasil* in the County of *Ardmagh*, and serv'd my time to a Black-smith, I liv'd very well by my Trade for some time, marry'd, but had no children by the Woman I took to Wife; but being seduc'd by the Devil and evil Company, I did quit both my Trade and Wife, took another Woman as my Wife, I chang'd my Sir-name to *Holland*, and ever since I did not stick to commit whatever Satan and Flagitatious Complices did suggest unto me, I had My hand in every wicked design that I could hear of, I was at the Robbing of one Alexander Drumgool in the County of Down near Newry, and do declare as I am a dying Man, that one Donnely, and some others that I am told, are accus'd and bound over for the same, are innocent of it, and were neither Parties in it, nor privy to it. I deserve death for a great many Crimes, and among the rest for what I do now here Suffer; I do from the very bottom of my heart beg Pardon all that I did ever offend, and forgive all the World: I with all submission, with a contrite and sorrowful heart, O God which thou wilt not despise, do most humbly implore, with the Prayers of all good Christians, thy Forgiveness and Mercy, now dying in the 36th Year of my Age.

Patrick Illan.

I Was born at Killuckin in the County West-Meath, have follow'd making of Bodies and quilted Caps: I have been twice marry'd, and liv'd by my Labour and Industry well enough, till the Devil of discontent seiz'd me, made me flight my trade, follow loofe and idle Company, wherein I took too much delight, to my now shame and Sorrow, I have done Evil enough that deserve death, now alas in the 58th year of my Age, I must justly suffer a reproachful death, for this and all my other Sins, for which I do heartily Repent, and beg Christ Jesus my Saviour Forgiveness and Mercy, and Pardon of all that I have ever Offended, in Thought, Word or Deed, and do forgive all the World, craving the prayers of all the Faithful.

Lawrence Halpeny

MY parents liv'd at a Town called Clostogher in the County of Galway, where I the Unfortunate wretch had my Birth. I learn'd the Glew makers trade, by which I might get honest Bread, had not an Abhorrence of Labour and pains and an Aspiring Spirit rais'd in me thoughts of becoming a Trooper; having serv'd in the Horse for some time, I quit that Service, and Listed in Colonel Gustavus Hamilton's Regiment, Serv'd him in the West Indies, and in Spain; after escaping all the Dangers of War by Sea and Land, I now, through a continuation of Habitual

Wickedness, must Die a Violent, which does not so much Trouble Me as a Scandalous Death, a just reward for my manifold past Iniquities, as well as for the least Crime, which makes me now being 44 Years old, an Age fitter for Repentance than contriving mischief, be brought here to this Place of Execution. I have naught to say but crave the Great God's mercy, Pardon for the many Mischiefs I committed; I forgive all mankind, and beg the prayers of all that sees me suffer or reads these my last Dying Words.

James Quin

I Was born at Cregan *in the Barony of* Fews *in the County of Ardmach, I wrought Bread and had for some time a little Farm, but loving Idleness and a Lazy life rather than Labour, I soon met with Companions that did not stick to Steal, Robb and commit any Wickedness whatsoever, to whom I joyn'd my self. I deserved Death for this, and very many more Crimes for which I am heartily sorry, and beg my Saviour's forgiveness and mercy, and Pardon of all, which are very many that I offended, I forgive all Mankind, and confess I am justly brought here to Suffer, now in the 45th Year of my Age, and I beg the Prayers of all Good Christians, I call'd myself by the name of* Johnson, *but my right name is* Patrick MacShane.

If any other Speech be Publish'd concerning these Persons, it is Extorted and a Sham, just reason being for a Caution, this City being daily Impos'd on in many respects.

FINIS

Dublin: Printed at the Union *Coffee-House* on *Cork-Hill*, 1708.

(Location: Trinity College Library, Press A.7.3. No 178)

6

THE LAST SPEECHES AND DYING WORDS OF

Thomas Renals, and Richard Perry Alias Barry

*who were Executed at Kilmainham,
on Wednesday the 7th of May 1712*

Taken from their own Mouths by a Friend, to prevent Counterfeits.

Good Christians.

'TIS the General Method of Persons under the Sentence of Death, to Satisfie the World by making a formal Speech at the Place of Execution, therefore I *Thomas Renals* do think it Requisite to inform every Body of the Truth of my Present unhappiness, and what fatal Consequences brought me to this untimely End.

I was Born within a Mile of *Navan*, in the County of *Meath*, of Mean but Honest Parents, and might have advanced my self in the World on better Grounds than Villany, had not the Seducements of Vicious Company perverted my Youthful Intentions, for in my Infancy I was Educated a Roman Catholik, but falling off from Vertue, I forsook Religion, and run into all manner of Intemperance. I am about 26 Years of Age.

Now as touching the Fact for which I am to Dye is for Robbing of Mr. *James Rickerson* of one Hundred Pound in Plate, and a Parcel of Linnen and Several other Goods, which fact I confess myself to be Guilty, and Guilty of Robbing of Mr. *Robert Bulger* of Nineteen Pounds in Money, and likewise I Robbed his Maid of her Money, and I do hereby confess, that I am Guilty of Several other Robberies, but I do hereby declare as I am a Dying-man I never Murdered any Body, and I Listed in the Honourable Colonel *Creaton's* Regiment of *Foot* in Captain *Maleeds* Company, and served 7 *Months*, this is all I have to say, and do Desire the Prayers of all Good Christians at my

Departure. I Dye a Roman Catholick. This is my True Speech and no other.

Thomas Renals.

The SPEECH of *Richard Perry Alias Barry.*

Good People,

I was Born in the County of *Cork*, and Listed in the Honourable Colonel *Creaton's* Regiment of Foot, in Captain *Maleeds* Company, and Served about 3 Months, and am about 23 Years of Age. Now as Touching the Fact for which I am to Dye, is for the same Robbery of Mr. *James Rickerson*, and likewise I do confess, that I am Guilty of Robbing *Thomas Barton* of several Goods, and another Robbery in *Bray-Road*, and several other Robberies. Now Christians as I am upon the Point of Expiring, I think myself Bound to give Warning to others, that they take Example by my wretched End. Fate has permitted me to Spin out 23 Years, in one continued Scene of Sin and Villany, But the Heavy Hand of an All-Powerful and Avenging Deity has Scourg'd me at last; and were it not for the Hopes of a Merciful Saviour, my Soul as well as Body would be Lost: There! There's my Redemption, through the Intercession of good Christians, and my own Sincere Repentance. I Dye a Roman Catholick, and Desire the Prayers of all good Christians, and the Lord have Mercy on my Soul. Amen

This is my True SPEECH.

Richard Perry.

DUBLIN: Printed in *Channel-Row*

(Location: Trinity College Library, Press A.7.3 No 301)

7

Ensign Edmund Budd's

Speech Who Suffered near St Stephen's Green, on Saturday the 8th of November, 1712.

Gentlemen

Were it only to justify my self against a most *Scandalous Paper*, Printed *in School-House-Lane*, and Published on the 25th of October last, I should not (my time being now very short and but a Step between me and Death) have thought of Publishing This: But to satisfy the few Friends I have in this Kingdom, and my many and dear Relations in *England*; I do solemnly Declare, as I am a Dying Man, I had no Design of killing the Deceas'd *Robert Watts*, which the Judges by their Reports seem also to believe; neither can it enter into my Thoughts that the Blows I gave him were the Occasion of his Death; for he afterwards appear'd very well, undress'd me and put me to Bed; and after that, was with the rest of the Company for some Hours whilst I was asleep; But what they did to him, or how he manag'd himself afterwards, God and they only know. And I pray God Forgive me (if I say or think amiss) they were more accessary to his Death than I was.

But to do Mr *Lambert* (who I am inform'd is severely Censur'd in this Matter) right, he left the Company before I went to Bed; And in all my Conversations with him, which was very frequent, I never saw or knew any harm by him.

As to my Self, I was Born at *Parsenham* near *Stony-Strafford* in *Northamptonshire*, in the Month of *May*, 1691. And tho' my Father in the Sham Speeches before-mentioned, is set forth as an Under-Keeper to my Lord *Wharton* (whom I pray to God to bless, as my great and good Benefactor) yet that Representation is both false and spightful : It's true he is not in any Great or Publick Employ, but a Gentleman that is Respected and Beloved by the best in England.

As to my Education, it was Gentleman-like; and I hope all such will pity rather than Censure this shameful Closure to my life.

And to satisfy the World yet further, I do solemnly Declare upon the Word of a Dying Man, I knew nothing of the young Woman that was thrown over the Wall on *Usher's Key* into the River, for which it seems I was suspected, tho' at that time I was in *England*; nor did I ever play any such vile prank on the Body of a Woman in *Cook-street* or elsewhere, as the said Scandalous Paper mentions.

What Sins I have been Guilty of, were more to the Prejudice of my own poor Soul, than any ways Injurious to others, which I hope God of his infinite Mercy will Pardon; And 'tis only the Thoughts of an Almighty Saviour and Merciful Redeemer that revives my Hopes, and gives me Assurance, that as I Trust I am in a great measure Innocent of the Fact for which I Dye, so he will intercede for me, that my Sufferings here by virtue of his Merits may contribute to the Attonement of my other Sins, and advance my Happiness in these Regions of Bliss, where I trust I am now going. And I do sincerely from the very bottom of my Heart Forgive all my Enemies and all Mankind, that has either directly or indirectly done me any ill Office: And I do as sincerely upon my bended Knees beg the Forgiveness of all those that I have any way or at any time injur'd or offended.

I do humbly and earnestly by the fervent Prayers of all good Christians for my poor Soul, and the great God of Heaven hear them, and reward those that are so Charitable to afford them.

If any other Paper be Publish'd, 'tis Counterfeit.

Edm. Budd

This is a true Copy of the Paper left with me by Mr. Edm. Budd *and by him desir'd that Mr* Dickson *might Publish it.*

Jo. Finglasse

Dublin, Printed by *Francis Dickson* at the *Union* on *Cork Hill*, 1712

(National Library of Ireland, LO P30)

8

THE LAST SPEECH AND DYING WORDS OF

Charles Donnell

of the City of Dublin Gent, who was Executed near St Stephen's Green, on Saturday the 8th of November, 1712.

As the End of Execution and Corporal Punishment are designed to deter others from Committing the like Crimes; so Speeches and the last Dying Words of every Christian ought to be for Instruction and Amendment of Life; and therefore wish that my Suffering, and what I am now going to say, may answer these Intents.

I was Born at *Ballymenagh* in the County of *Antrim*, a Son to *Robert Donnell* Esq; I was Educated and now Dye a Member of the Established Church, and have only two Brothers living, both Clergymen.

My dear Father's Inclinations were that I should follow my Study as my Brothers had done; but to my great Sorrow and Grief, I did not observe his Paternal and Good Advice in that, and many other Occurrences of my Life; And before I proceed further in this Speech, let me Advise and Admonish all young unthinking Men, to be Obedient to their Parents (more especially where such are Men of Sense, being best Judges of what is proper for them) who cannot be supposed to have any Design upon them to their Prejudice.

When my Indulgent Father perceiv'd, that I did not nor would apply my self to College Learning, or other Studies, he bound me an Apprentice to Capt. *Robert Macarroll* Merchant of this City; during which time I went in a ship of his to *Virginia*, but some Misfortune happening in that oyage, I was necessitated to stay 3 years on my

Master's Account, and soon after my return home, he Died, so that I quitted that way of Living.

My Father endeavour'd afterwards to Instruct me in his own Office in Order to succeed him in his Registry of the Diocese of Conier; but alas! I was Deaf to all his Wise Admonitions, and gave too much way to the Follies of Youth, by which this good Design of my Father was also frustrated.

Soon after my Father's Death, I came to this City and Married Mrs *Esther Pullman*, without consulting my surviving Mother, Brother or Relations; and here I lived 2 years. About the 2d of *April* last purposing to go to the North to see my Friends, and taking leave of my Acquaintance here in town, that Day I happened to be so overtaken with Drink, that as I am now a Dying Man, I do not remember how that unhappy Accident happen'd betwixt me and that unfortunate Gentleman Mr *Briton*, who lost his Life.

This I do assure and declare to the World, that I had no Malice to him, nor ever saw him before to the best of my knowledge. And when it was discovered that the said *Britton* had been the only Support to his Father and Family, my Friends offered in my behalf to grant them an Allowance to live upon in lieu of the great Loss sustained by his Death, which with regret was Rejected.

My Relations were informed by their Lawyers inquiring fully into the Case, seeing no Malice Propense cou'd be prov'd against me, and both Swords Drawn, by an Impartial Jury that it was improbable to find me Guilty of Murther. The High Sheriffs were Ordered in Regard the Subsherriff was of the Same Name as the Dead Man to strike a Jury, which was accordingly done; but the Return (as I have been told) was afterwards Alter'd. The Tryal came on; and there being Two Indictments against me, the one for Murther and the other upon the Statute of Stabbing, I was found Guilty at Large; but that Mistake of the Jury was Amended by the Court, and I acquitted of the Latter; the which with other things, as I was inform'd, wou'd have been Ground for Plea in Arrest of Judgement, only for fear of incensing the Court, which altogether seemed inclinable to Mercy, and the more especially when my Friends Moved only for Transportation.

Afterwards my Brothers applied for a Report from the Judges, which they Granted, and most men were of Opinion it left some Room for Mercy. With this Report my brother *Robert* a Clergyman went to *England*, where he has continued ever since; and as his many Letters express he had Obtain'd a Pardon, if not prevented by some ill offices done me here. The many Scandalous Stories and Reflections industriously spread abroad, as it is presum'd to make me Odious, not only to the City, but to all my Friends were such as are not fit to be Named; but Thanks be to God they are all False, as for Instance, I thought proper to have the following Affidavit Annexed; and for such Calumnies and all other Injuries done me, I freely forgive all Mankind, and though with Sorrow I confess I did not employ my whole time so well as I ought to have done, yet I appeal to the Clergy, who frequently visited me, whether they ever saw or heard any unbecoming Carriage since I was put into Goal.

And now I conclude, with committing my poor Soul to God who gave it, and hope only for Mercy in and through the Blood of my Blessed Saviour Jesus Christ, and heartily beg the Prayers of all Good Christians that I may obtain the same.

Signed *November* the 7th, 1712.

Charles Donnell

This the true Speech as Delivered to the Reverend Dr. Finglass

C.C. Dub. ff.	Thomas Pullman *of* Caple-street *in the city of* Dublin, Tallow-Chandler, *Father-in Law* to Charles Donnell *now a Prisoner in Newgate in the said City, came Voluntarily this Day before Me and made Oath, That ever since the said* Charles *was Marryed to this Deponent's Daughter he never Assaulted, Beat, or Abused this Deponent or this Deponent's Wife, as has been Scandalously reported; This Deponent further Deposeth that since the said* Charles *has been confined in* Newgate, *he never was unthankful for any Victuals or other things*

sent to him from this Deponents House, nor ever abused the Meat or the Vessels that the same was sent in, and further this Deponent Saith not.

Jurat Cor.   Me 22 die Octobris, 1712

Thomas Pullman   Thomas Quin

N.B. It is left to the Publick to Judge how Notoriously they have been Impos'd on by Sham Speeches, as well as the Two Unfortunate Gentlemen.

Dublin: Printed by *Francis Dickson* at the Union on Cork-Hill, 1712.

(Location: National Library of Ireland: LO P30)

9

THE LAST SPEECH AND DYING WORDS OF

Peter Dalton

Who was Executed near St. Stephen's Green, on Saturday the 23d of August 1712.

Good Christians,

I *Peter Dalton* was born in the County of *Meath*, in the Parish of *Kilkarn* near *Naven*, Descended of Honest Parents out of the Country of *West-Meath*, and was but 12 Years of Age when my Father Dyed, and by the loss of my Father my Mother being a Widow, and having several more Children, she was reduced and the Children were Separated; whereupon I went to *Dublin*, and Bound my self to one Mr. *Crowler* a Brewer, where I did live in Splender and Request, until I thought fit to Marry, and being Married in a short time after, I came in Credit and took a House and Sold Ale, given to no Ill Vice during that time, and kept House Selling of Ale four Years, and got the Handling of other People's Money, I took Frolicks of Drinking, and Spending in all Sorts of Company, till I run my self in Debt, and was forced to quit Selling of Drink, my Wife and I were forced to Separate out of this City, and found Friends in the Country very Cold. I got into a Gentleman's Service in the Country to one Captain *Netterfield*, and out of his Service, became Servant to Captain *Wade* my Prosecutor, and lived with him about Three Months, and during that time I suffered great Hardships, which I complained to Alderman *Quinn*, who ordered me to quit his Service, the said *Wade* being displeased at my Parting, he threatned to put me in Bridewell, the Alderman fearing I should be sent to Bridewell, he ordered I should go Home and Serve my Time to *Wade*. I did accordingly, and while I was Serving him after, I had worse Usage then I had before, and I told, I wou'd not serve him any longer, and said I wou'd chuse to suffer his Displeasure than serve him, this happened a Year and a half ago, and I parted with him before my Time was Expir'd a Fortnight, this is well known by several in City and Country, then came to Serve Captain *Warren* of *Corduff*, lived with him Three quarters of a Year in Credit, being given to Drink I affronted my Master several times, his Honour seeing my failing, he has taken the Affronts with great Patience, very Honourably, I being always waiting of his Honour to Town, was troubled with so many Persons craving Debt of me, that I was asham'd, so that I quitted his Service by his Consent, and Honourably paid me, and more then my Wages, and gave me a favourable Discharge, and soon after Discharging me, I came to my last misfortunes, which brought me to this my shameful End, meeting one *William Warren* and one *James Dalton*, about Five Months ago the said *Dalton* lately came out of *England*, I being glad to see him, being long out of this Kingdom, told he was bare of Money, he knowing the said *Warren* in *London*, the said *Dalton* demanded of me if I knew him, I told him I did, then we concluded to take a Pot of Ale, and we all complained the want of Money, *Warren* sends one abroad, and got as much Money as paid the Reckoning, and I said it was a pitty so many free Lads should want Money, and the rest said the same, but *Warren* said which way shall we come by it.

The said *Warren* knowing I lived with an able man meaning *Wade*, asked of me if any Money was to be got in his House, I told him I could not well tell, he said I know the House and no body dwels there, and let us attack it this Night and see what we can get, I think it is no Sin to take from him or from such Misers, then we did atack the House, and took Several sorts of goods away, and divided them even, and then parted one from the other, where they Disposed of their shares.

I do not know, but what I had I Discovered it, and directed *Wade* to find them, which was the only Material Evidence he had against me on Tryal, and for the same was Convicted, that the said *Warren* took a *Bed* and two *Looking Glasses* to one *Mulloy's* House in *Thomas Court*, and he borrowed Eight Shillings from the Landlady, being late he went out to find a Broker to buy them, he came in and brought one to buy the said Goods, but could not sell them, and told the Land lady that the said Goods belonged to me and came out of the Country, and I telling to the contrary, caused Suspicion that the Goods was unlawfully got, so that I was immediately Secured, and brought me before Alderman *Page*, and was Committed on Suspicion, and he ordered the Prosecutors to put the said Goods in the Gazette, *Wade* soon came to Town and heard the same and Straight came to me, and I directed him as aforesaid by his promising me before Witness he would not harm me, only to tell where the Goods were, after receiving Sentence, I have prevailed with Judge *Nutley*, that his Honour gave me a Favourable Report, whereby I got Order of Transportation which I have by me, and the said *Wade* has prevailed with the Government to revoke the said Order of Transportation, and such Orders are given that I should Suffer the *23d* Instant.

I was 30 Years of Age last *June*, this is my last and true Speech, the said Wade Informed the Government If I should Escape Death, I wou'd let the *Inns* on Fire for Spite to his House that is there, as I am a Dying Man I never thought of any such thing, I desire the Prayers of all good Christians. I Dye a Roman Catholick, and the Lord have Mercy on my Soul.

This *is* my True SPEECH , *Peter Dalton.*

DUBLIN : Printed in *Channel-Row* 1712.

(Location: Yale University, Beinecke Library, Br Sides By 6, 1712)

10

THE LAST SPEECHES AND DYING WORDS OF

John Davis, James Demsye, and William Ledwidge

Who were Executed near St. Stephen's-Green, on Saturday the 27th of June, 1713.

Good Christians.

I *John Davis* Son of *Richard Davis*, I was Born in the County of *Limerick* of mean but Honeſt Parents, and am now about 35 Years of Age, when I was about 15 my Father put me Prentice to one Mr. *Caddel* a Weaver in *Limerick*, for the space of seven Years, I stayed with him a Year and a half, and then came home to my Father and quitted the Trade, I went from thence to *Cork* where Liv'd my Foster-Sister who kept a Coach, soon after I became her Coach-Man, I Liv'd there in Credit and Repute until I left her, then I Hired my self to a Gentleman in the Country and undertook the same Imployment, and Liv'd there in Love with all People until I Placed my fancy on the Cook-Maid and Married her, ſoon after we was both Diſcharged, and came to this City Nine Years next St. *James's* Day.

I hearing that 'Squire Rantford at Stephen's-Green wanted a Coachman, I was immediately Entertained in his Service by producing my Certificate, I ſerved there two Year, and was diſcharged according to my Deſire. I was Recommended by a Gentleman to 'Squire Boucher's as a Coachman. I ſerved there five Months, the Gentleman going to the Country had no further occaſion, he Recommended me to Captain Kelly in the ſame Employment, I ſerved him there for the ſpace of three Year true and honeſt, and when the Captain was going for England to the Baths, left me in

THE LAST SPEECHES

AND DYING WORDS OF
John Davis, James Demsye, and William Ledwidge;

Who were Executed near St. Stephen's-Green, on Saturday the 27th of June, 1713.

Good Christians.

I *John Davis* Son of *Richard Davis*, I was Born in the County of *Limerick* of mean but Honest Parents, and am now about 35. Years of Age, when I was about 15 my Father put me Prentice to one Mr. *Caddel* a Weaver in *Limerick*, for the space of seven Years, I stayed with him a Year and a half, and then came home to my Father and quitted the Trade, I went from thence to *Cork* where Liv'd my Foster-Sister who kept a Coach, soon after I became her Coach-Man, I Liv'd there in Credit and Repute until I left her, then I Hired my self to a Gentleman in the Country and undertook the same Imployment, and Liv'd there in Love with all People until I Placed my fancy on the Cook-Maid and Married her, soon after we was both Discharged, and came to this City Nine Years next St. *James's* Day.

I hearing that 'Squire *Runtford* at *Stephen's*-Green wanted a Coachman, I was immediately Entertained in his Service by producing my Certificate, I served there two Year, and was discharged according to my Desire. I was Recommended by a Gentleman to 'Squire *Boucher's* as a Coachman. I served there five Months, the Gentleman going to the Country had no further occasion, he Recommended me to Captain *Kelly* in the same Employment, I served him there for the space of three Year true and honest, and when the Captain was going for *England* to the Baths, left me in charge with 'Squire *Donnellàn* until he would return, upon some difference of words my Master discharged me, and then I hir'd to Colonel *Eyres* of *Escourt* and served in his Family two Year; likewise I served Doctor *Reymond* in *Trim* two Year faithful and honest, and served in Credible Services all my Life, and has all my Discharges to show, until this last time I came to 'Squire *Boucher's* to my great Sorrow, and all by the means of this *Mary Hamock* that is now in Newgate, she Deluded me, and brought me to this untimely End." I own that I was Married to this *Hamock* last St *George's* Day, though my Lawful Wife lives upon the Strand in this City, which I had four Children by her: As for the Fact that I am to Dye, is for Robbing 'Squire *Boucher's* Clerk which is Mr. *Green*. I own I got into my Hands about Seventy odd Pound of the Money. And now I repent with the greatest Remorse and Sorrow, that all good Christians may Interceed for me to the Almighty for my Pardon and future Happiness. I Earnestly beg all your fervent Prayers, but especially, those of the Establish'd Church, in whose Principles I unworthily Lived in, and now as Submissively Dye in. This is my true SPEECH. *John Davis.*

Sign'd. N. *Jones.*

The SPEECH of *James Demsye.*

Good People,

I *James Demsye* Son of *Kelip Demsye*, I was Born in the County *Wexford* of mean but Honest Parents, and am 17 Years of Age, and about Seven Years ago came to this City to my Sorrow, and served Two or Three House-Keepers in *Channel*-Row true and Honest, until I met with Ill company that Deluded me, especially my fellow Sufferer, who is to Dye along with me, and as I am a Dying Man I never was Guilty of any other Robbery, but this of Mr *Cooke's* in the whole course of my Life, I Desire the Prayers of all Good Christians, I Dye a Roman Catholick, and the Lord have Mercy on my Soul. This is my true SPEECH. *James Demsye.*

The SPEECH of *William Ledwidge.*

Good Christians,

I *William Ledwidge*, Son of *Thomas Ledwidge*, I was Born at *Tara-Hill* in the County *Meath*, of Poor but honest Parents, and am about 18 Years of Age, I came to this City about Eleven Years ago, got my Living by Cleaning of Shoes and going of Arrants, until I got acquaintance with Pick-Pockets and Thieves, and followed the same but never was brought to Justice until now, I own I Robbed Mr *Cooke* of his Plate, though I got but about Thirty Shillings of the Money, and for which fact I own my self Guilty. I Dye a Roman Catholick, and the Lord have mercy on my poor Soul Amen. This is my true SPEECH, and no Other. *William Ledwidge.*

DUBLIN: Printed by *Sarah Sadleir* in School-House-Lane, 1713.

charge with, 'Squire Donnellan until he would return, upon fome difference of words my Master discharged me, and then I hir'd to Colonel Eyres of Escourt and ferved in his Family two Year; likewise I served Doctor Reymond in Trim two Year faithful and honest, and served in Credible Services all my Life, and has all my Discharges to show, until this last time I came to 'Squire Boucher's to my great Sorrow, and all by the means of this Mary Hamock and that is now in Newgate, she Deluded me, and brought me to this untimely End. I own that I was Married to this Hamock last St Georges Day, though my Lawful Wife lives upon the Strand in this City, which I had four Children by her. As for the Fact that I am to Dye, is for Robbing 'Squire Boucher's Clerk which is Mr Green. I own I got into my Hands about Seventy odd Pound of the Money. And now I repent with the greatest Remorse and Sorrow, that all good Christians may Interceed for me to the Almighty for my Pardon and future Happiness. I Earnestly beg all your fervent Prayers, but especially thofe of the Establish'd Church, in whofe Principles I unworthily Lived in, and now as Submissively Dye in.

This is my true SPEECH.

John Davis
Sign'd *N. Jones.*

The SPEECH of *James Demsye*

Good People,

I *James Demsye* Son of *Kelip Demsye*, I was born in the County *Waxford* of mean but Honest Parents, and am 17 Years of Age, and about Seven Years ago cane to this City to my Sorrow, and served Two or Three House-Keepers in *Channel-Row* true and Honest, until I met with Ill company that Deluded me, especially my fellow Sufferer who is to Dye along with me, and as I am a Dying Man I never was Guilty of any other Robbery, but this of Mr *Cooke's* in the whole course of my Life, I Desire the Prayers of all Good Christians,

I Dye a Roman Catholick, and the Lord have Mercy on My Soul. This is my true SPEECH. *James Demsye.*

The SPEECH OF *William Ledwidge*

Good Christians,

I *William Ledwidge* Son of *Thomas Ledwidge*, I was born at *Tara-Hill* in the County of *Meath*, of Poor but honest Parents, and am about 18 Years of Age, I came to this City about Eleven Years ago, got my Living by Cleaning of Shoes and going of Arrants, until I got acquaintance with Pick-Pockets and Thieves, and followed the same but was never brought to Justice until now, I own I Robbed Mr *Cooke* of his Plate, though I got but about Thirty Shillings of the Money, and for which fact I own my self Guilty. I Dye a Roman Catholick, and the Lord have mercy on my poor Soul. *Amen.*

This is my true SPEECH, and no Other.

William Ledwidge

DUBLIN: Printed by Sarah Sadleir in School-House Lane, 1713

(Location: Cambridge University Library, Bradshaw Collection, Hib.0.713.14)

II

THE LAST SPEECH AND DYING WORDS OF

James Hamilton

In the Parish of Kilmore in the County of Down;
who was Executed at Downpatrick for the Bloody and Hainous
Murder of William Lammon, the 17 of April, 1714.

Giving a True Account of his Birth, Life and Conversation, Parentage and Education. Wherein he desires the Ministers to give it to the Printing-press, to be publish'd for the Good of all Young People, desiring them to lead a pious Life, and to refrain idle Company. Whereunto he puts his Hand.

James Hamilton

The Last Speech and Dying Words of James Hamilton, &c.

I Was born in the Parish of *Kilmore*, of sober & Religious Parents, who took an early care of my Education, and had me taught to read the Scriptures and to write, by which I though my self fitted to gain a Lively-hood in the World. And therefore about three Years ago I began to travel with the pack; for about half the Time I was pretty Sober and Industrious in my business, till being puff'd up with the little stock I had, I begun to be very saucy, and proud, and was so vain as to go to dancing and pushing Schools: Upon which I became careless of my Affairs; and straight fell to keep very Idle and graceless Company, by which I was soon brought to be as vitious as 'emselves. For we spent our time in sotting & drinking, in horrid Swearing, & gaming, and especially at Cards, and now I very well remember, that it was my wicked dreadful imprecation, the Devil take me if I play any more for a Twelve-month but when I met with my Comerades again, I was as ready and eager to play, as they could wish. This was my sad life and practise till I became so levish and extravagant, that I thought nothing to spend a crown a day, and thus was I hardned in my wickedness and wholly casting off the fear of God, did not withold my self from any degree of debauchery, tho I was often warn'd by my Parents, and other Friends, what bad company wou'd bring me to: But I disreguarded all they said, and still cloacked my evil courses as well I as cou'd from 'em & put 'em of with fair words of falshood & deceit which were indeed very habitual & customary to me: to such a shameful height of intemperance & profainness was I quickly carried being left to my self & forsaken of God; but I must own not till I had forsaken him, for he seldom or never was in my thoughts no duty did I make conscience of unto him, But even the very day which is set a part for his service and worship, was often the time of my closest drinking and many other enormous practises; such a cursed trade of expensive sinning soon run thro' the greatest part of my small Substance, and I easily saw then my stock & credit must quickly sink. Upon which I sometime considered what method I should take for recovering & supporting 'em but alas! not one honest project came in my head; for a while I thinking to travel up the Country & Sell off my goods there, that so I might the better pretend I was robbed of what I had, and in this manner might get my own extravagant spending at once made up & concealed but at last not liking this contrivance tho' God knows bad enough, a more hellish and desperate one entred into my mind, even that horrid murder: for which I am now to suffer by the hand of Justice, and to be made a spectacle of horrour to you all, I was tempted to execute it in this manner.

 On the 5th of *March* last I met the poor unfortunate *William Lammon* in *Killeleah* & he had a pretty store of goods & money, I thought with my self the shortest way to make up my stock again, wou'd be to kill him and secure that to my self, with that view I waited upon to carry him a long with me, and accordingly when I cast my eyes upon his pack, which he had on a peice before him, I was then violently tempted & inclined to have dispatched him with a Sword, which I had in my hand, but recollecting my self how inconvenient the place and opportunity was to divert the temptation for that time, I begged him to take my Sword and give me his staff, because I was tired & it would ease me in the way.

We sleept together that night in my Fathers house, and the most of the time the bloody execrable design was still in my head, and strongly urged and bore in upon me by the suggestions of the divel, who was a murderer from the beginning, Nixt morning at breakfast any little misgivings of mind and fear of so black a guilt, which had somewhat shoked me before, were quite banished and driven from me, And with my whole heart was set upon the accomplishing the barbarous and cruel slaughtring of him, and so I straight rose up and drew ane old charge out of a Gun which was in the house, and clapt a new one in when he was ready to go, in Pretence of friendship to him, would convoy him to Mr *Johnstons* of *Redemmon*, in our passage thro' the wood in the middle and thickest part of it, the poor Creature sat down to rest himself; which I looked upon as the fairest occasion for my Devilish purpose and so straight shot him in the breast either thro' the surprise or that his life & strength was not quite gone, he made an attempt to get to his feet; but I knock'd him down with the Gun, upon which he lookt up to me most ruefully, and said O *Jammy* are you going to kill me! but this it self did not move me, nor made my cruel heart to relent, for I redoubled my blows upon his head, with so much rage and fury, that I broke the stock and bended the barrel of the Gun, and when I saw that I had killed him outright I dreg'd him a small way into a bog, and covered him with the top of a bush, having searched his pockets and found only about eight pence in them; but I go to death with it I neither cut his pocket nor his flesh as was fancied I did, & having thus inhumanly destroyed & disposed of the innocent owner, I eagerly returned to my prey & having refled his box, I found there about 40 Shillings sterling, one pair of small silver buttons, and a bad Dollar, all which I carried with me, and having dashed his box in pieces, I hid it in a bush & the rest of his goods in another; and having thus finished the dreadful murder, I was straight making off, but fear immediately sized me, and my imagination being disordered with my terrible guilt made me apprehend I saw a man coming just down upon the place, which seemed so real to me that I run a little piece before, I durst look back, but then saw nothing.

    I was not gone much further till passing by some Cows, they

roared and bellowed, and this my guilty mind soon suggested to me, was out of abhorrence of my worse than brutish murder. At once I was filled with frightful and ghastly horrours, and my conscience began to tear and distract me with the apprehensions of Divine as well as human Justice. I made straight for Down my frequent haunt and Scene of wickedness, and thought to overlay and smother the a Wakened sense of my guilt in the Croud of my old Companions, and drive away the uneasie forbodding thoughts of punishment by excessive drinking, but I found all these but miserable Comforters; my Spirit was too deep wounded to be eased of its smart & pain by such slight and false remedies as these. For still my mind was full of horrour and confusion, and tho I ply'd, 'em hard enough during my stay there, yet for the two nights space I tarried, got I no rest at all, but on the Munday morning went to my Fathers house, with a mind so racked and tortured, with a sense of my heinous Crime that I cou'd continue no longer, but sending for my Mother, with whom on Thomson a Tailour came out, I was forced to divulge and confess the horrid Fact unto 'em, my Sorrowful Mother gave me 4 Crowns, my Aunt & Sister, a Crown and an half more; and thus I went directly to *Newry*, where also I confessed my guilt in a little time, and stayed 6 days to take shipping for *England*, before I was apprehended by *James Stewart*, who found 8 Crowns in my Pocket, brought me to a Justice of the Peace, who wrote my Mittimus; and he the said *Stewart* guarded me to the Goal, where I have been keept ever since, I was still flattered with some hopes of life, tho' very groundless and unreasonable; and therefore stood my Tryal & boldly pleaded not guilty, tho the Fact was Notorious & Evident by the most undenyable Circumstances, I own my condemnation Just, and my Sentence in its outmost Severity, deserved by me. And here I must not forget to acknowledge my disposition was always fierce & cruel, apt to break out into all the Extravagancies of Rage & Madness, ready to fight and quarrel upon the most triffling Occasion.

But yet however infamous my cruel deliberate shedding of innocent blood, may justly render me in the Eyes of all good men I must beg of them to judge of me no worse than I deserve, & no to believe that I either killed any other Person, or had a design upon the life of, one Dixion, for I solemnly declare before that awfull Judge, to whom I must soon give ane account of my doings, that these reports are false and groundless. And now beging forgiveness of God I mean for all my offences committed against them, I humbly resign my Spirit, to God who gave it, & do cast my self, on his mercy, trusting and depending on the Merits and Mediation of Christ Jesus our Lord and dearest Saviour, for blotting out my sins, delivering me from blood guiltiness, & reconcealing me to God the Father, whose Laws I have broken and whose Image I have struck at, and destroyed in that innocent Person, whom with a hard heart and bloody hand I murdered, and now all Reparation I mean to make for this horrid Fact, is to beg and intreat with my dying words, that all that behold or may hear of my Fatal end may take warning from my sad Example, to watch and guard themselves against those Sins, which have at length brought me to such Deepths of wickedness. And in a special manner, I wou'd address my self to all my Companions in Youth, that they wou'd carefully shun these things which, I have here confessed to have been snares unto me, as they wou'd not desire to be Companions with me in guilt and Punishment. Let this my publick Execution with all its shame and torment, strike horror to your minds and not only convince you of the depth and dreadful guilt of Murder, but let you see how much you are concerned to keep at a distance from the first beginnings of vice, for if once you give way to sin, you know not where you shall end, you may be assured from me who thought as little of coming to such an ignominious death when I first entred, upon a Course of Sin, as any of you can do. And now I hope, out of a deep Compassion to such a wretched Person, you will join with me in recommending my poor Soul to the Mercy of God through the Merits and Intercession of our Lord and Saviour Jesus *Christ Amen.*

FINIS

Printed by HUGH BROUN, in the *University of Glasgow.* M.DCC.XIV.

(Cambridge University Library, Bradshaw Collection, Hib.8.714.1).

12

THE LAST SPEECHES AND DYING WORDS OF

John Riley, Alexander Bourk, Martin Carrol, James Commins, Thomas Neal, Neal Lacy, Michael Cleary, alias Mc. Daniel

Who were Executed on the 26th of June, 1714.

Good Christans.

Finding it but folly to make any long Speeches at this Juncture, being sensible that no Printer would be troubled to publish what we would speak, therefore we only acquaint you, that the four Persons who swore at our Tryals, have gone beyond the bounds of Truth and reason in their Evidence; purely for the lucre of a reward from the Government, upon which account we lay nothing to the Charge of the Government nor our Jury, but that according as the Evidence swore against us (if they swore Truth) we all desearve to die by the Laws of the Nation, for that we were under Her Majesty's Government as quiet and easy as any Subjects in the world. I the said John Riley was born of very honest good Parents in the County of Ardmagh and am now about 44 years of Age. I Alexander Burke was born at Portumna in the County of Galway, and the said Martin Carroll near Philips-town in the Kings-County, and never before now Guilty of any crime before this; therefore we do expect the hearty Prayers of all good Christians, and do pray you all to take example by our untimely end, and to be contented to live happy and easy under the good sound Laws of the present Government. The said Burke is about 28 years of age, and the said Carroll about 38, we all die Romon-Catholicks, and the Lord receive our Souls

John Riley, Alexander Bourk, Martin Carroll.

The last Speech and Dying Words of James COMMINS.

I was born in the County of Kildare, on the Estate of Old Esq; Keating. I am now about the Age of Forty Eight Years, now I am brought to this untimely End, for the burning of a Houfe and the murdering of one Nicholas Leneham, I do declare as I am a Dying Man, and that I cannot expect to fee the Face of Christ, with a Lye in my Mouth, that I don't know whether I Committed the said Fact or not, not that I Charge unjustice done me but that fame Day I took the Convulsion Fits, which took my senses from me. Therefore I am sorry for all my Transgressions in this world, and begs the Prayers of all Christians.

I die a Roman Catholick, and the Lord Receive my Soul.

James Commins

The Last Speech of Thomas Neal

I Was born in Ardmale in the County of Tipperary, did serve my time to one Nicholas Casey Butcher in Clonmell, and being out of mytime, I came to Dublin and began to set up for my self upon the Glibb, where I lived very honest for several Years, untill I happen'd to break then I Listed my self in my Lord Montjoyes Regiment of Foot, and being Disbanded out of the said Regiment, I Unfortunately met with one Michael Cleary, One of my present Fellow-Sassets, who was a Loose wicked Liver, and who brought me to this Dismal Doom. I own I justly die for the present Fact, I forgive all the World, and I beg the Prayers and Forgiveness of all People, I die a Roman Catholick and the Lord have Mercy on my Poor Soul

Thomas Neale.

The Speech of Neal LEACY.

Good Christians.

I Was born at Portlanone in the County of Antrim, I came from thence to Dublin when I was but 2 years of age, I lost my Father at the Fight of Aghrim, after his death I went to live with one George Pain, formerly Merchant in High-street, who liv'd that time in the County of Wexford; from thence I went and livd with one Derengy Esq; with whom I liv'd for a 11 years, afterwards I was recommended by Capt. Miller to Brigadier Steerns, with whom I liv'd but a short while, from thence Mr George Walton recommended me to Ralph Gore Esq; then Lord Mayor of this City, from thence to John Ormsby Esq; of this City, from thence to Mr Walton, who most unfortunately employ'd me to take one Roony upon Action on the 24th of October last, but the said Roony, strugling and striving to get away from me by saying that he had a Protection, whereupon I having a Pistol charg'd in my hand which accidentially fir'd, and which I believe shot the Person for whom I am to die for, being one Stephen Young, who as I expect to appear immediately before the Judg of Heaven and Earth, was shot without any design of mine, tho' it was sworn aginst me at my Tryal that my then Mrs. Walton gave me orders to shoot the said Young, which as I hope for salvation was false, I lay my blessing with all my said Masters, Misteres's and their several Famelies, and Lord forgive the said Roony's Wife and Youngs widow for what they have sowrn against me. I beg very heartly for the Prays of all good Christians, I am about 39 years of Age, I forgive all the World, as I beg they'l forgive me, I die a Romon-Catholick, and the Lord have mercy on my Soul.

The Last Sppech and Dying Words of Michael Cleary, al. Mc. Danniel

I *Am Son to Hugh Cleary, and was born near Portumna in the Parish of Lorha and County of Tipperary. I liv'd all my Life-time very honest, untill some few years ago, that I unfortunately met with one Charles*

Carroll a Highway-Man who was Executed at Phillipstown for the same, but prevail'd on me to be one of his Companions, and to follow his own wicked Course of Life, but after the faid Carrol's Execution, I unfortunately came to Dublin, to one Antisles House in James's-street, knowing that to be the sd-Carrol's Lodgings, and the said An - le and Family hearing that there was 50 pounds Reward for Apprehending me, who in hopes of getting the same, he betray'd me in his own House, which said sum I wish my bloody Prosecutors may never Receive.

I am about 40 years of Age, I own that I have deserv'd Death for several Reasons. For that I have been concern'd in several Robberies and Fellonies, for which I beg the earnest Prayers of all good Christians. I forgive all the world, as I hope they'll forgive me. I Die a Roman-Catholick and the Lord Receive my poor Soul.

WHEREAS the several Speeches of one (Neal Lacy, Tho. Neal, Michael Cleary alias Mc. Donnell and Jam. Judge, have been falsely Printed in this City about 3 Months ago; These are therefore to give Notice, that the Printers of the said Speeches never did see the sd. Persons Faces, nor had he any person concern'd for him. And that any Printer who shall for the said Attempt to Publish such sham Speeches, shall be Prosecuted according to Law.

Dublin Printed by C. Carter, in Fish-shamble street, 1714.

(Cambridge University Library, Bradshaw Collection, Hib.O.714.22)

13

LAST SPEECH AND DYING WORDS OF

Richard Lawler, Jeremiah Farrel, James Quin, and Alexander Mac Cann

who were Executed at St Stephen's-Green, on Saturday the 10th of December, 1715.

I *Richard Lawler,* Son of *Edmond Lawler,* was born in *Castle-Town,* in the County of *Carloe,* of honest Parents, who gave me good Education; I am about 31 years of Age. The manner of my being brought into this dreadful Misfortune, is as follows. One *George Lesly,* and one *Richard Wilson,* sent for me from my Shop in *Thomas-street,* to one Mr *Kelly's House,* at the lower end of *New-Row,* and ask'd me whether I had made the two Smoothing-Irons they had agreed with me for; I reply'd I had not; but they made Answer, that was not the bus'ness they sent to me for, but to get them a Customer for a parcel of Brass they had to dispose of; I told them I did not know where to get them one; but they desired me to go to Mr *Shurlock,* Brasier in *Back-Lane;* and if I could sell the Brass for them they wou'd make me drink; So by their direction I went to the said *Shurlock,* and desired him, or one for him, to go down to the said *Kelly's-House* and make a Bargain, with them, for the said Brass.

The said *Shurlock* sent a Servant with me to the said Place, which Servant weigh'd the said Brass, and carried it to his said Master, and I went with him to Mr *Shurlock,* in order to receive the Money; but Mr *Shurlock* told me he wou'd call upon me at my Shop, and pay me; but I told him I had nothing to do with it; and what I did was upon the Entreaty of the said *Leisly* and *Wilson.* Mr *Shurlock* immediately came to my Shop, who ask'd me, *Are you at Work.* I answer'd, I am. I am making two Smoothing Irons for the Persons that I had the Brass of. He invited me to go to my Landlord's and take a Glass of Ale; which I did. And he seem'd to be concern'd that his Servant was so long before he brought the Money to pay for said Brass. I said to him the Money was not to be pay'd to me, but to the said Persons that were at Mr *Kelly's* House, at which I went down to see if Mr. *Shurlock's* Man was at *Mr Kelly's*; but when I came there, I found one had made his Escape, and the other in Custody; And at my Approach a Constable seiz'd me; but telling the Constable I was but a Minuit ago with Mr *Shurlock* at my Landlord's, and was just going to him again, so that by that Means I made my Escape and left the Town for Eight Days, for Fear of being made an Evidence against the other Person. And as for Stealing the said Brass, or having any Hand in it, than what is before recited, I declare to the World I am intirely Innocent of it, tho' I suffer'd for it.

Some little time after, late at Night, going home, I unfortunately met with one *Hanlan*, who was talking with a Quaker at the *Tholsel*, and as I was passing on, *Hanlan* call'd after me, and desired me to affront, and pick a quarrel with the said Quaker, which I refus'd to do; After which denial, Hanlan went himself to the Quaker, and gave him a stroke on the Head, and after run away; And the said Quaker turning to me, thinking, I suppose, I had given him the blow, knock me down with great Violence, and after I had got up, I drew, and run him in the Right Arm. I went of, towards *Nicholas-Gate*, and he persuing me very close, I begg'd very often of him, for God's sake, to keep off, but he refusing, I gave him a thrust in the left Breast, to my great grief. I suffer for this Fact (tho' the Surgeon testify'd he did not dye of the Wounds I gave him).

I dye a Roman-Catholick, and desire the Prayers of all good Christians. And the Lord have Mercy upon my Soul.

This is my true Speech, deliver'd to the Printer, on *Friday* Night December the 9th 1715. And what I intend to deliver at the Place of Execution. And if any other be Printed, they are False and Spurious.

Richard Lawler

Jeremiah Farrel, His Speech

I *Jeremiah Farrel*, was Born in the County of *Westmeath*, of honest Parents. I kept a House of Entertainment in the County of *Kildare*, between *Carloe* and *Castle-Dermot*. And lived in Credit and Repute in a Place call'd *Furmell's-Town*, for several Years; till about two Years ago I came to *Dublin*, and unfortunately fell into bad Company, and spending what Money I had, betook my self to Evil Courses. I was Condemned for Driving a Parcel of Sheep, (belonging to a Dover) which Fact I confess, and justly suffer for the same.

I dye a Roman Catholick, and desire the Prayers of all Good Christians. And the Lord have Mercy upon my Soul.
This is my true Speech.

Jeremiah Far[rel]

James Quin's Speech

I *James Quin* was born in the County of *Kilkenny*, of honest, Parents. I have lived in Creditab[le services]. I served the Bishop of *Ossory* for several Years, and during my Service, behaved my s[elf true] and honest, till about Seven Years ago I came to *Dublin*, and fell unfortunately into wicked C[ompany] living a leud and vicious life, as Swearing, Thieving, breaking the the Sabbath, and keeping of ill [and bad] Company, and many other Crimes. And at length being Tried for Robbing one Mr Thomas N[of] Back-Lane, for which I Dye.

I Dye a Roman Catholick. And the Lord have Mercy on my Soul.

Ja[mes Quin]

Alexander Mc. Cann's Speech

I Was Born in the Highlands of *Scotland*, and coming to *Dublin* some Years ago, to receive [work] for some time, but falling into ill Company, leading a wicked Life, and prone to all Vices [brought] my self to this untimely Death. I Dye for the same Fact, my Fellow-Sufferer (*James Quin*) [suffers].

I Dye a Protestant. And the Lord have Mercy upon my Soul.

Alexander M[c Cann]

(Location: Cambridge University Library, Bradshaw Collection, Hib.0.715.1).

14

THE LAST SPEECH AND DYING WORDS OF

Garret Landergan

who was Executed at St Stephen's-Green on Saturday the 19th of this Inst. January 1716-17.

Good People.

I Was Born in the County of Corke of very Honest Parents who gave me Reasonable Education according to their Ability untill I was about ten Years of Age, that my Father and Mother came to live in Dublin, where alas! to my Wonderful Grief and sad Surprize, I soon embrac'd the Loose, Idle Pickpockets and Vagabonds, in whose Wicked Conversation, I took so much Delight, that I never could be Wean'd from such tho' my Parents have done their Duty in Binding me to the Paving Trade, by which I might a got Honest Bread, if I had the Grace to Live Honest and follow the same, but Lackedea, what I find to be the greatest Burthen to my Conscience at this Juncture is, that by my Lewd way of Living I brought the Grey Hairs of my Honest Father with Sorrow to the Grave, which together with the Tears and Curses of my Mother who is still alive in this City, I fear has brought me to this most Shameful End, by which I pray you all my Spectators to take Warning, and especially the Younger sort that you pray to your Heavenly Father to give you Grace to Live in the Love and Fear of God and to keep you out of such Company as brought me to be a publick Example to you all, and that you also Comfort, Cherish, Love and Obey your Parents.

I declare here, in the Presence of you all, That I had the Misfortune, at several times e're now, to be concern'd in a great many Robberies, and other Debaucheries, for which I find to my Shame and Disgrace, that the Vengeance of Heaven, has justly overtaken me, and for which I heartily beg God Almighty's Pardon, and the sincere Prayers of all good Christians. I *cannot not don's deny, but that I was accessary to the Robbery of Capt. Rose, for which I justly loose my dear Life, tho' as I expect very soon to appear before the Searcher of all Hearts, I took none of his Wine, tho' I believe the Men that were in my Company took some Bottles of Wine, and I believe I might have taken some for my share if the Watch had not come into Captain* Rose's *Cellar so soon, where they found me standing with my Paver's Rule in my Hand, but my Company being apprehended by the Watch as well as I the rest made their Escape, and I was unfortunately left in the Lurch, to be made an Example to you my Spectators. I forgive all the World, as I expect they will also forgive me. I most particularly beg the Prayers and Blessing of my dear ancient Mother. I am about 36 Years of Age; I die a* Roman Catholick, *and the Lord have Mercy upon my poor sinful Soul.* Amen. *This is my True Speech and no other.*

Garret Landergan.

Dublin, Printed by C. C. 1716-17.

(Location: Cambridge University Library, Bradshaw Collection, Hib.0.716.3)

15

SPEECHES AND DYING WORDS OF

James Nowlan, and John Fitz-Symmons

who were Executed near St. Stephens-Green, on Saturday the 23d of February, 1716- 17.

To all good Christians

Tis the general Method of Persons under the Sentence of Death, to satisfie the World, by making a formal Speech at the Place of Execution. But because Artful Printers often foist Imperfect and Sham Accounts of the Town; I think it requisite to inform every Body of the truth of my present Uphappiness, and what fatal Consequences brought me to this Untimely End.

I was Born in Church-Street in the Parish of St. Michans of honest Parents, but notwithstanding they gave me all manner of good Education becoming a Gentleman, and might have advanc'd my self on better grounds than Villany, had not the Seducements of vicious Company perverted my youthful Intentions. For in my Infancy I was Educated a Roman Catholick, but falling off from Virtue, I forsook Religion, and ran into all manner of Intemperance.

That I was bred a Surgeon-Barber, and truly served an Apprenticeship to the same, after which time I gave my self to Gaming, Drinking, Whoring, but never was prone to any manner of Theft or Defraud, till by my Gaming I fell into Company with Daniel Costikin, who is now in the Black-dog, likewise with Robert Twadle and James Crookshanks, who were Soldiers in Colonel Price's Regiment of Foot, who brought me to all manner of Gaming at Cards and Dice. Likewise to Preach the Parson, a false notorious Cheating Game at Cards, from thence I came to Travel in pretence of Selling Wiggs, and carried the like with me to hide my design, and pretended to buy Hair, but the Head of which I Preached the Parson,

SPEECHES AND DYING WORDS

Of *James Nowlan*, and *John Fitz-Symmons*, who were Executed near St. Stephens-Green, On Saturday the 23d of February, 1716-17.

To all good Christians,

'Tis the general Method of Persons under the Sentence of Death, to satisfie the World, by making a formal Speech at the Place of Execution. But because Artful Printers often foist Imperfect and Sham Accounts of the Town ; I think it requisite to inform every Body of the truth of my present Unhappiness, and what fatal Consequences brought me to this Untimely End.

I was Born in Church-Street in the Parish of St. Michans of honest Parents, but notwithstanding they gave me all manner of good Education becoming a Gentleman, and might have advanc'd my self on better grounds than Villany, had not the Seducements of vicious Company perverted my youthful Intentions. For in my Infancy I was Educated a Roman Catholick, but falling off from Virtue, I forsook Religion, and ran into all manner of Intemperance.

That I was bred a Surgeon-Barber, and truly served an Apprenticeship to the same, after which time I gave my self to Gaming, Drinking, Whoring, but never was prone to any manner of Theft or Defraud, till by my Gaming I fell into Company with Daniel Costikin, who is now in the Black-Dog, likewise with Robert Twadle and James Crookshanks, who were Soldiers in Colonel Price's Regiment of Foot, who brought me to all manner of Gaming at Cards and Dice. Likewise to Preach the Parson, a false notorious Cheating Game at Cards, from thence I came to Travel in pretence of Selling Wiggs, and carried the like with me to hide my design, and pretended to buy Hair, but the Head of which I Preached the Parson, and learn'd to Frap, a deceiting way of Cheating all whom I dealt with, by Changing a Piece of Money, and being more Nimble-finger'd than ordinary, out of the Change of a Crown, would Cheat them out of 3 Thirteens very often, by which and the like, I Travell'd most part of this Kingdom, then when well acquainted in this Kingdom of Ireland, I went for England, where I followed the like unjust Dealings, till I came acquainted with some of the Padders in England, with whom I made no scruple to stand on the Road several times, till I had put my self in pretty good order, then I could not be at Ease till I return'd from where I Travell'd as before, a considerable Playing, Gaming, and Frapping, and the like, but the greatest of my misfortune proved by my proud haughty Spirit, which occasion'd me several times to fall out with several, even with my own Companions, which bent them and several Gentlemen against me.

I then resolv'd to go back for England, but meeting with one Robert Harley who was also on the same design, which said Harley brought me to his Lodging in St. Francis-Street, where we both were Apprehended for Stealing a Silver-Tankard belonging to Mr. Jeremy Cash in Cutpurse-Row, which said Tankard was stole by the said Harley, who made his Escape out of Newgate, with Rice and Carrol. As I am a Dying Man I am Innocent, and never was in his House, nor never saw him or his Wife, or the Boy, or Girl, until the day of my Tryal.

I Dye a Roman Catholick, the Lord have Mercy upon my poor Soul.
This is my true Speech and no other, James Nowlan.

The SPEECH of John Fitz-Symmons.

Good Christians,

I John Fitz-Symmons was Born in the County of Meath, within seven Miles of Drogheda of Poor Parents, but honest, they never gave me any Education, but brought me up to hard Labour, till at last I went as a servant to Mr. Marvin ; who gave me some Money to buy some Cattle, which Money I Embezeled, and for fear of incurring my Masters displeasure, or loosing my Place, and knew not how to raise this Money again, I set me down to consider what I had best for to do, the Devil Prompt me on to steal a Horse and so I did, and sold the same to a Pinn-maker, which Fact I own I am Guilty.

I Dye a Roman Catholick, and the Lord have Mercy on my poor Soul.
This is my true Speech and no other, John Fitz-Symmons.

DUBLIN: Printed by Elizabeth Sadleir, in School-House-Lane, 1716-17.

and learn'd to Frap, a deceiting way of Cheating all whom I dealt with, by Changing a Piece of Money, and being more Nimble-finger'd than ordinary, out of the Change of a Crown, would Cheat them out of 3 Thirteens very often, by which and the like, I Travell'd moſt part of this Kingdom, then when well acquainted in this Kingdom of Ireland, I went for England, where I followed the like unjuſt Dealings, till I came acquainted with some of the Padders in England, with whom I made no scruple to stand on the Road several times, till I had put my self in pretty good order, then I could not be at Ease till I return'd from where I Travell'd as before, a considerable Playing, Gaming, and Frapping, and the like, but the greatest of my misfortune proved by my proud haughty Spirit, which occasion'd me several times to fall out with several, even with my own Companions, which bent them and several Gentlemen against me.

I then resolv'd to go back for England, but meeting with one Robert Harley who was also on the fame design, which said Harley brought me to his Lodging in St. Francis-Street, where we both were Apprehended for Stealing a Silver-Tankard belonging to Mr. Jeremy Cash in Cutpurse-Row, which said Tankard was stole by the said Harley, who made his Escape out of Newgate, with Rice and Carrol. As I am a Dying Man I am innocent, and never was in his Houſe, nor never saw him or his Wife, or the Boy, or Girl, until the day of my Tryal.

> I Dye a Roman Catholick, the Lord have Mercy upon my poor Soul. This is my true Speech and no other, James Nowlan.

The SPEECH of John Fitz-Symmons.

Good Christians.

I John Fitz-Symmons was Born in the County of Meath, within seven Miles of Drogheda of Poor Parents, but honest, they never gave me any Education, but brought me up to hard Labour, till at last I went as a servant to Mr Marvin; who gave me some Money to buy some Cattle, which Money I Embezeled, and for fear of incurring my Masters displeasure, or loosing my Place, and knew not how to raise this Money again, I set me down to consider what I had best for to do, the Devil Prompt me on to steal a Horse and so I did, and sold the same to a Pinn-maker, which Fact I own I am Guilty.

I Dye a Roman Catholick, and the Lord have Mercy
on my poor Soul.

This is my true Speech and no other, John Fitz-Symmons.

DUBLIN: Printed by Elizabeth Sadleir, in School-Houfe-Lane, 1716-17.

(Location: Cambridge University Library, Bradshaw Collection, Hib.0.716.4)

16

A PARTICULAR CONFESSION OF

Sarah Grew

just now going to Execution at St. Stephen's-Green, being the 13th day of July 1717 With particular Accounts of Thefts and Correspondants, and Receivers of the Goods, for which she was Convicted and Condemn'd.

SArah Grew, was born at Loughgall in the County of Ardmagh, of poor and dispiseable People; In the War time her Father became a topping Rapperee and being taken, by the Provoes, was Hang'd on the Road between Loughgale and Monaha, by order of the Provost Marshal, and left his Wife and 4 children to shift for themselves; Their Mother believing they wou'd find little Favour in their own Country, retir'd with her Charge Begging to Lurgan-Clonbrazil then the Town of greatest business and Wealth of all Ulster; where the Inhabitants in pitty, and supposing them Honest, took all the Children; and Sarah's Lot happen'd to fall in with Thomas Walker, Father to Mrs. Webb, from whom she stole the Goods, for which she was con-condemn'd, being in all to the Value of near 200*l*. with Mr. Walker she liv'd near 2 Years, when some of the other Children being detected at Lurgan of Theft, and receiving Stolen Goods, Sarah pretending to be asham'd, retir'd to Dublin about 7 or 8 Years since, where she addrest herself to Mr. Webb; who recommended her to the *Widdow Biven* in St. James-street, with whom she liv'd some Time, thence she went to live with Mr *William Dean* in St. Patrick-street, where she remain'd but a short Time by reason of a Cruel Tongue; thence she went to live with *James Hobson* In Brides-Alley; and remain'd there 2 Years afterwards went to, and liv'd about 2 Years with *Sam. Watson*, then at the Corner of Bride's-Alley, and after that liv'd with Mr. *Wm. Constable* in High-street, in all which Places she behav'd herself with the utmost Insolence and Impudence, and not without Suspicion of Theft and Whoredom, but more particularly at Mr Constables, who during her Being there, lost several Sums of Moneys and Parcells of Goods; but she always behav'd herself so Cuningly, and pretended so much Honesty, that he had no Mistrust of her, till detected by Mrs. Webb who had so good an Opinion of her, as always to Plead every where for her Honesty; and to confirm it, after all the rest entertain'd her as a Servant to herself, where she liv'd about a Year and 9 Months; and had always recourse to the Shop, Ware-house, and every thing therein, Mrs. Webb frequently mist her Goods, yet could not entertain an ill Opinion of her Servant Sarah, till after leaving her Service, she put some Muzling Head Cloaths to be made by one Phillis Allen, a young Woman in Arundal-Court, with whom she had insinuated herself to Lodge, and Phillis Allen asked her what the Muzling cost, and being told, thought it extraordinary cheap, went to, and asked Mrs. Webb how she would sell such Muzling and being told a much greater Rate than what Sarah said that cost; Told Mrs. Webb that was bought much Cheaper, Mrs. Webb thought it was very like Muzling she had in her Shop, ask'd whose it was, and being told Sarah Grews gave Mrs Webb cause to suspect her, and to Search her Trunk, where she found, 15 Ells of Holland, cut out for Shifts, which cost Mrs. Webb 9s. 6d. the Ell, prim Coft, and 7 new fine Muzling Aprons, not wash'd, then took her minion Sarah to task; upon which Sarah, discover'd several Parcels of her Mistresses Goods log'd with, several of her Associates: Particularly with one Devilin in Golden-lane near St. Bride's-street, 16 Pieces of fine Linnen, with Mrs. Webb's own Mark on them, and several Pieces of Holland cut into Sheets, and unsewd; and several other Pieces with one Devilin in Dromcondrah-Lane, and with one Jane Carr that lately before creept into the Service of Dr. Lewin in Arundal Court, for which the Doctor would have had prosecuted, but for the Perswasions of Mr. Webb, to the contrary; And Mrs. Gallahar in St Patrick-street having 9 Pieces lodg'd by Sarah with her, upon hearing Sarah was detected, as aforesaid of Stealing her Mistriss's Goods, supposed those Pieces might been Stole from her, brought them to Mrs. Webb, who in all recover'd but about 60 pounds worth out of near 200 pounds worth which she stole. And 'tis believ'd the rest was convey'd to her Mother and Sister, which last, is Alce Grew who liv'd some Time with one Fox at the Sign of the Wheat-sheaf and 3 Pidgeons, faceing Vicars-Street, and while there a Servant, contracted the French Pox, which Sarah well knew and took her from her Service and kept her in Lodgings, till Cured and paid for the Cure, and she lies now in Newgate for receiving from her Sifter Sarah part of Mrs. Webb's Goods. So that they are not only the Spawn of Thieves, but also themselves, both Thieves and Whores. When Sarah was reproach'd for Ingratitude, as well as Baseness, in so abuseing so good a Friend, and Mistriss, and to whose Family, she was oblig'd to in a manner for the Being she had, she to save and excuse herself, laid all the whole Charge upon Mrs. Webb's Daughter, and said she receiv'd all the Goods she Stole, from her. But the 15th of June being appointed for her Execution by her first Sentance; and seeing no hopes of Life, the Night before, own'd all she had Charg'd her Mistresses Daughter with, was utterly false. That she had from Time to Time Stole from her Mistriss to the Vallue of near 200 pounds, and wou'd discover where to be found, but for fear of bringing the Receivers to Trouble. And that the Charge she made upon her Mistriss's Daughter was in hopes by Criminateing the Girl, to get clear herself: But escapeing then afterwards chang'd her Notes, and as its suppose urg'd to it by some Enemy's to the Girl and the Mother, has since renew'd the Charge upon the Girl: Tho' no Body that knows Mrs. Webb or her Daughter, will give Credit, to any Callumnies rais'd against them by a notorious Thief and Whore, under Condemnation for her Crimes. And if I am not miss-inform'd by the Chyrurgeon that Cured her, the condemn'd Miscreant, was Poxt twice, and Miscarry'd in Dublin twice, and upon that Account left her last Service, to have the Opportunity for so doing, without Suspition.

Dublin, Printed John Whalley in Arundal-Court.

(Location: Cambridge University Library, Bradshaw Collection, Hib.0.717.4).

17

THE SPEECHES OF

Captain Maurice Fitzgerald, Charles Burn and Francis Burn

who are to be Executed at Blessing-town, on Friday the 27th of this Instant December, 1717.

I Maurice Fitzgerrald, was born in the County of Kildare, and bred in the County of Carlow, of very honest Parents; and that my Father Garrett Fitzgerrald was a Gentleman in King James's Army, who, by the Misfortune of the World, went for France, after the Surrender of Limerick; and that for the Want of Friends or Substance, I miss'd the Opportunity of Learning, or a Trade; that for that Reason, I was oblig'd to go to serve the several Persons following, viz. William Brown, William Bumbery, and John Humphries, of the County of Carlow, Gent. and Captain Sheperdson, of the County of Kildare, Gent. in whose several Services I behaved my-self very gentile and honest, until the 9th of May last, that Hugh Connor, a proclaim'd Rapparee, impeached me for being in some Robberies along with him, which, when I understood, to save my Life, I went to the Road along with my Fellow-Sufferers. I declare, before God and the World, that I never was guilty of any rogueish rascally Actions, nor of Murther, nor of Robbing any poor Traveller Man nor Woman, tho' I was betray'd by one John Reilly, my own Confederate, and unfortunately taken by Serjeant Alexander and his Company of Soldiers. I forgive the said Hugh Connor, John Reily, and all the World besides. I am about 27 Years. I die a Roman Catholick. And the Lord have Mercy upon my Soul. Amen.

Maurice Fitzgerald

The Speech of Charles Burn

I Charles Burn was Bred and Born at Logduff near the Seven-Churches, in the County of Wicklow, of very honest Parents, I do here Declare in the presence of Almighty God, and of you all my Spectators, that I have liv'd all my Life a Quiet Honest and Sober Life, having dealt between City and Country in several Sorts of Merchandizes, until about Six Weeks ago that one Hugh Connor an out-law'd Tory and Raparree did Impeach me for Receiving of Plate and other Robberies from one John Burn who was lately Shot in the said County, and who was a pretended Captain of Raparees, and that to avoid being apprehended for the same I took to the Road along with Captain Fitz Gerrald and the rest of my Fellow-Sufferers. I declare before God and the World, that the several Persons lately accused by the said Connor and Reily in the said County, for harbouring of several Highway-Men, and for receiving several Robberies from them, are falsly and wrongfully accused. I beg the hearty Prayers of all good Christians. I am about 20 Years of Age. I die a Roman Catholick. And the Lord have Mercy upon my poor Soul.

Charles Burn.

The Speech of Francis Burn.

GOOD People, I was Born in the Parish of Frabane, in the County of Wicklow, of very honest but poor Parents; I have lived in several good Services in the said County, and behaved my self True and Honest, until one Nicholas Burn had me taken up for an Assault, and for the fame Committed to Wicklow Goal, where, I met John Reily who betray'd me; along with whom I broke out of the said Goal, and being afraid of being confined again by the Indictment of Reily, I went to the Road, and have been concern'd in several Roberies, for which I ask my Saviour Forgiveness. I forgive all the World, as I hope they will forgive me. I earnestly beg your Prayers, I am above 22 Years of Age. I die a Roman Catholick, and the Lord receive my poor Soul, Amen.

All that Art Burn says, he met with John Riley near Blessing-town, and remain'd with his fellow Sufferers for the space of four Days, and made no other Speech.

I Do certify, that the above Speeches are the true Speeches of Maurice Fitzgerrald, Charles Burn, and Francis Burn. As Witness my Hand this 25th Day of December, 1717.

Morgan Field.

Last Night the Militia of Blessing-town came to this City, and this Day went to guard the Robbers thither, in order to be try'd this Day, they Rid two and two, their Legs being chain'd under the Horses Belleys.

(Location: Cambridge University Library, Bradshaw Collection, Hib. 0.717.1)

18

THE LAST SPEECH AND DYING WORDS OF

Daniel O Neal, Edmond Mc. Guire, and Henery Graham

who was Executed near St. Stevens Green, on Wednesday June the 4th 1718.

Good Christians,

I was Born in the North of Ireland, of very good honest Parents, who brought me up very Tenderly, and never speard any Cost to Instruct and bring me up in the fear of God, Alas! all was in vain, for tho' I took all the care that I could to attain to Learning but at the end I prov'd very Careless of the fame, for I neglected both the laws of God and Man, or else I had never been brought to this shameful End, it is true I was taken up for the Stealing of three Horses, and two Mares, and these my fellow Sufferers along with me, but as I shall Answer the great God, they Die Innocently, for as I was Riding along the Road, I overtook these my fellow Sufferers who seeing me leading 4 Horses asked me if I would let them ride, I tould them they should, now as I am a dying Man this is all they knew of it, which grives me to the Heart, and indeed I am more sorry for their Death, than my own.

I freely forgive all the World, and I beg forgiveness of all those whom I ever offended, I am now about six and thirty Years of Age, I die a of the Church of England, and the Lord have mercy on my Soul, Amen.

This is my true Speech and no other

Daniel O Neal

The Speech of *Edmond M'Guire.*

Good Christians,

I Was born in the North of Ireland, of Poor, but honest Parents, who with their Industry, Care and Labour, brought me to these Years, during which time, I behav'd my self true and honest in the World, and endeavour'd very hard for my Bread; but I being born to hard Fortune, I was taken up by one Mr. Legg, for being concern'd in stealing of three Horses and two Mares; 'tis true I had one of the aforesaid Beasts under me, but the way I came by it was in the manner following: I having been in Dublin for some time, was willing to return home to my Wife and Children, and overtaking Daniel O Neale, my fellow Sufferer; he having the Cattle abovemention'd, I ask'd him if he wou'd let me Ride, he said he wou'd oblige any Traveller as much as he could, and so bid me Mount one of the Horses, which I did, and was very thankful to him for his kindness; but to my great Sorrow, it has prov'd the worst rideing that ever I rid in my life: Now, as I am a dying Man, I was never guilty of stealing the value of two Pence in all my Life: nor had I any Hand in stealing those Beasts which I am to Dye for. I forgive all the World, as I hope to be forgiven. I am about 40 Years of Age, and Dye a Roman Catholik, and the Lord have Mercy on my Poor Soul. Amen, Amen.

The Speech of *Henry Graham.*

Good Christians,

I was born in the North of *Ireland*, of very honest Parents, who was very tender over me, and brought me up in the fear of GOD as much as in them Lay; but Fortune has been very Cruel to me, or else I had never came to this Place, for I liv'd with my Parents till I came to get a Wife; and indeed it was my Fortune to get a poor honest Girl, who endeavour'd very honest for her Bread as well as I, but the World frowning upon me, I went and listed in the Army, where I behav'd myself as became a good Subject, at lenth I was broak, and so return'd home to my Wife again, but my Business calling me home to Dublin, to my great Sorrow I went there, but having finish'd my

Business, I was going home again, where unfortunately I met with *Danel O. Neal*, and *Edmond M'Guire* a Ridnig along the Road, to whom I said, pray let me Ride, and indeed, they freely comply'd, but I had not Rid long before we were all taken and committed to Goal, and from that brought to Dublin, so Try'd and found Guilty of the same, and now brought to his Place to end my life, now as GOD is my Judge, before whom I hope to appear in short time, I had neither Act nor Part in stealing of the said Horses, or any of them, and I die in Charity with all Men, and do freely forgive those who Swore away my Life as I hope to be forgiven, I am about 30 Years of Age. I die a Protestant and the Lord have mercy on my Soul.

Henry Graham.

(Location: Cambridge University Library, Bradshaw Collection, Hib.0.718.5)

19

THE LAST SPEECH AND DYING WORDS OF

John Magee

who was Executed near St. Stephens Green this 18th, Day of February 1718-19 for stealing a Bay Gelding from Mr. Robinet the Attorney.

GOOD Christians, being now brought to this place of Execution where I have but a very short time longer to live in this world, I think it is my Duty to Discharge my Conscience, by declaring to you all my past Life and Conversation, which I hope shall be a warning to as many of you as did lead such a Wicked Course of Life as I did.

I was Born in the County of Monaghan of very honest but mean Parents who have shewed me a very good example, if I had the grace to follow their steps, and about Sixteen years ago being then about 20 years of Age I became so headstrong, in so much that I grew Disobedient to my Parents and forsaking them gave my self to playing Cards, Dice, and to keep company with loose idle Men, and Women who delighted most in cursing, & Swareing, Drinking and Stealing, and about ten years ago I came to live in about Dragheda, where I unfortunately married without the consent of any of my Parents; and being often pinch'd for wanu of Money I Stole several Horses backward and forward beetween Linster and Ulster, along with others of my Confederates.

But about 2 years agoe I was apprehended in the County of Dublin for stealing a Horse for which I was committed to Killmanham Gaole, where I was Tryed for my Life, Convicted and sentenc'd to be Executed but my Friends Expecting that I should change my course of Life and being moved with Pitty they got me a Reprieve which they brought the very minute that I was going to the Gallows and the Rope about my neck; and being so Repriev'd my

JOHN MAGEE

good Friends gott me a free Pardon paid all my Fees and procur'd my Liberty (but alais), I like an unfortunate, Stubborn wicked Liver, have turn'd to my former Trade again, by Stealing Horses from one Country to another.

But more particularly and unfortunately, I stole the said Mr. Robinets Horse from Glasnevin, out of one Mr. Burns Fied, which Horse was found in my Custody as the Pi'd Horse in Caple Street, where I was Apprehended and committed to Newgate for the same, and for which I was Prosecuted at the last Term, and justly found Guilty, and accordingly I am brought here to be a publick Example to you all.

Therefore I wish you may all take notice by shuning such Company as I Embrac'd being the Distruction of Mankind, I forgive the said Robinet; I also forgive my Wife who lives in Dragheda, but never came near me since my Confinement. I lave my Blessing with my three Children, and with all the World in General, as I hope to receive their forgiveness, and particularly theirs I have any ways offended, I hartily beg all your harty Prayers; I am about 36 Years of Age, I die a Roman Catholick and the Lord have Mercy upon my poor Soul Amen.

This is my last and true Speech given by my self to a friend in Newgate, any other Speech is false and Counterfit.

John Maggee.

Dublin: Print by G.N.

(Location: Cambridge University Library, Bradshaw Collection, Hib.0.718.13)

The Last SPEECH

And Dying words of *John Magee* who was Executed near St. *Stephens Green* this 18th, Day of February 1718-19 for stealing a Bay Gelding from Mr. Robinet the Attorney.

GOOD Christians, being now brought to this place of Execution where I have but a very short time longer to live in this world, I think it is my Duty to Discharge my Concience, by declaring to you all my past Life and Conversation, which I hope shall be a warning to as many of you as did lead such a Wicked Course of Life as I did.

I was Born in the County of Monaghan of very honest but mean Parents who have shewed me a very good example, if I had the grace to follow their steps, and about Sixteen years ago being then about 20 years of Age I became so headstrong, in so much that I grew Disobedient to my Parents and forsaking them gave my self to playing Cards, Dice, and to keep company with loose idle Men, and Women who delighted most in cursing, & Swearing: Drinking and Stealing, and about ten years ago I came to live in about Draghada, where I unfortunatly married without the consent of any of my Parents; and being often pinch'd for want of Money I Stole several Horses backward and forward beetween Linster and Ulster, along with others of my Confederates,

But about 2 years agoe I was apprehended in the County of Dublin for stealing a Horse for, which I was committed to Killmanham Goale, where I was Tryed for my Life, Convicted and sentenc'd to be Executed but my Friends Expecting that I should change my course of Life and being moved with Pitty they got me a Reprieve which they brought the very minute that I was going to the Gallows and the Rope about my neck; and being so Repriev'd my good Friends gott me a free Pardon paid all my Fees and procur'd my Liberty (to whom) I like an unfortunate, Stubborn wicked Liver, have turn'd to my former Trade again, by Stealing Horses from one County to another.

But more particularly and unfortunately, I stole the said Mr. Robinets *Horse* from *Glasnevin*, out of one Mr. *Burns Feed, which Horse was found in my Custody at the Pi'd Horse in Caple Street, where I was Apprehended and committed to Newgate for the same, and for which I was Prosecuted at the last Term, and justly found Guilty, and accordingly I am brought here to be a publick Example to you all.*

Therefore I wish you may all take notice by shuning such Company as I Embrac'd being the Distruction of Mankind, I forgive the said Robinet; I also forgive my Wife who lives in Draghada, but never came near me since my Confinement: I lave my Blessing with my three Children, and with all the World in General, as I hope to receive their forgiveness; and particularly theirs I have any ways offended, I hartily beg all your harty Prayers; I am about 56 Years of Age, I die a Roman Catholick and the Lord have Mercy upon my poor Soul Amen.

This is my last and true Speech given by my self to a Friend in Newgate, any other Speech is false and Counterfit.

John Maggee

Dublin Printby G. N.

20

THE LAST SPEECH AND DYING WORDS OF

Charles Calahar alias Collmore

who was Try'd on Tuesday the 17th Inst. Feb. 1718/19 at the Sessions of Dundalk, for being a Proclaim'd Tory, and was the next Day Hang'd, Quarter'd and his Intrals burn'd.

Deliver'd at the Gallows to Will Moore Esq. High Sheriff of the County of Lowth.

Good People,

ALMIGHTY God has by a just Providence brought me to this untimely End, He has been Mercifully pleas'd not to Cut me off in the midst of my Sins, but to allow me some Time to reflect on my unhappy mis spent Life, and to Implore Forgiveness for my many Iniquities, which I trust he will graciously Pardon.

And as my Crimes have been of publick crying Nature, so I think myself Bound to make a publick Confession of them both to God and my Country.

And first with Shame and Confusion of Face I confess I have been Guilty of many Robberries and Thefts, and have also Seduced and Encouraged others to do the like.

I Barbarously and Unjustly Embru'd my Hands in the Blood of my Fellow Creatures, and in particular I Murder'd Martin Grey and Christopher Betty, and suffer'd that worthy honest Gent. Mr. Edmond Reily to be wrongfully Executed at Cavan Assizes for the said Murders; He being no ways Privy or Accessary to them, but entirely Innocent of that bloody Fact which was the ruin of his Wife and several small Children.

I likewise Confess I was at the Inhumane Murders and Butchery of Bryan O' Hanlan, and M 'Gibbin, for all which I most humbly beg the Almighty's Pardon, and the Pardon of all whom I have in any way Injur'd, and declare I have a thorow sence of my former Impietys and an utter Abhorence and Detestation of them, and hope God will please to look on me, and accept of my Blood, tho' a most unworthy Offering, since my Punishment is not half what I deserve.

I die a Member of the Church of Rome, tho' an unworthy one, and do freely forgive every one that have Injur'd me, especially John M'Keoine who betray'd me, and I declare I wou'd have Fought my way thro' the Soldiers who surrounded the Cabbin where I was, and had new Charged and Prim'd my Pistols in order to it, but was prevented by the Entreaties of my Nephew, and am now thankful to God for it since I have by that had opportunity to think of my Soul. I humbly Recommend into the Hands of my most Merciful Redeemer, and beg the Prayers of all good People.

After he was Executed there was 3 Kishes of Turff lighted, wherein his Harts Livers Lights and Members were Burned, and his Head set on the Goal, Two Yards higher than any of the rest, with His Hat and Wigg on; his Nephew James Mc Caraghar and 3 more are to be Executed on Saturday 21st.

Dublin Printed, by C. Carter 1718-19.

(Location: Cambridge University Library, Bradshaw Collection, Hib.0.718.12).

21

THE LAST SPEECHES OF

Patrick Carraghar, Nephew to the great Collmore, and Two Arthur Quinns

who were Executed on Saturday the 21st of this Instant February 1718-19 at Dundalk. Together with the Tryal of Capt. Collmore.

The Speech of Patrick Macallaher

Dear Christians,

I Patrick Carraghar am the Nephew of that Collmore who was Executed last Wednesday, who was the Ruin of me, who am but Eighteen Years of Age now, tho' of these Tender years, I am very sensible of the great Follies and Sins that I have been Guilty of, my Father and Mother Liv'd in the Place call'd Loghross, in the County of Armagh, as for my Father People may say what they please of him; for he is Alive, but for my Mother she was never charg'd with any-thing that was ill, and the Neighbours in the Country knew her to be an honest good Woman she dy'd when I was very young, nevertheless I was bound Prentice to a Taylor, but did not serve my Master long, but followed my Uncle, which is the Cause of my coming to this untimely End, tho' I was Try'd for keeping Company and assisting one Gillaspy M'Culum, a Proclaimed Tory, for my part I was neither Guilty of Murther nor Robbery of my self, but I have been by when Robberry was committed, I have no more to say but that I die a Roman Catholick, and I beg of thee O my great God to have Mercy on my poor Soul. Dear Christians Pray for me.

The Speech of the Two Quins.

Good Christians,

FOR our Parts we have but little to say for our selves, only that we were born in the Fews, in the County of Armagh, and our Parents Lived Poor and Honest, but many honest Parents has had Wick'd Idle children as we both have been very Disobedient to our Parents or Friends, which gave us good advice, but we follow'd too much of our own, which Brings too many young Fellows either to the Gallows or to be Transported, and as we are Dying Persons, we desire all young People to take the Advice of their Parents and Friends, here we die for Robbing a poor honest Man's House in the County of Cavan, his name is one Coleman, we can't deny the Fact, it being prov'd so home on us, though we thought what we took there did not deserve Death, but this with other wicked Sins and Crimes is the Cause of our being Brought to this shameful End, O great God we Crave Mercy, and begs of thee O merciful Father to receive our Souls, O good People pray for us, for we die Roman Catholicks, and sweet Jesus receive us Amen. One of the Quinn's had the Impudence of Curse and Abuse the High Sheriff, the Grand Jury and the whole Court, and told them that they Murdered him.

The Whole Tryal and Examination of Capt. Collmore a Proclaim'd Tory, and was Noted for being Guilty of Bloody Murthers, Rapes and Robberies in the County of Armagh

WHen Collmore was brought to the Bar to be Tryed, he denied himself to be the Man, then the Clerk of the Crown was obliged to Swear to the Proclamation where he was nam'd; so when the Jury was call'd and Sworn, he was asked several Questions, but answered to no Purpose, then one Andrew Thompson appear'd, and the Book was given him, who Swore that he was the same Charles Carraghar who Liv'd formerly with Mr. Blykes of Darcy in the Fews, and that he Stole Two Heffers from Aldarman Grimes, and was for the same Indicted and

Proclaimed at Ardee Collmore objected against the Evidence, because he said that Thompson had formerly forsworn himself, to which the Evidence answered, that as he was coming home late to his House one Night, that he was met by this Collmore, and was forced in Defence of his Life, which was so much threaten'd by him, to Swear that he never Presented him, the Jury immediately brought him in Guilty.

Councellor Townly gave him the following sentance, That he should be Hanged; and be Cut down before he was dead, his Privy Members to be Cut Off, his Bowels burn'd, and his Quarters to be dispos'd off at the King's Pleasure.

When Collmore was brought to the Gallows, he Hang for a small Time, he was Cut down while alive, when the Hangman was cutting off his Privities, he cry'd out, then the Sheriff ordered his Throat to be Cut, the Hangman could not do it readily, for he strugled very much, his Head was afterwards Cut off, his Chops open'd and shut, tho' his Head was a Yard from his Body, his Carcass was divided into 4 Parts, and set up in 4 several Parts of the Country. He died very obstinately.

Dublin: Printed by C.C. 1718-19

(Location: Cambridge University Library, Bradshaw Collection, Hib.0.718.14)

22

THE LAST SPEECHES AND DYINGS WORDS OF

Darby M'Cormock, James M'Manus; Hugh Ferloy, Edward M'Mahan, Anne Buttler alias Morris; Rose Gorman and Sisly Burke

who are to be Executed near St.Stephens-Green on Saturday the 12th Instant. 1720.

The last Speech of Darby McCormock

Good Christians,

I was born in the County of Meath of very Creditable Parents, who gave me good Education, and afterwards sent me to a Trade, a Silk Weaver, and there served my Prenticeship very Honest and Just; and afterwards attained my Trade to Perfection, and set up for myself a considerable Time; unfortunately meeting with Idle and bad Company which has brought me to this untimely End. I have been presented by one Eleson for several Robberys, I Confess I have bin guilty of some; and several other Corporable Crimes in my Life, Elleson is the Man that Swore away my Life. I ask forgiveness of all the World, begging all your Earnest Prayers to God for me. I am about 30 Years of Age and dye a Roman Catholick, and the Lord have Mercy upon my poor Soul, Amen.

The last Speech of Hugh Ferloy

Good People,

I Was bred and born in the County of Lowth; of poor but honst Parents who were very tender of me, alass were not able to give me education, nor was I willing to go to any Trade, tho' often advised by them, yet all their Advices were in vain, for I would not harken to any thing that wou'd part me from my Parents wing; at length coming to the years of Maturity, I began to be ashamed to be Lurking at home, and not knowing where to go, wander'd like a lost Sheep, till at length to my Sorrow I became acquainted with my present Fellow-Sufferer, and several others, with whom I joyn'd in all manner of mischief, as Stealing Horses, Cows, Sheep and the like which, Trade I follow'd for several Years, till now the just wrath of God hath at last overtaken me, and now I am brought to this Place, to be made a publick Example to you all, and I hope that you'll take warning by me, and let not the Temptation of the Devil over power you, least you Reprent like me when 'tis too late. This being all I have to say, begging all your Eearnest Prayers to God for me, I am 34 Years of Age and dye a Roman Catholick, and the Lord have Mercy upon my poor Soul Amen.

The last Speech of James Mc Manus

Good Christians,

I Was Borne and bred in the City of Dublin of poor and honest Parents who was very tender of me and put me Aprentis to a silk Weaver and when my Aprentiship was out (I having attain my Trade to Perfection) my Mother bought me Two lumes and I set up for my self but at last meeting with Idle and bad Company, I spent my litle Substance and Compel'd to Earn my bread from another at my trade. I was Prosecuted by one Ellston for some losse I declare I had nothing to doe with it, or any the like Crime, he is the man that Swore away my life, I forgive all the world and beg the Earnest prayers of all good Christians. I am thirty years of Age and dye a Roman Catholick and the Lord have mercy on my poor soul.

The last Speech of Bryan Mc Mahon

Good Christians,

I Was Born in the County of Monaghan of very Poor parents, who had no means to give me Learning yet they too all the Care they could for to maintain me untill I was able to doe for myself, when I arrived to the Age of Fifteen Years, I took upon me a shift for my self so I went and wrought Laboureing work such as Hedgeing and Ditching, but finding Labour to hard I soon thought of some other project to get my bread with ease which is this, I haveing the Misfortune to meet with some fellows that followed nothing but Horse Stealing, and giveing me advice to go along with them and unfortunately their advice which has brought me to this Pass, for Stealing of two Mares. I forgive all the world and Desire the Prayers of all good Christians. I am about twentyeight Years of Age. I die Roman Catholick and the Lord have mercy upon my Poore Soule.

The last Speech of Rose Gorman

Good People,

I Was bred and born in the County of Antrim, of very honest Parents, but gave me no Learning. I left them at the Age of 12 and was at Service in the Country, where I continued till about 19 and go several good Creditable Services, till unfortunately I was Debauched by a Gentleman which was my first Misfortune and then meeting with one John Millington, kept him Company for 7 years and Married him after, we were both Extravagant and had nothing to support it, which witht he Love I had for him seduced me to take all senister Methods to get Bread for us both, tho' against his will. I Confess I have ever since kept Lude Idle Company, who brought me to this untimely End as for the Crime I am now to die for and was Convicted for the same at the King's Bench last Candlemas a Twelve-month, I own myself guilty which is Robbing a Sailor of nine Guineas, which I was Robb'd of next Day, by Honora Reily, Anne Williams and her Daughter, Thomas Singon, was the Man that swore away my Life for the Lucker of gains and I leave my Blood at his Door, tho' I forgive him and all the World, and likewise ask forgiveness all that ever I have Offended, I die a Roman Catholick and desires the Prayers of all good Christians, I am 21 Years of Age, anbd the Lord have Mercy on my Soul.

The last Speech of Sisly Burke

I Was Born and bred in the County of Gollway in the Barroney of Ballymore of good Credable and Responcable Parents, who gave me sufficient Education and were very Carefull and tender of me and brought me up in the fear of God till I was Eighteen Years of age then I of my own accord (without thire consent) went to seruce where I behaued myself just and honest till aboute two Years agoe being then at seruis in the Country my Cloths were burnt and Distroy'd by fire and soon after I got into my Lord Newtown seruis where the house Keeper and I could not agree and for that Reason was for turning me of and then one Mary Harper who was House-Maid incorraged me to take a sute of Cloths of my Lady's sister's but missing them and fetching the said Mary Harpers, she had me brought before my Lord Chife Justice Witched where I Confess'd the Fact, and was sent to New Gate. Last Michaelmas Term was a 12 month, where I was but 3 days when I was brought in Guilty by the prosecucion of Mary Harper, who swore against me and was ever since Respited to the last day of Term. I am 26 years of age, and Dies a Roman Catholick, and the Lord have Mercy on my Soul. Amen.

The Last Speech of *Anne* butler, alias *Morris*

I was born in the County of Tiperary and bread in the County of Cork of Poor but oonest onest Parents who were Tendder and Careful of me till I was 16 years of Age, but were not able to give me Learning, my Unckles Servant Maid, one Hannah Humpheries who brought several besides me to Distruction, she deluded and brought me to this City, where by her Contrivance, I met my first Misfortune, being Debauch'd here, and brought me from hence to London, where to my great grief, I follow'd a very liew'd Life for a considerable time, and then Return'd to Dublin, where I betook my self to Service, and was in serveral good Services, and contiru'd so for a long time, but to my sorrow my tormenter followed me and perswaded me to leave my Service and go to my former Trade, which I have followed and Confesses before my Great God I have been guilty of several Culpable Crimes, which I ask God's pardon, and am sure 'tis by them that brings me to this untimely End, I hope all my Sex will take Ezample by me.

As for the Crime I die for, is a Robbery of 21 pounds, which as Maliciously sworn by one Judy Quin of aof Swisns Ally against me, I Declare before my great God, as I am a Dying Woman, I am as Ignorant of it as a Child unborn, I forgive her, and God forgive her, and do likewise forgive all the world, and hope they'll all forgive me; and especially such as I have offended in the least.

I Die a Roman Catholick, and desires the Prayers of all good Christians. I am about 21 yeers of Age, and the Lord have mercy on my poor sinful Soul.

ANNE BUTLER
This is my True Speech and no other

'Tis said that Keating being young his Frinds much ado, got him a Repeief.

I do acknowledge the above Speeches to *be* True, and no others, As witness my Hand this 12th of March 2720,
Tho. Foulks Keeper in New-Gate.

Dublin Printed by C. Carter.

(Location: National Library of Scotland, Crawford Miscellaneous Broadsides, 1196)

23

THE LAST SPEECH AND DYING WORDS OF

Robert Malone,

late Informer of the City of Dublin who was Executed at Tyburn the 30th of April 1723: For the Robbery of a Clergyman, near London:

Dear Strangers,

THere is a time appointed for all Men to once Dye, so it is, that Providence has allotted my unfortunate end, this Day to come and suffer in a strange Country to me:

In falling out so, I am willing to give you all my Spectators a small Narrative of my past Life; when I was in Ireland, I was one of those Persons who was concern'd in Prosecuting the Pretenders Men, and Impeach'd a great many honest Men wrongfully; but being guilty of some Crimes, I was and my Comrade apprehended by the means of one Mr, Costigan and Mr, Collins, which we had Impeach'd wrongfully; but my Comrade to serve himself, swore that I had a design to Murder Mr, Costigan, on that I was committed to Kilmainham Goal near Dublin; being there a considerable time, and not knowing what wou'd become of me having so many Enemies; at last I got my poor Sister to get me some Bail, as she did, and paid my Fees, and when I got my Liberty I left my Wife and Friends, so came for England, Expecting to meet with good Encouragement; but I found to the contrary being so much reduc'd, I alter'd my Name, and went into the Army, under the Command of Coll Phillips, and Capt.Grimes my Commander, I was not long there before I was discover'd, and how I follow'd the Trade of Impeaching People in Ireland for High Treason, on that the Capt. Order'd me to be Strip'd and Discharg'd, so not knowing what to do, and my necessity being great, I undertook to Rob a Clergyman on the Road.

I must Confess that I got as much by that Booty as wou'd maintain me for one Month, if I had the luck to keep it; for in two Nighs after I was apprehended, carried before a Justice of the Peace and they swore heartily against me and sent me to Gaol, where I remain'd till the Assizes, where I had a fair Tryal for my Life, was found guilty and to Die now for the same,

I do declare as I am a Dying Man, that I have been very wicked and have Impeach'd several honest Men in Ireland, for being concern'd for the Pretender, as for what I swore against Mr, Collins; and Mr. Costigan was false and Malitious; so that every one must expect that the Vengeance of God must follow those that used my way of Living.

As for the Fact for which I Dye here, I can't deny; but I have been Guilty of several henious Crimes before. I was born in a place call'd Drimon in the County of Dublin in Ireland.

My Parents being Honest and Poor People, brought me up very tenderly and took a great deal of pains to make me serve God, and when I was fit to go to a Trade, they bound me Prentice to one Mr. Moony a broad Weaver, but did not stay long with him, but betook my self to bad Company; which I caution all young People to Refrain, Whoring & Drinking which brings most People to my End, as it has done me, being about 35 years of Age, I beg prayers of you my Spectators, I forgive all the World and I heartly beg that they'll forgive me.

I Die an unworthy Member of the Church of England, and the Lord have Mercy on my poor Soul. Amen.

London Printed, and Re-printed in Dublin, by P.K. 1723.

(Location: National Library of Scotland, Crawford Miscellaneous Broadsides, 1229)

24

THE LAST SPEECH AND DYING WORDS OF

Captain Collins

Who was Executed at Kingston in Surry, the 4th, of October Inst.

Dr. Spectators,

I Cannot say that it is an unusual Thing for a person to be brought to so untimely an End as you now are come to behold me Suffer; but this I say, that I little thought once to Suffer so ignominious a Death, yet, alas! how shou'd I expect better, having led a Life worse than the vilest Wretch that ever Suffer'd, being often guilty of Whoring, Gaming, Blaspheming, Sabbath Breaking, Perjury, Uncleaness Debauchery, Cheating, Tricking, nay, what is worse, coveting to deflour my own Daughter; which I own to be a Crime that loudly calls to Heaven for Vengeance, and which, I believe, might be the only Furtherance of this my untimely End. In my Prosperity I scorn'd those in a meaner Condition than myself; and (Heaven forgive me for it now) the Lives of many I have been Instrumental in dispatching unjustly, and turn'd Causes that were lawfully clear the contrary Way. O Heavens! What in this World can be depended on? Nothing is certain but Uncertainty, Prosperity to Day and Adversity to Morrow: yet I wou'd advise all that now beholds me entring upon the Brink of Eternity, either to enjoy everlasting Happiness or Misery, to shun those wicked Vices I have been guilty of; particularly I wou'd recommend to you to love and live with your lawful married Wives, and never stain your Marriage Beds. I am (as I may say) just in the prime and Vigour of my Years, which makes me desire all round me to shun this my untimely Fate; and continually pray to Heaven to keep them from what I have been Guilty of, to which my Aspiring Ambition only led me to.

At my first Arrival in this Kingdom I brought sufficient to have maintain'd me handsomly, but following my trade of Gaming, I was cut down at my own Weapons, and lost all that I had, so that being put to my Shifts I was forc'd to bethink of some way to Recruit my self; which I did, but after an unlawful Manner. But being in my second endeavour taken by one James Kingston, Esq; and his Servant, who seiz'd and brought me before Sir William Grimston Justice of the Peace, who at the next Sessions had me Try'd and Condemned. This is all at present I have to say; but deliver the Copy hereof to the Sheriff, and desire he may after my Death Communicate it to the Publick in Print, as a Terror to all Evil Doers.

Dublin: Re-Printed by John Harding in Molesworth's Court

(Location: National Library of Scotland, Crawford Miscellaneous Broadsides, 1248, 1249)

25

THE LAST SPEECH, CONFESSION AND DYING WORDS OF

Henery Watts, Philip Reily, and Edward Fox

a Boy, who are all to be Executed near St. Stephens Green, this present Saturday being the second of this Instant November 1723.

Good Christians,

I Was Born in Mass-Lane in *St. Francis-Street*, of poor but honest Parents, who tenderly brought me up in the love and fear of God, and gave me as good Education as ever a poor Lad in the Parish could have. But the 28th of *December* 1721 I took one *Elizabeth Williams* Daughters up for an Assault, and at the same time the Chapple of St. Francis was Robb'd of a Plate Box and Cup, and the said *Williams* having Received the said Robbery, said she had that in her Pocket wou'd Hangme; and went and madeOath against me thatI was thePerson that gave her the above named Goods; upon which I was Apprehended, and soon after I was Try'd and foundGuilty for the same; but theCourt finding what sort ofPersons they were, granted me Transportation, accordingly I was set on Board, but the Captain finding me Sickly, set me on shore again; then Iwent to Limrick whereIfollowed my Trade which is Weaveing, and by it got honest Bread; but Mr. *Hawkins* hearing I was there, sent an Order and Committal on me; and there I was Try'd for the Escape, and was acquitted. Then I came to Dublin in order to take Shipping and go to England, but seeing one *Conely* I call'd to him, brought him in to an Ale-house and spent thirteen pence on him, and then to requite my kindness, he took me Prisoner, and in the scuffel I cut his Cheek, being then Committed was lately Try'd and found Guilty, and now must die in a shameful manner tho' undeserved, for you may be sure (tho' Wicked enough) I would not be so Wicked as to commit Sacrelidge, for as I am a dyeing Man I am Innocent of the Fact for

THE LAST
SPEECH

Confession and Dying Words of *Henery Watts*, *Philip Reily*, and *Edward Fox* a Boy, who are all to be Executed near St. *Stephens Green*, this present *Saturday* being the second of this Instant *November* 1723.

Good Christians,

I Was Born in Mass-Lane in St. *Francis-Street*, of poor but honest Parents, who tenderly brought me up in the love and fear of God, and gave me as good Education as ever a poor Lad in the Parish could have. But the 28*th* of *December* 1721. I took one *Elizabeth Williams* Daughters up for an Assault, and at the same time the Chapple of St. *Francis* was Robb'd of a Plate Box and Cup, and the said *Williams* having Received the said Robbery, said she had that in her Pocket wou'd Hangme; and went and madeOath against me thatI was thePerson that gave her the above named Goods; upon which I was Apprehended, and soon after I was Try'd and foundGuilty for the same; but theCourt finding what sort ofPersons they were, granted me Transportation, accordingly I was set on Board, but the Captain finding me Sickly, set me on shore again; then Iwent to *Limrick* whereIfollowed my Trade which is Weaveing, and by it got honest Bread; but Mr. *Hawkins* hearing I was there, sent an Order and Committal on me; and there I was Try'd for the Escape, and was acquitted. Then I came to *Dublin* in order to take Shipping and go to *England*, but seeing one *Conely* I call'd to him, brought him in to an Ale-house and spent thirteen pence on him, and then to requite my kindness, he took me Prisoner, and in the scuffel I cut his Cheek, being then Committed was lately Try'd and found Guilty, and now must die in a shameful manner tho' undeserved, for you may be sure (tho' Wicked enough) I would not be so Wicked as to commit Sacreledge, for as I am a dyeing Man I am Innocent of the Fact for which I Dye, and also of the Escape, for 'twas the Captain that set me a shore.

My time being short I shall say no more at present but to let you know that I Dye in Charity with all the World, and begs the Prayers of all good Christians, I die a Member (tho' an unworthy one) of the *Roman Chatholick* Church, and in the 20*th* Year of my Age, and the Lord have Mercy on my poor Soul, *Amen*.

Good Christians,

I Philip Reily *was Born in the County of Cavin of very honest Parents, who took what care they could in bringing me up tenderly; but leaving my Friends, came to Dublin, and having no Trade, got to Work for Sir John Rogerson, in one of his Floats, by which means I got honest Bread, till James Reily lately Executed at Kilmainham, deluded me to go along with him to Robb his Uncle, after long perswasions I went with him, but finding no Money in the House, we took two Mares from him. But as for this Fact for which I Dye, it is for Robbing of one Mr. Byrn at Donybrook, but as I am a Dying Man I know nothing of it, nor of any other Robbery saving the two Mares. But I do believe that God has laid this Scurge on me, for slighting my Wife, for I am about six Years Marryed, and never kept above one Quarter of a Year with her, but took more pleasure in others, so for this and other my offences to God, he is pleas'd to punish me in this manner.*

Having no more to say but beging the Prayers of all good Christians, I dye in Charity with all Men. I am a *Roman Catholick* and in the 30*th* Year of my Age, and the Lord have Mercy on my poor Soul, *Amen*.

There is also *Edward Fox* a Boy of 14 Years of Age to Dye, for Picking the Pocket of one Madam *Broad-street* of 10 Pound but would make no Speech; but he Dies a *Roman Catholick*, and the Lord have Mercy on his Soul Amen.

This is our true Speeches given by our own Mouths to the Printer hereof, and if there be any other they are false.

Dublin Printed by C. Hicks, at the Rein Deer in Montrath-street 1723.

which I Dye, and also of the Escape, for ëtwas the Captain that set me a shore.

My time being short I shall say no more at present but let you know that I Dye in Chariry with all the World, and begs the Prayers of all good Christians, I Die a Member (tho' an unworthy one) of the Roman Chatholick Church, and in the 20th Year of my Age, and the Lord have Mercy on my poor Soul, Amen.

Good Christians,

I Philip Reilly *was Born in the County of Cavin of very honest Parents, who took what care they could in bringing me up tenderly; but leaving my Friends, came to Dublin, and having no Trade, got to Work for Sir John Rogerson, in one of his Floats, by which means I got honest Bread, till James Reily lately Executed at Kilmainham, deluded me to go along with him to Robb his Uncle, after long perswasions I went with him, but finding no Money in the House, we took two Mares from him. But as for this Fact for which I Dye, it is for Robbing of one Mr. Byrn at Donybrook, but as I am a Dying Man I know nothing of it, nor of any other Robbery saving the two Mares. But I do believe that God has laid this Scurge on me, for slighting my Wife, for I am about six Years Marryed, and never kept above one Quarter of a Year with her, but took more pleasure in others, so for this and other my offences to God, he is pleas'd to punish me in this manner.*

Having no more to say but beging the Prayers of all good Christians, I dye in Charity with all Men. I am a Roman Catholick and in the 30th Year of my Age, and the Lord have Mercy on my poor Soul, Amen.

There is also Edward Fox a Boy of 14 Years of Age to Dye, for Picking the Pocket of one Madam *Broad-street* of 10 Pound but would make no Speech; but he Dies a *Roman Catholick*, and the Lord have Mercy on his Soul Amen.

This is our true Speeches given by our own Mouths to the Printer hereof, and if there be any other they are false.

Dublin Printed by C. Hicks, at the Rein Deer in Montrath-street 1723.

(Location: Yale University, Beinecke Library, BrSides, By 6 1723)

26

THE LAST SPEECH AND DYING WORDS OF

James Casady

*Beggar Man who was Executed this Day,
being the 27th of this Instant January, 1724–5
at Kilmainham, for Robbing on the High-Road.*

Good People,

I was Born in Artlow in the County of Wicklow, and had very honest Parents, who gave me good Edication.

When I came to my Tryal before the Judge at Kilmainham, one Margaret Nowland and Owna Callahan, Swore I was a Robber these thirty Years past, and they also said that I was concern'd in Robbing the Bishop of Dublin, for which I was Try'd and Clear'd; the above Witness also Swore that I was concerned in a Robbery of a Gentlemans House in Great Britain Street, about three Years ago; The said Owna also Swore that *I*, one O Neil, and a Piper was concern'd the last Robbery, and that she was one of their Comrades then, and watch'd in the Street while the said Robbery was doing.

They also swore that I had Plates and Dishes in my Custody; which I brought out of the sd. House, Also that the above *Margaret* swore that when she heard the great dogg bark, that she came down stairs, and seeing me and above 3 *Men* coming out of Capt. Gratons House, she heard the sd. *Casady* speak to the rest of his Comrades to Murder her, to which the said Ona Cry'd out and spoke to 'em, and begg'd that there should be no murder, Committed where she was, this is what the above Per- swore against me at the Sessions-House in Kilmainham.

Now I do hereby Declare before God, the sheriff, and all the rest of my Spectators, that as I am here to suffer this untimely Death; tho' I cou'd not live much longer, for I am about 80 years of Age.

As for what Money I had by me, it was very honestly got, and I design'd it for my Son. but having an extravagant Wife, was the reason that I always carried the sd. money always with me, wherever I went a begging, or to work any where, which I am sure that the sd. money is the cause of this my untimely end.

I James Cassedy do further declare at this my Dying Minute, that I do not know any of these my Prosecutors, and on the Dying Words of one who expects Salvation I know nothing of the matter that Iam Charg'd with.

I do not blame the Judge nor Jury, and I forgive all the World, I would die a Roman Catholick, and the Lord have Mercy on my poor Soul.

He was buried under the Gallows in his Cloaths.

[Dublin, Printed by] C.C. , 1725

(Location: British Library, C.133.g.7(70))

27

THE LAST SPEECH AND DYING WORDS OF

Valintine Kealy, and Cornealus Svlavan

who is both to be Executed near St. Stephen's-Green, this present Saturday being the 13th, Inst. March 1724–5. For Robberys Committed by them.

The Speech of Valintine Kealy.

Good People,

I Am advis'd by several of my Acquaintance to give my Speech from my own Mouth to some Printer, in order to prevent others of that Trade, from Printing sham Speeches of me; therefore (*by their perswasions*) I sent for the Printer in *Montrath-Street*, to whom I made the following true Speech, and if any other Prints it, I assure you it is false.

 I drew my first Breath in the County of *Kildare*, of very honest Parents, whose Names and Trade I forbear to mention, because they are People of good Credit, and also took a great deal of Care of me; but when I found I was able to do for myself, I came to *Dublin* where I got very honest Bread by my Trade, which was by Killing and Hawking of Meat, the which I practic'd for several Years past; but I being void of Grace, not having the Consideration in me to remember what many Persons said, that I myself saw Die at this Fatal Tree; flung myself into the Company of loose Idle Women, in whose Company I took so much delight, that whatever I cou'd get I spent it on them. Thus I continued for some Time 'till I had Consum'd what little substance I had, and went in Debt with the *Drovers*, so that none of them would trust me; which put me into a study how I should Live, but more particularly how to please my former

Mistresses, who I knew, would not look upon me, had I not Money to spend upon them, which put me into a great Consternation to think what I should do.

But being one Day Sad and Melancholly, thinking of my own Folly, and Reflecting on myself for spending and squandering my Money away so Foolish, the Devil (who is like a roaring Lyon seeking whom he may Devour) put me on to Robb a Shop in *Bride's-Ally*, the which I Attempted to do, but was Timely Discover'd, so that I was taken and Committed to *New-Gate*, and now must Die for the same: But I must tell you by what Stratagem I contriv'd to Robb the said Shop; I went and took the Pin out of the Barr of the Window, but the Maid being aweak was soon betray'd, and brought to what you see.

Therefore let me beg of all both Old and Young, that they will beg of the great God above for Grace and Mercy, that he would be pleas'd to preserve them in the state of Grace, and that they may shun the Company of Harlots, and lead an honest sober Life, is the Hearty Prayer of your Dying Friend & wellwisher *Valintine Kealy*.

Having no more to say but beging the Prayers of all good Christians, I Dye a Roman Catholick, and in the *30th*, Year of my Age, and for the second fault I ever did Commit, and the Lord have Mercy on my poor soul *Amen*.

The Speech of *Cornealus Svlavan*.

Dear Christians,

I At first had no thoughts to make any Speech, by reason I am far from my Friends or Relations, but seeing my Fellow Sufferer doing it, I thought fit to do the same, which is in manner following. I was Born in the County of *Kerry*, of poor Parents who was not able to give me any Education, but took what Care they cou'd otherwise of me, 'till I was able to do for myself, then I came to *Dublin*, where I got honest Bread for some Years; but one Day a Gentleman of my own Name in *Essex street*, Intrusted me to get him a *Guniea* changed, but I went off with the same, then I was both a shame and afraid to show my Face in *Dublin* again, and therefore went to the Country where I continu'd for some Time, 'till all the Money was spent, then I came back, but was loath to be seen, by which means I had like to perish for want of Food, and Cloathing, and many Times bleaming myself for the same.

    Thus I continued bemoaning my own hard Fate, 'till at length I went to the shop of one Mr. *Gun* in *Essex-Street* a Book-seller, from whence I stole a Parcel of Books and got off with the same, and brought them to *Batchelor's-Walk*, and hid them among some Timber there, then I went back the second Time but was taken and [prosecuted for] the same. I Dye a Roman Catholick and in the *19*th Year of my [age. May the Lord] have Mercy [on my Soul. Amen.]

(Location: British Library, C.133.g.7 (40))

28

THE LAST SPEECH, CONFESSION AND DYING WORDS OF

William Dickson

who was Try'd and Condemned, for High Treason against his Majesty King George, for Counterfeiting the current Coin of Great Britain, at the General Assizes holden at Ardmagh, the 23d of March, 1725, and was Executed, Tuesday the 13th of April, for the same; with an Account of the Coller he had to save himself, as it was taken from his own Mouth in the Goal, &c.

GOOD Christians my time being very short, expecting a Reprieve from Dublin, this morning, it did not come according to Expectation I did not loose any Time in preparing my self for the World to come, and hopes that I shall Reign with my Blessed Redeemer.

First, I Recommend my Soul to Christ, my Lord and Saviour, to forgive me my manifold Sins and Wickednesses which I have committed from Time to Time, in not Obeying his Laws, nor taking my dear and beloved Parents Advice, in what they would have me to do, which I hope will be a warning to all Men, as I am a Dying Man, this Day, the Truth I will declare before God and the World, to whom, and through his great Mercy, I hope to merit Salvation.

I William Dickson was Born of very good Parents, and come of an honest Family and Married one of the Richisons, whom God preserve and keep them from all Danger Ghostly and Bodily, and all their Enemies. I am aged to the best of my Knowledge, about 29 Years of Age, and in all that Time, I thank my God, I never was guilty of any ill Vices in all my Life, nor, did any harm to any Body till I went to Live with Mr. Alexinder Hurdman as Overseer, near Kilalee in the County of Ardmagh, and in a little while, he sent me to lay out Five Guineas for him, but they were returned back again to me, the first Time I saw James Dunbar was at his House.

The first time that ever I saw any of the Molds was at Drum, where I went to get a Cavesson that I lent to James Glass, and they told me he was in the Garden, where I found the said Dunbar, James Gass, and Robert Gass, and when they saw me they thrust the Mold into the left side Pocket of Robert Gass, that I might not see it. The next Morning going to the Smiths Shop, and coming back again, I met Robert Gass in the Wood, and he told me that James Gass was going for Mettle and Fire, desiring me to stay till I saw them try the Mold. Soon after the said Gass cast two Crowns, and would have given one of them to Robert Gass for a Pocket Piece, but he would not receive it for fear I should discover them on him, he melted them down to Dross, and hid it in the Moss. As I answer before God and a dying Man, I never had any thing to do with the said *James Gass* in the whole course of my Life, nor did I ever Coin to the value of six pence in all my Life, nar had I any Moulds for that Use. As for *James Gass* that has sworn my Life away wrongfully, and not only so, but has most barbarously Murder'd me, and has been the occasion of making the best of Wives loose a Husband; for which I do not doubt, but the Lord of Heaven and Earth will do us Justice and Revenge my Cause.

As for Mr. *Francis Scott* who was Accus'd &c. I never knew any thing by him in all my Days. And likewise John Hurdman. I hope the World will not Reflect on any of my Friends for Dying this Untimely Death, I not being Guilty of what is laid to my Charge, I do desire my good and loving Wife, (that Lives in the Parish of Kildree in the County of Tyrone) to take good Heart and not to Pine for me, for I hope with the Assistance of my blessed Saviour to be with him in a very little time, which is better than this Worldly Wealth, for there is nothing in it but Trouble & Sorrow, And my Daughter whom I leave my Blessing, take heed to mind your Redeemers Commandments, and your Mothers Orders, and then the Lord will bless and prosper you in all your Doings, be sure to mind the Church and keep Gods laws, and every thing will prosper that you take in Hand, Likewise I begg all good People may not reflect on my Dear Father and Mother, that lives in Carinomoney in the Parish of Baleniscron in the County of Derry, brought me up in the fear of God, and gave me a good Education, may the Lord Prosper Them, and when they depart this Life, they may have Life Everlasting, and that the Lord May Crown them with a Crown of Glory.

O dear Brothers, mind to shun Bad Company, which was my Overthrow in this World and be Upright and Just in all your Dealings before God and Man, and you need not fear Living in the World. Mind your Father and Mother's Advice. My time is almost spent, and having no more to say, Sweet Saviour open thy Arms of Mercy, look down upon me, O Lord, and Shut not thy Gate against me, but take me to Thy Self, into Thy Heavenly Kingdom, where I shall rest in Peace, and all you who are Spectators of this my unfortunate and Tragick Scene, lift up your Hands and say, Lord, receive my poor Soul.

I die a member of the Church of England.

An Account of a Collar he had about his Neck to save his life
As the prisoner was going to the place of Execution, the Sheriff and High Sheriff, perceiving he went very stiff, the wonder'd what was the matter, but they never minded him till they came to the place of Execution, and when the Minister had done with him, then he went 4 or 5 steps up the Ladder very fast, but the Sheriff and High Sheriff perceiving his Neck very thick, desir'd him to come down, on searching they found a Collar of Iron well fix'd about his Neck, they call'd to the Gaoler to take it off upon that the Executioner took it off, it weighed about three pound, there was a Hinge in the middle and 3 hooks to it, one before and another at each side, it Clasp'd together, like a woman's Clasp for Shoes, with a Girth Web, before and behind which went between his Legs.

We testify the above is True, as Witness our Hands

Terence O'Neill Sub-Sheriff
Will. Watts Head Sheriff

Tomorrow will be publish'd the Last Speech of a Woman Cook Maid to the Bishop of Londonderry, who was Burnt alive at Derry for the murder of her own child.

Belfast Printed and Reprinted in Dublin by C.C., 1725.

(Location: British Library, C.133.g.7 (35))

29

THE LAST SPEECH AND DYING WORDS OF

Cap. Mc. Dermot

who was formerly concern'd in Listing Men for the Pretender; and was Hang'd and Quarter'd at Cavan, on Tuesday the 30th of March 1725, for most barbarously Murdering of one J. Dalley on the High-Road.

Good Christians Listen to my words.

MY Father lived on a Farm plentifully stocked, near Newtoun in the County of Farmanah, where my self and my Brethren took our Birth and Education; and might have been as happy a Family as any in that Neighbourhood, had our Father kept with us in our growing Years, as he did in our Childhood; but he gave himself over to Extravagancy, and other unwarrantable Practices, whereby our mother and we were put to our Shift: And I who was taught to read the Latin, English and Irish Tongues, and was naturally compusant to all mankind, am here made an Example for the Sins of my Forefathers. For I must confess that I knew of several that were carried for France, as it was reported, to serve the Pretender; but I missed of going, which I am sorry for: After which I betook my self to the Foly of Gaming, and became so expert in it, that for a while it was my Support of Life; but looking into the evil Consequences which attend ils as Swearing, Drinking, Quarrelling, and other Enormities against God and our Neighbours, I quit it, and betook my self to serve a Gentleman of my Acquaintance, in whose Service I studied to demean my self as became me: But not living after a religious manner, as I ought to have done, I was led into my former Foly; for my master sent me about an Affair of his, I took some other Persons of a vile Character for my Assistance, and we not meeting with Success, betook our selves to play Cards on the way, but not with my will.

And altho' I had the Advantage of the Game, yet I urged them to quit it, but they would not but bred a Quarrel with me, wherefore to prevent their farther Disturbance, I unsheath'd my Sword, and said I would injure the unruliest of them if he was not immediately quiet, meaning thereby no mischief further than to pacify them by force, but one of our Company carry'd the quarrel so high, that instead of moderating him, I was forc'd to stand on my Defence, and whether he threw himself on my Sword endeavouring to catch hold of me, or where I on my own Defence wounded him, I know not, neither could my Accusers say the contrary but when the Accident happen'd I sent part away for a Surgeon and whether he did Justice to that poor Wounded Man or me, I have the issue, to the Great God who knows the secrets of all hearts and as I shall presently answer before his tremendious Name. I did not design to either Kill or wound him, and my Innocence tyed me to that place untill I was Apprehended, for I could have made my Escape very easy: It was reported on me that I struck and abused my Parents, If the Words of a Dying Man may be beliv'd, and as I must shortly answer for all my misdeeds I am Innocent of that Report; it was likewise Reported I attempted a Rape on a Female Prisoner under the same Confinement, that scandal is false and groundless by the attest aforesaid.

I am in the midst of several hundred Persons who know me and my People, and I think, I know most of them, and I am Certain not one Can say I ever Stole to the Value of one penny since I was born, I Chalange even Millions it self, to Impeach me with a Crime of that Nature, therefore I forwarn all young Men, for my sake to Game no more, for altho' I never Stole any thing in all my Life: nor Countinanced it in others yet it Occasioned the Death of two Men, for one of which I am made a Publick Example, and I belive it is by GOD's apoyntment, for my good, least I should Live to be an instrument of greater Evils, and I take my Saviour to Wittness; I die in Charity with all Men, and I forgive all my Prosecutors, and Slanderers; and all Men principly Concerned in my Tryall, and all Men who have done Me wrong; and the Last Request of a Dying

Penetant is that no one, out of spite or otherwise will Reproach my Relations with their suppose and Crime which has brought Me to this Ignominious Death, for which I Humbly Request all good People will send their Prayers to Heavan for the Redemption of my poor soul, before I depart which I hope sweet Jesus of Heaven will Receive my soul into the Arms of his Mercy adue.

I Dye a Roman Catholick, the Lord have mercy on my poor soul.

C. Mac. Dermot

DUBLIN: Printed by C.C.

(Location: British Library, C.133.g.7 (60))

30

THE LAST SPEECH, CONFESSION AND
DYING WORDS OF

John Comber

who is to be Hang'd and Quarter'd this present Wednesday, being the 5th, of this Inst. May 1725. Near St. Stephen's-Green; for Murdering Councellor Hoar, in January last.

GOOD *Christians,*

MY Heart has been so hard hitherto, that I had no Manner of thought of either Soul or Body, but now I seeing Death plainly before my Face, causes me to consider of my latter End; and praise God for giving so much Grace so to do; therefore I am resolv'd to make a Publick Confession of my past Life and Conversation, which is as follows.

As to my Birth and Parentage, it is but a folly to relate, yet I can say I came from very honest Parents, who took what Care they could to bring me up in the Love and Fear of God, but I contrary to the Laws of God and Man, have gon astray, and follow'd Loose Idle Company, which brought me to this untimely Death; and how it came to pass was thus.

I being Entimitly Acquainted with one *Patrick Freel*, and *David Mc. Clure*, with whom I went to a House in *New-street*, where we then (after several meetings) made a Plot to get Money, by reason it was scarce with us, at length we Consulted the 19th, of *January* last, to Robb the first we wou'd meet with, and being over perswaided by the Devil, I went to the House of Mr. *Carter* and meeting a Child of his, bid him fetch his Dady's Pistol, and I would fetch him some sweet things, upon the same promise, the Child brought me a Pistol, and then I, in Conjuction with the above Named Persons, went towards *Stephen's-Green*, where we met with Mr. *Kennedy*, Mr. *Leeson's*

THE LAST SPEECH

Confession and Dying Words of *John Comber*; who is to be Hang'd and Quarter'd this present *Wednesday*, being the 5th, of this Inst. *May* 1725. Near St. *Stephen's-Green*; for Murdering Councellor *Hear*, in *January* last.

GOOD Christians,

MY Heart has been so hard hitherto, that I had no Manner of thought of either Soul or Body, but now I seeing Death plainly before my Face, causes me to consider of my latter End; and praise God for giving so much Grace so to do; therefore I am resolv'd to make a Publick Confession of my past Life and Conversation, which is as follows.

As to my Birth and Parentage, it is but a folly to relate, yet I can say I came from very honest Parents, who took what Care they could to bring me up in the Love and Fear of God, but I contrary to the Laws of God and Man, have gon astray, and follow'd Loose Idle Company, which brought me to this untimely Death; and how it came to pass was thus.

I being Entimitly Acquainted with one *Patrick Freel*, and *David Mc. Clure*, with whom I went to a House in *New-street*, where we then (after several meetings) made a Plot to get Money, by reason it was scarce with us, at length we Consulted the 19th, of *January* last, to Robb the first we wou'd meet with, and being over perswaided by the Devil, I went to the House of Mr. *Carter* and meeting a Child of his, bid him fetch his Dady's Pistol, and I would fetch him some sweet things, upon the same promise, the Child brought me a Pistol, and then I, in Conjunction with the above Named Persons, went towards *Stephen's-Green*, where we met with Mr. *Kennedy*, Mr. *Leeson's* Clerk, whom we Robb'd of a Ten Peney Piece, from that we proceeded to *Henry-street*, where we met the Deceased Gentleman, to whom I went up, and Demanded his Money, he only said what do you Mean Gentlemen, I have no Money, with that he moving his Arm, and I having the Pistol Cock'd, caused the same to go off, tho' as I shall Answer my God I did not think of being his Butcher; and when I found the Pistol went off, I never staid to know whether he had Money or no, but took to my Heels as fast as I could.

Then I went to the Sign of the Black *Swan* in *Mary's-Lane*, where I and my Comrads met; from that my Profocuter *Patrick Freel* and I, went to the Country where we staid for some small Time, then I came back, and as God, who never suffers Murder to be Conceal'd, I was soon Apprehended and put to Goal, upon Suspission, where I lay as good as a Month, but a Proclamation being Issued out, concerning the Murder, he came in and made Oath that I was the Person that Shot the Councellor, which to my sorrow is True.

Having no more to say but beging the Prayers of all good Christians, I Die a *Roman Catholick*, and in the 22d. Year of my Age, and the Lord have Mercy on my poor Soul *Amen*.

Dublin: Printed by C. P. 1725.

Clerk, whom we Robb'd of a Ten Peney Piece, from that we proceeded to *Henry-street*, where we met the Deceased Gentleman, to whom I went up, and Demanded his Money, he only said what do you Mean Gentlemen, I have no Money, with that he moving his Arm, and I having the Pistol Cock'd, caused the same to go off, tho' as I shall Answer my God I did not think of being his Butcher; and when I found the Pistol went off, I never staid to know whether he had Money or no, but took to my Heels as fast as I could.

Then I went to the Sign of the Black *Swan* in *Mary's-Lane*, where I and my Comrads met; from that my Prosocuter *Patrick Freel* and I, went to the Country where we staid for some small Time, then I came back, and as God, who never suffers Murder to be Conceal'd, I was soon Apprehended and put to Goal, upon Suspission, where I lay as good as a Month, but a Proclamation being Isued out, concerning the Murder, he came in and made Oath that I was the Person that Shot the Councellor, which to my sorrow is True.

Having no more to say but beging the Prayers of all good Christians, I die a *Roman Catholick*, and in the 22*d*. Year of my Age, and the Lord have Mercy on my poor Soul *Amen*.

Dublin: Printed by C. P. 1725.

(Location: British Library, C.133.g.7 (51))

31

THE LAST SPEECH, CONFESSION AND
DYING WORDS OF

John Coamber

who is to be Hang'd, Drawn and Quarter'd this Day, being the 5th of this Instant May 1725. For the Murder of Councellor HOAR in Henry Street the 19th of Jan. last.

Deliver'd to the Printer hereof C. CARTER the 5th of May, and to no other, By me John Coamber. And All others are Imposing on the Publick

All you my Spectators,

THIS is to give you the following Account, I was born in the Town which is Call'd Thurles, in the County of Tipperary in Munster, of very honest Parents, that brought me up in the fear of God, and Wou'd give me good Learning, but I was too Head-strong, and wou'd not be Rul'd or Guided by my tender Parents, but left 'em and went to serve a Tobacco-twister, which I work't at for about 5 years, being weary of that I came for Dublin, being a stranger, I turn'd Porter about Cork-hill, where I stood and follow'd that business for near 3 years, all this time I behav'd my self very honestly, and was well belov'd by all that knew me, especially in the above Neighbourhood, being weary of that, I took a fancy to Cry News about this City, which in a little time, I began to get a great many pence by it, and in sometime after, I became Acquainted with Idle and loose Company, Viz. and in process of time I came to be acquainted with particular Persons and some others who first brought me in Company among Whores to Drink and spend my Money &c. Which was the first Cause of my Destruction.

    Afterwards I went of my own Accord, and follow'd the said Evil Custom and other ill Actions, then I became as obdurate and as Wicked as the worst of my Ring-leaders.

I have Reason to Curse them Idle fellows which made me first acquainted with the whores and Pick-pockets in this City, of which there is abundance too many.

But finding Money not Answering to keep the above Company, being acquainted with one David Mc Clure who was my chief Comrade, and who made his Escape to France after the Murder was Committed, he and I stuck together, and followed a very Idle Course of Life, and we Committed several ill Facts in this City and Liberties thereof.

All our shifts not Answering, I, Mc Clure, and Patrick Freel (who was the first Evidence against me) Resolv'd to turn Robber, but never did design to be Guilty of Murder, and did design when we got a Sum of money that was worth While, to leave the Country.

I Confess, that Patrick Freel, David Mc Clure and I went on the 19th of January last at Night, to Henry Street, with a Design to Rob, or Plunder the first Gentleman that came that way; which was the luck of that worthy honest Gentleman Councellor Hoar, though I declare before God I did not design to hurt him, or any Man else that time.

I do also Confess that I did own to the Blind Boy, Lawrence Dugan, (who was the t'other Evidence against me) that Patrick Freel, David Mc Clure and I my self, were all Guilty of the Murder for which I now suffer, but I wonder he did not Discover, it when one Pitts and another one Hand, had like to suffer for this Murder.

I further Declare, tho' it was falsly and Scandalously Publish'd in Print, by one Mrs. Needham and her Son Dickson; that I had got Mr. Carter's Pistols from his young Son about 8 years of Age, (we had but one Pistol among us) and as I am a Dying Man I got no such thing from the said Child, nor none of his Family, neither did I steal any such thing out of his House in my Life time.

I accused one Daniel Field and Michael Tankard falsly, which I am heartily sorry for, but it was by the Advice of Winfred Dunn and Patrick Dunn the 2 Informers, that swore against Pitts and Hand that was Try'd the last Term for this Fact.

I beg of my great God to forgive my Prosecutors, and all my Enemies, as I do forgive them from the bottom of my heart.

I hope this my untimely End will be a Warning to my Comrades, and also to all young Men, which I pray to God it may. For my own part I own I am Guilty of the Fact for which I Die, And I hope the Lord of his infinite Goodness, will have Mercy on my Soul and forgive me.

I am about 19 Years of Age I dye a Roman Catholick, and Desires the Prayers of all good Christians, and the Lord have Mercy on my poor Soul. Amen.

JOHN COAMBER

DUBLIN: Printed by Corn. Carter. 1725.

(Location: British Library, C133.g.7 (54))

32

THE LAST SPEECH, CONFESSION AND DYING WORDS OF

Mr. J. Dunbar

who was Try'd and Condemn'd, for High Treason against his Majesty King George; at the Assizes, of Oyer, Terminer, or Goal Delivery, holden, at Carrickfergus, for and in the County of Antrim, the 17th Day of Ma. 1725. And was Executed Saturday, April 10th for the same together with his last Advice to his Children prov'd by Scripture Texts, &c. As it was taken from his own Mouth in the Goal, and desir'd to be Printed.

Courteous Readers,

INTO whose Hands those my Dying Words shall come; they may not be look'd upon as a Form, because it is Customary, for unfortunate Persons under my Fate so to do; No, but with a sincere Heart to clear my Conscience, as I am a Dying Man. First to my Creator & Redeemer, by whom and thro' his great Mercy I hope to merit Salvation.

I JAMES DUNBAR, was born in the Town land of Grogan, in the Parish of Drummal, near Ronaldstown, in the County of Antrim of honest Parents; My Father was a Farmer, Liv'd in the fear of God, attended the Meetings constantly with his Family, doing to the best of his Knowledge as became a Man in his Station; brought up all under his care in the fear and service of God. To this Day I well remember when I was about Eleven years of Age, I had amongst others learned a great Word to swear by my Conscience, and in his hearing, he finding it became practice took an opportunity to Chastize me for it, but with that pleasant Fatherly Correction, that he perfectly sham'd me out of it, the same was so Imprinted in my mind, be in what Company soever, I never was any way addicted to that Sin of Swearing to this Day. He taught me the Catechism and Psalm Book; brought me up to the Age of Sixteen, then I stray'd away from him and Listed in the Service, where in Flanders and Ireland I served seven years under King William, in which time I receiv'd three Wounds, during my whole Travels my mind was always bent upon the Genuine part, casting Molds of several sorts, each exceeding the other.

Upon my return I settled, Marry'd a Wife, and got things necessary about me: But in process of time, hearing such a Character of New England, what great Advantage was to be made by those that could carry some Money with them, I resolv'd for that place: In order thereunto I made Sale of all I had, & proceeding forward at Newtown-Stuart chang'd my Mind, which I now dearly repent. Settles again there about three Years. At Leisure times to recreate my self with an Innocent Pleasure I took delight in Fishing; but once too often, for by an unhaypy fall, there was a Knife with the point towards me, stuck into and gave me a Wound six Inches deep, the same I lay by sixteen Weeks. Even upon my Recovery, came three Idle Fellows, knowing me to be an Ingenious Artist, desired me to make them a Crown Molud in Steel for the use of Coyning, I told them in Horn, Brass, Pewter, Silver or Gold I could; but because I had never try'd in Steel I should spoil it, they not fearing told me that I should have twelve pence per Day if I did, not being of Steel as I said, I did notwithstanding they paid me twelve Shillings. Sometime after they came to me again to do the same the which I dextrously Perform'd to a truith, and [for] the same receiv'd forty Shillings; Some of the same 3 [men] have been Executed on that Head since: As for In[stance] David Denniston at Omey the last Affizes. For my [own] part my Genious so far exceeded other Men that I have [no] occasion for help but for Company sake; I ca[n make] Molds and could Perform all that Art requir'd; [but because] the Laws of the Land are so strict I must own an[d confess] myself Guilty of what is laid to my Charge, a[nd I am] willing to resign my Vital Breath and Soul to hi[m, my God,] for the same, in whom I trust thro his great Me[rcy, with] sincere Repentance I have made my Peace, and s[eek out] the Kingdom of Heaven, forsaking this Life for [that of the eter]nal. I Die in Charity with all People, freely fo[rgiving] those that was the cause of this my untimely Dea[th and any] others that ever wrong'd me in Thought Word [or Deed] and for all those that I have wrong'd Directly or [Indirectly] I ask Pardon and Forgiveness. First of my Grea[t and Glo]rious GOD, the which I hope to obtain for all [my off]ences; next of them, hoping they will do the s[ame, I] do expect to be forgiven at the latter Day.

My dear Friends and Countrey-Men, and all [people that] hears of my Unhappy Fall to take Warning in t[his; let it] be an Example to all; especially Young People, w[hatever walk] of Life it is the go on in, and to their utmost En[deavour] shun all lewd Company. Besure first choose the [compa]ny, than their Liquor, and then not to Dabauch [ ] with it, so as to be bereft of Sense; it is the f[irst step to] Destruction. Next to shun all lewd Women, [ ] Total Overthrow, and nothing but the Works [of the Devil] proceeds from them. Thirdly be not Covetous of [ ]stance. And fourthly, If the LORD is pleased to [endow us] with a Talent to be more Ingenious than any other [to put] it to that Use that the great Giver of all Design[s ordains.] I leave behind me one Son and three Daughters [; Grant] them Grace to lead their Life and Conversation u[ntroubled be]fore God and Man. I hope there is no Person w[ill put] either upon my Wife or them after my Decease. T[o] all that knew me in my Settlement in the County of Derry; and all others, that knew me else where, what a Value and Esteem all People had for me, for my Ingenuous Performances in that Trade of Horning. How I lived in my Family is well known for many Years together, performing the Duty as becometh a Professor or Christian to do, I could inlarge: But let no Man boast in his own Strength least he Fall, they are well kept whom the LORD keeps.

I have laid down some Scripture Proofs to shew the Error of Man, and the Scourage that attend it, which I hope may prove of some Use after my Decease, as follows

Jeremias 17: 14 17 18. Heal me O Lord and I shall be heal'd, save me and I shall be saved for thou art my praise.

V. 17. Be not a terrour unto me thou art my hope in the Day of evil. V. 18. Let them be confounded that presecute me, but let not me be confounded. Let them be dismayed bring upon them the day of evil and destroy them with double Destruction.

I will look unto thee O Lord for Deliverance from all my Troubles: For there is no Power like unto thy Power, who delivered thy People from all the Power of Egypt, and with a strong Hand brought them through the Red Sea.

Mat. 9,10. And it came to pass as Jesus sat at Meat in the house behold many Publicans and Sinners came and Sat down with him and his Disciples; And when the Pharisees saw it they said unto his Disciples, Why eateth your Master with Publicans and Sinners. But when Jesus heard that he said unto them, They that be well need not a Physician, but they that are sick. Now go ye and learn what that meanet, I will have Mercy and not Sacrifice; for I am not come to call the righteous, but Sinners to Repentance.

[Some] Advice from a Father to his Children,
when he was near to his Death.

[My] Son James Dunbar, I Charge thee in the Name of [the L]ord thy God, that thou keep thy self from the Unlaw[ful, Lewd] Women strong Drink, and Sabbath breaking for [they d]raw away thy Heart from the Lord thy God, & [follow the w]ay of his Commandments. [Proverbs 5 V.]3. For the Lips of a strange Woman drop as a Hon[eycomb an]d her Mouth is smoother than Oil. V.4. But her [end is bitter] as Wormwood, sharp as a two edged sword. V.5. [Her feet go] down to Death, her steps take hold on Hell. V.6. [Lest thou sh]ouldest ponder the path of Life, her ways are move[able th]ou canst not know them. V.7. Hear me therefore, [o sons], and depart not from the Words of my Mouth re[move thy way] far from her, and come not nigh the door of her house.

[Keep thy]self from all Woman kind, except thy own [wife (if] you live to have one) for that Unlawful Use of [them an]d strong Drink hath been the Ruin of me, and [others], and so it will be of thee and thine, if ever thou [follow that pr]actice.

[Hear m]e my dear Children, hear the Instruction of your [dying Fa]ther, from the Word of God, receive them and [take them dee]p in your Hears, for they will be an Ornament [ ] to your Hands, and

Chains of Gold about your [wais]t as They will render you Beautiful and Accept[able to Go]d and good Men. When you are in Trouble, God [hears y]our Cries when ye pray unto him, and will deliv[er you ou]t of all your Distresses, if you be not in the wrong; [These a]re the Troubles that Afflict the Just but the [good be]ereth them out of them all. My dear Children, [let your e]yes be fixed on the Lord your God in all your [actions;] if you offend in one you are guilty of all; there[fore keep e]qual Regard and Respect to them all, and when [you have d]one all that you can, say you are Unprofitable [ ].

[But] be not Lifted up, nor High in your own Eyes, but fear least ye be Tempted to Sin and God be provoked to cast you down again, as he has justly done to me. Therefore I beseech you for your Saviour's sake, beware of vain Glory and high Mindedness but Contrarywise of be Humble and Meek and Lowly, and God will lift you up, but if he do not be Content he is well worth the trusting for he is not Unrighteous to forget your Work and Labour of Love for when he seeth you Diligent and Sincere in your Christian Course he will help you with his Blessing in the Work of your Hands and he will encourage you and strengthen your Hearts with the gracious of his Spirit, but if it be his Will to keep you Low and Mean in the World be Content and do not fret nor repine at the Dispensations of God, for that is the way to keep you Low and Mean still, but contrarywise be thankfull, and say with Paul I have learned in whatsoever State or Condition I am therewith to be content. For if you be content and have but a Morsel of dry Bread or Herbs you have a good Feast. For Contnetment is great gain, Likewise I beseech you my dear Children set your Hearts to seek the Lord with all your might.

Thess.5: 16, 17. Rejoice evermore Pray without ceasing. V.18. in every thing give thanks, for this is the Will of God in Christ Jesu, concerning you. V.19 Quench not the Spirit. V.20. Dispise not Prophesying. V.21. Prove all things hold fast that which is good V.22. Abstain from all appearance of evil, V.23. And the very God of Peace sanctifie you wholly, and I pray God your whole Soul and Body be preserved blameless unto the coming of our Lord Jesus Christ &c.

Consider my Children, these words, *Pray without Ceasing*. It is not that you should always be upon your Knees at Prayer, but that you shall be always in a Praying Flame of Spirit, But more particularly, dear Children see that ye neglect not to Pray in secret every Morning, and at Night, for that is the Duty of all others. That you may pour foth your Hearts to God, in the most familiar way without Bashfulness or Confusion, and expect most of the Presence of the Holy Ghost.

Eph. 6 16, Praying always with all Prayer and Supplication in the Spirit and watching thereunto with all Perseverence and Supplication for all Saints.

And now my dear Children, I might have Recommended you to many more Places of Scripture, but I rather Recommend you to the search of the whole Old and New Testament, which is able to make you Wise unto Salvation.

I humbly beg leave of thee, O Father, of Heaven and Earth, to return thee my hearty thanks, for inspiring a Spirit of Remorse & Pity, into the Hearts and Minds of those Learned Gentlemen the Clergy of the Presbytery of the Town of Belfast &c. Who was pleas'd to remember me in their publick Service, joyn'd with their Congregations, on Sunday last. Humbly rendering their Prayers to thee O GOD to have Mercy on me, a poor lost Soul, without thy help; hoping thou was pleas'd to hear the same, and that I may find the Sweetness, Joy and Comfort of it, at this my Sudden Departure; altho' I was no ways deserving of such a Compassionate Christian Favour, being a fallen Member and Transgressor of the same; That they will be pleased to receive this as in obedience of thanks Paid to them as true Professors obedient to God's Holy Word, and Teachers of the same; and all those that joyn'd with them in that Charitable Act.

Also those Worthy Gentlemen of the Church of England, who hath since offered up their Prayers for me.

My time is spent my Glass is run, sweet Saviour open thy Arms of Mercy, for unto thee I come. O Lord, shut not thy Gate against me stretch forth thy Almighty Hand, and take me to thy self and let not SATAN have Power over me; now I launch into Eternity in full Hopes of Assurance to be with thee in thy Heavenly Kingdom, there to remain with thee and thy holy Angels, World without end.

I Die in the Presbyterian Communion, and upwards of Fifty Years of Age.

Have Mercy on me O LORD sweet JESUS I COME I COME, Mercy I crave at this my last Minute, Grant it for thy dear Son's sake Amen.

JAMES DUNBAR.

[Dublin, Printed by] C. Carter, 1725

33

THE LAST SPEECH AND DYING WORDS OF

Ellinor Sils

who is to be Burn't alive this present Wednesday being the 19th of this Instant May 1725. For Murdering her own Child.

Good People,

AT first I had no thought of making a Speech, had I not heard a false and scandalous Paper cry'd about, call'd my Speech, Printed by one *Brangan* but as I am since Inform'd, it was done by one C___r in *Fishamble-Street*; the which was an Imposition on the Publick; therefore that causes me to makea Speech which is as follows (*viz.*)

I drew my first Breath at the Place call'd *Lisnaw* in the County of *Kerry*, of very honest Parents, (my Father having the Honour to be Coach-man to the Lord of the same) who brought me up very tenderly, 'till I was fit for Service, and I praise God for it, had always the good Fortune to get a Service amongst the best, and thro' my Industerous Care, Learned to be a Cook-Maid, and had the Honour to be among the best of People. Thus I continued for a long while, and kept my self free and Chast from all Men, till about this time three Years, that I was deluded, and got with Child, the which soon after Dy'd.

Then I made a firm Resolution never to have another, nor would I, had not one *Mc.Cormick* (that he and his Wife were among my fellow Servants) deluded me, and got me with Child, which pass'd for a long Time undiscover'd, but drawing near my Time, my Mistress seeing me more large, and more unhealthy than usual taxed me about it, but I alas! poor wretch had no mind to have the Name of any such thing it deny'd to her, by Reason the Devil prompted me so to do, on purpose to hide my shame; but my Mistress Insisted still it was so, but the more she said it the more I Curs'd and Swore it was not so.

Thus I continued under sensure of my Mistress, who kept a Watchful Eye over me, until the unhappy Day came I was deliver'd, which Day I stuck more close to my Business, than I did for a Month before, in hopes there should be no Suspicion of me, but when Night came, I went to my Chamber, but being missed, my Mistress sent her waiting Maid up after me, but to no purpose, for I fastned the Door very well within side, and said I would not admit any one into the Room at all, for that I was Sweating, and would not get up.

Thus I spent the most part of the Night in great Sorrow, Grief and Pain until I was Deliver'd, then I poor wretch, having not the fear of God or Man in me; took my tender Babe in my Arms, and went down Stairs, and threw it into the Privy, in the Dead time of the Night, and the next Morning I got up and was as strong as if nothing ail'd me, but when my Mistress saw me, asked me how I was; and whether I was Deliver'd or no, I told her I was well, but as for being Delivered, I told her I had nothing to be Delivered off; upon which I was immediately Discharged.

About 3 or 4 Days after my poor Babe was found where my own Hands laid it, by the Servants of the House, who got one *Mackelroy* a Porter, to take it up, (and who was a very great Evidence against me at my Tryal) then serch was made after me until I was taken, and now am made a Publick Example to the whole World; now I beg of God, that this my untimely Death my be a Warning to Young and Old, for realy the sin of geting a Child by a deluding Man is enough, but far more greater in the Murdering of it.

Thus Christians have I given you a true Narative of my past Life and Conversation, likewise of my base and cruel Astions concerning the Murder of my Child, the which I hope, will be a means to deter others of my Sex from doing the like.

Having no more to say, my Time being so short, but beg the Prayers of all good Christians, while I am alive. I fereely forgive both Judge and Jury, because they did nothing but according to what Evidences Swore. I also forgive my Prosecutor, but I can scarce forgive Mc. Cormick who got me with Child, but as I am Commanded to forgive my Enemies, I obedient to that Command, do freely forgive him also. I am now about 28 Years of Age, and am an unworthy Member of the Church of England as by Law Establish'd, and the Lord have Mercy on my Soul, Amen.

(British Library, C133.g.7(56))

34

THE LAST SPEECH, CONFESSION AND DYING WORDS OF

John Mc.Coy, Thomas Barnet, John Smith, and Owen Geoghegan

who are to be Executed near St. Stephen's-Green, this present Wednesday being the 13th Inst. October 1725. For Robbing Mr. George Scrivener, the 25th of September last, of a Silk Purse vallued one Shilling; with Sixteen Moydors in Gold.

The Speech of *John Mc.Coy.*

Good Christians,

SInce it is my Fortune to come to this Untimely End, I think it proper to give the World a true Account of my past Life, and Conversation, which is as follows (*viz.*) I was Born in the County of *Derry* of very honest Parents, who gave me what Education they could, 'till I was able to do for my self, and then I Bound myself an Apprentice to Learn to twist *Mohair*, being out of my Time I soon after Listed in the Army, where I behav'd myself true and honest as became a Soldier to do, untill I was Discharg'd for being an *Irishman*; then I betook my self to be a *Porter*, and kept about *Fishamble-Street* attending and going of Errants, and Carrying of Loads for several of the Inhabitance there, and behav'd my self true and honest, as many of them declar'd at my Tryal; but being at last deluded I went along with my fellow Sufferers to *Grafton-street*, where we met Mr. *George Scrivener*, and took from him 16 *Moydors*, for which we now Dye.

This being all I have to say, but begs the Prayers of all good Christians, and leaving my Blessing with all Youngmen to beware of Temptation; I Dye a Roman Catholick, in the 24th Year of my Age, and the Lord have Mercy on my poor Soul *Amen.*

The Speech of *Thomas Barnet*.

Good People,

I Drew my first Breath in *England* of very honest Credible Parents, and coming here to *Ireland*, I met an Uncle of mine who put me an Apprentice to a *Shoe-maker*, with whom I liv'd for some Time, 'till I was at length Tempted by the Devil to go along with these my fellow Sufferers to Commit the Fact for which I now Dye. Having no more to say, but Desiring the Prayers of all good Christians, I Dye a Member of the Church of *England*, in the 18th Year of my Age, and the Lord have Mercy on my Soul *Amen.*

The Speech of *John Smith*

Dear Christians,

I Was Born in the County of *Catherlough*, of very honest Parents who took all the care they could to bring me up in the Fear & Love of God, but coming here to *Dublin*, I came acquainted with several Idle Persons, which brought me to this Fatal Death, which I must Confess we are all Guilty of, but as I am a Dying Man I never was Guilty of any other in the whole Course of my Life. Having no more to say, but Earnestly beging the Prayers of all good Christians, I Dye a Roman Catholick, in the 18th Year of my Age, and the Lord receive my Soul *Amen.*

The Speech of *Owen Geoghegan.*

Dear Neighbours,

I Was Born at *Glosmbonoug*, of poor but honest Parents, with whom I liv'd for sometime, and was well belov'd by all that knew me; the Fact for which I Dye, is for Robbing Mr. *Scrivener*, the which I own I justly deserve, by Reason I am Guilty of it; but never Stole the value of one Farthing in all my Life before.

Having no more to say, but do Forgive the whole World from the Bottom of my Heart, hoping God will Forgive me, I Dye a Roman Catholick, in the 19th Year of my Age, and the Lord have Mercy on my Soul *Amen.*

Dublin : Printed at the *Reign-Deer* in Montrath-Street, 1725.

(Location: British Library, C.133.g.7 (37))

35

THE LAST SPEECHES AND DYING WORDS OF

John McCoy, Tho. Barnet, Owen Geohegan, and John Smith

who are to be Executed this Day being the 13th of this Inst. Octob. 1725, for Robbing the Lord Chancellors Gentleman in Grafton-street;

We all Four do Declare, that we gave our Speeches to Carter and to no other.

The SPEECH of JOHN Mc'COY.

GOOD PEOPLE,

I Should have made no Speech more than what I have made to my Father Confessor; only to prevent other false Speeches that might be Publish'd in my Name on this Subject.

I John Mac Coy was Born in the County of Londonderry in Ulster, and Parish of Rilre, of very honest and tender Parents, who gave me good Education, and brought me up in the fear of GOD, wherein I did continue untill I came to the Years of Discretion, and then I came to the City of Dublin, where I got very honest Bread, and behav'd my self very honestly to all that employ'd me, and in all places that I was, I behav'd my self very faithful in all things Committed into my Charge, untill I came acquainted to my great sorrow with Daniel Ross, and others who was the cause of this my untimely end; for on or about 18 Weeks ago, I and the said Dan Ross, and Owen Geoghegan my fellow Sufferer was coming thro' Aron Street, we chanc'd to meet one Mr Martin, they took his Sword and Cane from him, I declare before God and the World that I knew nothing of the Sword and Cane at that time, but finding after that they took them, and I being in the Company, was afraid that they should be discover'd, made me keep out of the way and not come near the place where I was known. Then the said Daniel Ross and my fellow sufferers did agree to go on some design of better Moment, there remain'd in the State they were in, upon which their chance was to meet Mr. Scrivener, whom we did Rob of Sixteen Moydores, a Pistol and his Sword. Good People, Last July was two years I had some words with one of the Fuzineers, which was Sworn to be Treason and Plasphemy, and it was Sworn against one Mr. Robert Joy that he was the Person that did speak the said Treason, but as I am a dying Man I am the Person that did say it, for which I am very sorry. I am 24 years of Age, in Peace and Charity with all the World, I die a Roman Catholick and the Lord have Mercy on my Soul.

JOHN Mc' COY.

The Speech of THOMAS BARNET.

Good Cristians,

I THO. BARNET was born in London in the Parish of S. Martin, of very good Parents, not of the meanest sort, where they gave me good Education and brought me up in the fear of God, I came over into Ireland with my Uncle Person Upton, and did leavehim in Anger, but I came to him again, and he being then in the Conuty of Longford, I came to this Town along with him where he bound me Apprentice to one Mr. Vantardillo a Shoe-maker on Hogg'Hill; I run away from him after serving him three Years and a half, when I began to take up with idle and loose Company. I do Confess before God that I was concern'd in the Robbing Mr. Martin. I confess also that I was one of them that Rob'd Mr. Scrivener my Lord Chancellor's Gentleman, for which I now dye. I am about 25 years of Age, I Die Member of the Church of England, and in peace with all People, the Lord receive my Soul. Amen.

THOMAS BARNET.

The Speech of OWEN GAUGHAN.

Dear People,

I Owen Geohegan was born in the County of *Clare* and bred in this City of *Dublin* of very honest Parents who brought me up in the fear of God, and by Trade a *Slater*, and made it my business to avoid all ill Vices, till one *Margaret Butler* did falsely swear, that I Robb'd her of a Gold Locket, and had several Constables after me, my Parents hearing of it, I was a fraid to go near them, and having no way to subsist my self, nor could not follow my Trade for fear of her, so I fell into bad *Company*, which caus'd me to Transgress against the Laws of God, and never went near my dear Parents; but the said *Margaret Butler* is the cause of this my untimely End, and as I am aDying Man, I do Declare before the Almighty God, towhom I am to Answer my Trespasses I never knew either Act or part of it, God for give her.

As for being concern'd in the Robbery of *Mr.* Screvenner belonging to the Lord High Chancellor of Ireland, I confes that I was in it with my fellow Sufferers and am Guilty thereof; *My* Prosecutor Daniel Ross which was one of the chiefest Instruments of the said Fact that God may for give him hoping through his infinite mercy to pardon my Sins. I am about 19 years of Age, I *D*ie a Roman Catholick, in charity with all the World, begging all your Prayers, and the Lord have mercy on my poor Soul.

and so took his leave of his Brother sufferers,

Owen GEOHEGAN.

The Last SPEECH of JOHN SMITH.

You my Spectators,

I John Smith was born in Lucan near Dublin, wherein I was bread of very honest Parents, woich took a great deal of care to bring me up in the fear of God and I got very honest bread, and serv'd a good

Master, one Mr. O Hara an Apothecary till I came acquainted with one Margaret Butler, who swore that I was the Man that Robb'd her, and took a Gold Docket from her, which she accus'd Geohegan my fellow sufferer for the same, and swore against us both, and said she wou'd Hang me, so that I forc'd to keep out of the way for fear of her, on that my parents and Neighbours hearing of this ugly odium, then nobody would Imploy or give me any business, then I met with Ill Company which I went along with to Robb and do other ill things, and I do Declare before God and the World that I never knew anything of taking her Locket.

I am 18 years of Age and die of the Church of Rome, Lord have mercy on my Soul.

(Location: British Library, C.133.g.7 (59))

36

THE LAST SPEECHES AND DYING WORDS OF

Cornet Joseph Poe, and Nicholas Cox

who are to be Executed near *Kilmainham* on *Wednesday* the 20th, of this Instant *October* 1725. Cor. *Poe* for the Robbing of *Michael Hall* and *Anthony Costolow*, two Frizemongers, on the 25th of *September* last, on the High Road near *Tallow-Hill*. And *Nicholas Cox* for Cow Stealing.

The Speech of Joseph Poe.

Good People,

THere are many of you come here this Day, on purpose to see me Dye, and like-Wise to hear what Linage I came from; as for to see me Dye you are welcome, but for Naming of my Parentage I hope you will Excuse me, by Reason they are Persons of great Credit and Worth: But where I was Born, and what I Dye for, likewise the perticulars of my Life and Actions, I am very willing to Inform you. I drew my first, but unfortunate Breath, in the County of *Tiperary*, of Credible Parents as above mentioned, who gave me a Gentlemans Education as behov'd me, and being come to Maturity I Enter'd into the Horse, and got to be a Cornet, in which Station I remain'd till the Regiment was broke, and then I was glad to live on half Pay, which is one Pound one shilling *per* week, but I being a Person that lov'd to live in Splender, I found that my half pay would not do; therefore I began to consider within my self how to Augment my Living, at length I unbethought of the most Beasest and Cruelest Contrivances, that none but my self would be Guilty off, which is as follows.

When ever my Money grew short, I would go to the Ale-house or Tavern, and there would Enter in Company, with whom I would sit and Drink, 'till they would be Fuddeled, and then I'd begin to

Drink Treasonable Healths, and Swear if they would not Drink the same, I would be the Death of 'em, which they would no sooner do, but I would go and Swear the same against e'm, [but if they gave me Money, I'd Swear nothing against e'm] Thus I continued for some Time to the great Determent of many of the Inhabitants of this City, who knows it to their great Sorrows, as some in St. *James's-Street* by Woeful Experience can justly tell, insomuch that I became the whole Scorn of all that knew me, and often times repremanded by well meaning People, one of which I had like to have been his Butcher, by giving him a mortal wound, for which I was put into *Newgate*, where I remain'd along Time; I was no sooner set at Liberty but I was put into the *Blackdog* for Debt, where I remain'd a considerable Time, but agreeing with my Creditor I was set at Liberty; I had not been long abroad before I was put into the City *Marshalsea*, on an Action of 2 *l.* 5*s.* and rather than pay the Debt, I gave Bail to the *Marshal* Keeper of 10 *l.* to be a Prisoner at large, so that I had my Liberty abroad all Day, but lay in the *Marshalsea* at Night. Thus I continued till the 25*th*, of *September* last, (hearing the Night before that the above *Hall* and *Costolow*, was to go and buy some Frize) and then took Horse at one Mr. *Dunn's* in *Pill-Lane* near the *Fishmarket*, where myself and another went to *Tallow-Hill*, and there we met the afforesaid Persons, and took 40 *l.* from one, Seven Moydors Eight Guineas, half a Guinea, and half a Pistol from another, which Fact I am realy Guilty of.

Thus Spectators, have I given you a true Account of my Wicked Life and Actions, which is all I have to say at present, only to Inform you that I am a Member of the Church of *England*, and in the 56th Year of my Age, and the Lord have Mercy on my poor Sinful Soul *Amen.*

The Speech of *Nicholas Cox.*

Dear Christians,

I Was Born in the County of *Westmeath* of honest Parents, who brought me up tenderly, with whom I liv'd 'till I was Married, and geting a few Cows with my Wife, I took a small Cabin and four or five Acres of Land to Grease my Cattle on, but going behind hand of my Rent, my goods and Cattle were Distrained, and I finding where they were put, went and Stole 2 of them, and sold them to buy Bread for my Family, and finding that I Escap'd with that, I went to *Palmerstown* the last Fair Day, and there Stole 5 Cows, but was Apprehended when Selling the same: Now as I shall Answer God, this is all the Theft I Committed in the whole Course of my Life.

Having no more to say, but Begging the Prayers of all good Christians, I Dye a Roman Catholick, in the 30th Year of my Age, and the Lord receive my Soul *Amen.*

(Location: British Library, C.133.g.7 (63))

37

LAST SPEECH AND DYING WORDS OF

Anne Pepper

who is to be Executed at St. Stevens-Green on Saturday the 22d of this Inst January 1725

Good Christians,
SINCE it is my hard Fortune to come to an untimely end, I will give the Publick an Account of my past Life, which you may take as followeth, Viz.

I was Born in Dublin, in the Parish of St. Brides, of poor and honest Parents, who gave me Education suitable whereby I might have got honest Bread. I was desirous to go to Service, and I had my wish, The first place I went to was to Mr. Paris's in York Street, and after to Mr. John Wards, and several other Credible Services; At length I unfortunately Married to one Pepper, who was Cooke to an Honourable Gentleman; This Marriage was the beginning of my Misfortunes, and the chief Cause of my coming to this shameful, untimely end; As I am a dying Woman, I never knew Man before my Husband, but God forgive me I have known several since, and for the most part other Women's Husbands, once I turn'd loose I embrac'd what came in my way, as Roberies, &c. The first that I Rob'd was my Master a French Minister and made off with the Robery to Holly-Head in Wales, from thence I went to London; and remain'd there five Years, where my Husband follow'd me, and brought my Mother and Brothers and Sisters with him, where they all remain (except my Husband) to this Day, if alive, it is now about two Years and a half since I left them. I by the time of my return to Dublin, came acquainted with Several Thieves and Robbers, and was concern'd in Several Roberies; and in particular this for which I dye.

ANNE PEPPER

I was Encourag'd by one Sarah Kenny a Running Broker, who promis'd that any Thing I brought to her, should never be brought to Light, after I had Committed this Robbery for which I justly Die. I was going Directly to the said Sarah Kenny's Room in Patrick's Close, and was met by one Patrick Hoy, Butcher a Notorious T_____se, just in the Close, who took by Force from me a Petticoat belonging to the Robbery, and said he would have it for his share, and so he took it to the said Sarah Kenny before me:

The said Petticoat is the Reason of my loosing of my Life, for all that was taken was Return'd except that Petticoat, and if they could have got that Petticoat, the Gentle woman that own'd it would not have prosecuted me.

Tho' I have seen several persons suffer here for varieties of Facts, yet it did no way daunt me, nor made no impression in my obdurate Heart, till now. I heartily begg of my Great and Merciful God to Bless me and save my Soul, I hope this will be a warning to all ill People.

Having no more to say, I begg the Prayers of all good Christians. I Dye a Protestant of the Church of England in the 33d Year of my Age, and the Lord have mercy on my poor Soul, Amen.

I leave my blessing with good Mr. DERRY, for the great care he took of my Soul.

This is my true Speech given by me to the Printer hereof, and all others are false, and Scandalous.

Ann Pepper.

Dublin. Printed by C. Carter 1725.

(Location: Trinity College Library, Press A.7.4 No 11)

38

THE LAST SPEECH AND DYEING WORDS OF

Thomas Craven and William Anderson

who is to be Executed this present Saturday being the 29th of this Instant January 1725–6. near Killmainham.

The Speech of Thomas Craven.

Good Christians,

I Had no thought at first to make any Speech, but being told if I would not, that Some Printers would, and I thereby made more blacker than I am, and the Publick impos'd on by a parcel of Lyes and Nonsence; in order to prevent the same, I have sent to the Printer hereof, to whom I related the whole truth of my past Life and Conversation, which is as follows, *viz.*

I drew my first Breath at a place call'd *Ballgee*, in the County of Meath, of very honest Endeavouring Parents, but so Poor, that they could not give me either Learning or Trade, but growing up to Years and Strength, I went to live with one Mr. *Boylan* a Miller, living at a place call'd *Moorehead* in the said County, with whom I liv'd for the Space of five or six Years, during which time I behaved my self true and honest, as many in them parts can tell, but leaving him about some few Months ago, took upon me to go to *Dublin*, but unfortunatly meeting with Mr. *Elisha Charles* at a place called *Swords*, and he having three Cows that he bought, desired me to drive them to his House, and I being one that always bore a good and honest Name, took no thought of me, but left me to my self, thinking that I would leave them at home, but he no sooner left me, but I turn'd the Cows and drove them to *Dublin*, and thought to have sold them the next Day; but Mr. *Charles* thinking I stay'd too long, he made an Enquiry about me, and being inform'd that I went to *Dublin* with the Cows, he took Horse and rid after me, and got me selling the Cows in *Smithfield*, for which he had me Apprehended and committed to *Killmainham Goal*, and now must justly Dye for the same, and now as I am a dying Man this is the first fact that ever I Committed. Haveing no more to say but beg the Prayers of all good Christians, I dye a *Roman Catholick*, and in the 36th Year of my Age, and the Lord have Mercy on my poor Soul, *Amen.*

The Speech of William Anderson

Good people,

I Seeing my Fellow Sufferer giving his Speech to be Printed, I thought it would be proper, since we are to dye together, that I should do the same which I did, and is as follows, *viz.*

I was Born in the County of *Cavin.* of very honest Parents, who brought me up very tenderly till I was able to go to a Trade, and then they bound me to a Courier, to whom I serv'd seven Years true and honest, being out of my Time, I wrought at my Trade, and by it got good honest Bread, but my time being so short, that I shall not trouble the reader with any long stories, but tell you the cause of my Death. I being acquainted in the House of Mr. *Tyeror* in St. *Patrick Street*, went there when I thought they were all a sleep, and went to the Window and took down the Glass and so got in, but got nothing for my pains but a small silver Cup, but indeed I thought to get a good parcel of Mony, but cou'd not, by reason they paid it away.

Having no more to Say, but begs the Prayers of all good Christians, I dye a *Roman Catholick*, and in the 27th Year of my Age, and as this is my first Fact, I hobe my God will forgive me my Sins, and receive my Soul in the Hour of my Death, and I hope all good Christians will say *Amen.*

Printed at the Rein Deer in Montrath Street, 1725–6.

(Location: Trinity College Library, Press A.7.4 No.13)

THE LAST SPEECH, CONFESSION AND DYING WORDS OF

Francis Mc. Cabe, William Cunneen and Edward Fox

who are to be Hang'd this present Saturday being the 14th, Inst. May, 1726. near St. Stephen's Green; the two Former for Robbing Mr. Delamain, the Latter for picking Mr. Smith's Pocket in Newgate.

The Speech of *Francis Mc. Cabe.*

AS 'tis expected I should say something for the Quietude of my own Conscience, and the Satisfaction of the World being now to be made a Dreadful Example and Warning to ill designing Persons, I shall refer you to the under Written.

The County *Cavan* gave me Birth and Education, where after I had spent my Youth, I came to Dublin, where I saw my unhappy Brother Executed for Robbery, which griev'd me so much that I return'd to my Native Place, but after two Years came again to Dublin, fell into the Company of some disolute Young Fellows, particularly my Fellow Sufferer; this soon reduced me to such necessitous Circumstances, that I was obliged to Rob for my Subsistence, and in this manner I lead a wicked Debauch'd life, till I Robb'd Mr. *Delamain* for which I was Apprehended and am now to Suffer. I desire your Prayers, I am about 23 years of age, Dying an unworthy Member of the Church of Rome.

Francis Mc. Cabe,

The Speech of William Cunneen

I Was born in the North in the County of Dunegal, my father Dy'd when I was Young, and my Mother being left poor was oblig'd to come here to Dublin at 14 Years of Age, I came after and got an acquaintance with those who have proved my ruin; in Seven Years I have committed 80 Roberies, of which Mr. *Delamain's* is the last; and for this I am condemn'd to Dye, I confess I deserve Death, and desire all who hear me, to avoid and shun all concerns with B...Y W...ms the Q—n of the S—ts in St. Francis-Street, the Ruin and Destruction of thousands. I beg you would Testify my Repentance to the World, and grant me your Prayers for my poor Soul.

William Cunneen

The Speech of Edward Fox,

Brother Pick-pockets among the Crowd,

I Was born and bred a Pick pocket, in the County of Cork and now am to Dye one in Dublin; I grieve the less at my misfortune for all my relations had the same Fate before me, I have been guilty of the Crime for which I now suffer in every part of the Kingdom, but my youth inclined the Jury to savour me, at fifteen years of Age I was committed to Newgate tried and Condemned, and there I have remained these two years under Sentence, I now dye for robbing Mr. Smith who came to see a Friend of his in Confinement, I am about 17 Years old, and dye a true Roman Catholick; beware good People of my Fate and your Pockets, and the Lord have mercy on my Soul.

Edward Fox.

N.B. Brian Sweeney alias Pig Sweeney in Montrath Street, has no Speech of mine all being feigned by scandalous fellows, but what is publish'd by the Printer hereof: I hear that fellow has a Speech ready to Print upon all occasions, and only changes the Persons Names. He has been already severely whipp'd through this City for an Imposition of the like Nature.

Dublin: Printed by G.F. in Castle Street, 1726

(Location: Trinity College Library, Press A.7.4. No 54)

THE TRUE LAST SPEECH, CONFESSION, AND DYING WORDS OF

Mr. James Stevens and Account of Patrick Barnwell

who are to be executed at *St. Stephen's Green*, on *Wednesday* the 25*th* Inst. *May*, 1726, being condemn'd for feloniously taking from Mr. *Philip Kennersly* of *Dame-street*, a Glass-case, Value 50l.

GOOD PEOPLE

IF it were not usual for Men of every Degree, in my unfortunate Circumstances to make a Kind of Declaration at their Death of their past Behaviour, I shou'd not, as at this Day, nor even should the above mention'd Considerations move me to make this, my *Only* and *Last*, were I not sensible of the many *Villanous Falsities*, which might be publish'd concerning my unhappy Fate, by Persons of the vilest Characters themselves; such as one *Hoy* in *Pembroke-Court*, who publish'd a scandalous and wicked Paper on the last poor Wretches that suffer'd, under the name of G.F. or *George Faulkner*, a Person known to have no Being in this Kingdom, this long Time past, altho' make his Tool and Screen for scandalizing the Chiefest of our Just and Good Governours, as vilely as the poor undone Wretches: Beside him, there is another as notorious for the like Villainy, living at the *Rein Deer* in *Montrath-Street*, unworthy, and noted for the above named wicked Practice. On these Considerations only, then I say, I the unhappy and unfortunate *James Stephens*, have thought fit to tender to *Richard Dickson* of *Dame Street*, *Printer*, THIS, for Publication, as he thinks proper.

FIRST, Then, since I see it is the Will of the most High God, whose Name be for ever Blessed, That in this World I should be brought from my Former happy, to this Wretched state, I submit, beseching humbly for his most Gracious mercy and Forgiveness for my manifold Transgressions in the Follies of my youth, and misspent Time, which began in the City of London, where I first Drew my Breath, being an entire Stranger here, of Creditable and Honest Parents, who Bred me Tenderly and well, till I was able to go Apprentice, which Time I serv'd to an Image-maker, after I had done with him, I Work'd for my self, and growing worth money, after I had spent some of my untainted Youth, in the Service abroad, belonging to the Ordnance, I set up to keep Hire-Horses, for the Court, in Nature of the great Mr. Blount, in the Parish of St. James, having Licenc'd coaches, and dealing for upwards of 500*l*, a year, till many Misfortunes comming on me, I was oblidg'd to leave my Native Country, and on a Woful Day, I came for Ireland with some small matter of Money, about a year since, where I follow'd making Images, till I came acquainted with the vile Woman *Eleanour Fenly*, who to save her Life at Tryal falsly said she was my Wife, Poverty forceing me to keep first with her, she pretending to have Friends who would make my Fortune, which alas! they have, it being her Brother, *Fernando Fenly*, and his Accomplice who swore my Life away, in declaring T*hat about the 25th of March, last I have a Box of Goods, which were Mr. Kennersly's, afterwards found in his Custody, and that I paid him 2 Shillings for carryage from the Sun Inn*, in Francis Street, *to Ross*, which I vow all False, nor was I e'er Guilty of what was sworn, tho' for it I must dye, having no Friend to appear for me, yet with the Constancy of a Christian who can accuse *himself*, of no great Crimes I go to meet my Fate, Dying in Charity with the World.

But this I further for my Innocency declare, I ne'er had Intention to rob Mr. *Kennersly*, nor e'er sold any of his Goods, but going into the Country with the Aforemention'd *Eleanor Fenly* to her Brother's in *Loghreagh*, where he lives well; she came in Company with one Byrn, a Fellow did not like and who resolv'd I suppose to do us an Injury, upon which I quarrel'd, and happening to be damag'd by some People in *Caterlogh*. I resolv'd to get Justice of which, being by 'em suspected, they got me apprehended on Suspicion of an idle Person, and *Nell Fenly* getting some Toys to sell there, she was discover'd at that time, on which her Brother made the Examination aforesaid, against me, which caused me to be transmitted and tryed upon it, to save his own Life; she as I before said, escaping by alledging she was my Wife &c. I may likewise add, that had not my Fellow Sufferer hop'd to have sav'd his Life, he cou'd have clear'd me, for which I pray God forgive him, And now Dear Christians, I have nought to say, but heartily beg that some of you, who shall see me dye, out of mere Pity to my unhappy State, (an entire and poor Stranger) will cover me with Earth, an Hindrance to those Men whose Business it is, to keep forlorn Wretches from their Graves, for private Practice o'er their mangled Bodies. I now conclude begging your Prayers to God for my Forgiveness, being about 37 Years of Age, A Protestant Member of the Church of *England*.

James Stephens.

PATRICK BARNEL Who is to dye with Mr. Stephens, on the Persuasion of some Friends has declin'd making further Confession, than to his Ghostly Father, which he desires so might be forth, lest any imprudent Person should pretend he had made any Speech, giving no further Account of himself, than that he was pritty well educated, and when young, that he serv'd Major Arthur, to whom he owns great obligation, that after he left him, he went to serve a Weaver, whose Business he after, follow'd, dating his Misfortunes to begin in being concern'd in Mr. Kenerslys Robbery; to whom he afterwards gave up several Things in hopes to save his Life. He Dies a Roman Catholick, begging the Prayers of All good Christians.

Mr. *Gray* having by Gracious Mercy, obtained a Reprieve, 'tis hop'd no notice will be taken of the absurd Pieces, design'd and *publish'd*, by the said *Hoy* in Pembroke Court, or under any feign'd Name whatever, which is *notoriously known* to be intended by *Hoy*, who surely will cheat the Publick with some scandalous and lying Paper, intitled a Speech to the abovenamed unfortunate Men, in prejudice and defamation to the Printer hereof, who unwittingly gall'd him, in saying th'other Day, *He look'd like Death*, when a Person affirm'd to his Face, in the open street, *he said he was a MOLLY*, (term well known for Sodomite) a charge so bold, that it might be wished, before he strives to taint another's, he'd clear his own Character, from *that Aspersion*, if so it may be term'd.

Printed by *Richard Dickson*, and *Gwyn Needham* in *Dames-Street*.

(Location: Trinity College Library, Press A.7.4 No. 55)

41

THE LAST SPEECH, CONFESSION AND
DYING WORDS, OF

Patrick Barnel, and James Stephens

who are to be executed at St. Stephens Green, this present Wednesday, the 25th of this Inst. May, 1726. For the Robbery of Mr. Kinnersly in Dames-Street.

The Speech of James Stephens.

Good People.

I James Stephens, was born at Cheswick, about five Miles from London: my Parents put me to a free School to learn to write, where I had the Character of an unlucky Boy. At 14 Years of Age, I was entertained by the celebrated *Jonathan Wilde*, under whom I arrived to such Dexterity in Picking Pockets and Impudence in barefac'd Robberies, that I robb'd on a Play Night in *Drury Lane Edward Martin*, Esq, of 75 Guineas and a Gold Watch. My honest Master for the sake of a Reward of ten Pounds for the Discovery of the Persons who committed the Robbery, made Oath that I was the Person.

But I having Timely notice of it, fled to *France*, where I with some others Rob'd and Murder'd Mr. *Lock*, and the English Gentlemen in his Company, then I took Shipping at *Calais*, and landed at *Cork*, where Information in a little Time was given against Me, for several Robberies; this obliged me to come to *Dublin*, where I most impudently perform'd that unparalleled Roguery of Stealing a Glass Case with Rings, Silver Spoons, Snuff-Boxes, &c. to the Value of Seventy, Pounds from Mr. *Kinnersly* Goldsmith in *Dame Street*. I heartily and sincerely repent of my horrid Crimes, and desire the Prayers of all my Fellow Christians. I dye an unworthy Member of the Church of England.

James Stephens.

The Speech of PATRICK BARNWELL

Good Cristians,

I *Patrick Barnel* was born in the County of *Dublin* of Poor, but Honest Parents; their mean Circumstances was in a great Measure, the Cause of my Present Misfortune, for they could not give me any Education, and I was often obliged to take away from the little Children of the same Town their Victuals to satisfie my Hunger, when I was a Boy, I stole several little Things, and escaped without Punishment.

I was induced to commit great Rogueries; I became acquainted with a Gang of Tories who kept their Rendevouz in the County of *Kerry* with whom I committed such Cruel and Barbarous Actions, that we were all Obliged to disperse and shift every one for himself, it was my Fate to come to this City where I had not been above Six Months, before I introduced into the Company of my Fellow-Sufferer, who was the Head of a Gang of about a Dozen, having no Manner of Subsisting myself.

I committed several petty Thefts with him and others, and at last that most notorious one for which I now die, I cannot deny that I am guilty, but having a true sence of my Crimes, I repent of them, and I desire your Prayers for my soul, I die a Member of the Church of Rome in which I was bred, and the Lord have mercy on my poor Soul.

N.B. On Sunday last, one *Dickson* a Printer, who publishes Papers under the Name of G *Needham*, came to us in Newgate, and we not thinking him a proper Person to make any thing publick from us. We desire the publick to beware buying any Speech of ours from him, for whatever is printed by him is an Imposition of the Town, and can only be excused by his saying, *He is a poor Boy, and must endeavour to better his miserable Circumstances,* and maintain himself and his little Family. He had already advertised, that he has the Speech of one who is not to die.

Dublin: Printed by G.F. in Castle Street.

(Location: Trinity College Library, Press A.7.4 No 56)

42

THE LAST SPEECH, CONFESSION
AND DYING WORDS OF

Moses Nowland

who is to be hang'd at St Stephen's Green, for inlisting Men for the Service of the Pretender, on Wednesday being the 6th of July, 1726.

Dear Countrymen,

IT is my hard Fate, and indeed I can scarce complain of it, to be here, exposed in the Eyes of the whole World to a shamefull and ignominious Death, about which I doubt not, there are, and will be, various Conjectures, some inclining to pity and compassionate my Suffering in this Manner, others again asserting it to be my Desert. To ease therefore your Minds of all doubts, and satisfy you of my true Crime, I will lay before you the real Nature of it. The Crime for which I was apprehended, tried, condemned by the Laws of this Land, and am now to dye in a publick Manner is the Acting contrary to the Duty incumbent upon a loyal subject, by inlisting Men for the Pretender's Service; and had this been truly the Nature of my Crime, I should not have regretted my Folly to that great Degree, I at present do, tho' I had been equally found guilty, but have had a more plausible Pretence, than I have, for my Crimes, and perhaps have drawn the Compassion of some of my Spectators on me, for the deluding Insinuations of cunning, designing and self-interest Men might have perswaded me, or the Dictates of mine own Erroneous Conscience told me, that, what I did, was but my Duty, being designed for the service of my lawful Sovereign, and the entire Good of my own Country. But, Alas, this is not what I am guilty of, tho' laid to my Charge; for my real Crime is so heinous and wicked in it's own Nature, that I cannot in the least excuse it to God, my Conscience or Country; no false and mistaken Zeal for my Country guided and over rul'd mine-Actions, but I was wholly swayed by damned Avarice and

Cursed Ambition, and not content with mine own Wickedness, I tempted and prevailed with others, I say many others, to follow the same destructive Paths, and be Partakers with me in mine Iniquity. I believe there are very few here, who are not sensible, that some Foreign Potentates entertain Natives of this Kingdom as Soldiers in their Service, and that the Kings of France, and Spain have several Regiments composed solely of Irish, and as it is next to an Impossibility, but that these Regiments must from time to time be deficient in their Number, so when ever a Compleating is necessary, they send here for that Purpose. About February last, I was ignorantly Employ'd by an unknown Gentleman, well dress'd, to carry some of these Recruits under the Notion of Passengers aboard a ship than at Anchor in the Bay where dreadful Time and Place, which with Horror I reflect on, I was made privy to the fatal Secret, and for a few pieces of Gold, and the promise of a Capital Commission to satisfy my ambitious Spirit, not only bribed to Secrecy, but employ'd as an Agent, to seduce more to enter themselves in the King of Spain's Service under the Notion it was for the Pretender; a Bait which the Ignorant readily swallow, and by which they are easily deluded. But what Recompence will this trifling Sum be to me, or what can Millions of Millions benefit me; tho' it were possible I could have bribed the impartial Law in my Favour, and escaped the Punishment I am now justly doom'd to suffer, yet how could I asswage the Tumults of my Mind, and still the Rebukes of my Conscience, which never ceaseth to reproach me with the Deformity and Blackness of my Crime, with what Arguments could I clear and excuse myself before the just Tribunal of an enraged and All-seeing God, before whom I am in a few Minutes to appear? Where then shall I hide my guilty Head to avoid that most dreadful Sentence, that He'll pronounce upon me? How shall I cry to the Rocks to fall on me, and the Hills to cover me? How shall I approach his awful Throne, when the Consciousness of my Guilt overwhelmes with Confusion, and criminal Blushes pronounce my Sins to be as read as Scarlet, and my Transgressions as Crimson? To furnish a Monarch of another Kingdom, a Monarch, who has always shown an inveterate Hatred towards these Kingdoms, with Men to fight against us, and destroy our Country, to tread down our Corn, and devour our Palaces, whom nothing, but the Terror of our Fleet, and Courage of our Admirals, hinders from invading us, Reason tell me is not only base, treasonable, and deserves a Punishment less favourable than our Laws admit of, but also directly repugnant to the Laws of Nature, and the Duty I owe to a just and merciful Creator. Had I been Guilty of Sewing Sedition in the Minds of the Ignorant, of stiring up the disaffected and Disloyal to Rebellion, I might then, as well as others, have had the Common Plea of Liberty and Property and only had some to think 'twas done for the Good of my Country, and so not have fallen unpitied, but likewise wherewithal to stop the Gnawing of my revilling Conscience.

But to be subservient to the Designs of a Foreign Potentate, whose Actions have always tended to the Subversion of our growing Commerce, and the flourishing Estate of these Kingdoms, who continually looks with a jealous Eye on our Felicity, who grieves at our Prosperity, and rejoices at every little Accident, that lessens and Diminishes it, is such a villainous and diabolical Action, that should the merciful Diposition of Gracious Governors grant a full and perfect Pardon for my Crimes, I should live under the incessant stings of my Conscience, be ashamed ever to appear in a free Society, whose Constitution I undermined as far as lay in my Power, and think myself not only the work but the scandal of Human and reasonalbe Creatures.

And now Vengence has overtaken my Crimes, and I heartily repent and grieve for them, yet nothing troubles me more than the Thoughts of the Grief it will give my poor Parents at Carlow; whose gray Hairs will come with Sorrow to the Ground. How shocking it will be to them to see that my Education tended only to corrupt my Morals and render me more Wicked, with what Sorrow will they hear of my Crimes, and Trouble of my shameful Death? How will the News of these Things pierce their aged and tender Hearts? I faint at the Thoughts and die at the Reflection of it. I desire you will all joyn in your Prayers for my poor Soul and beg of our God and merciful Father to have Mercy on me, and forgive my enormous Sins, of which I repent with the most sincere Contrition, and die an unworthy Member of the Church of Rome, trusting in my Redeemer who died for me, that he will save me from the wicked One, and Redeem my Soul from everlasting Wrath and eternal Damnation.

Dublin: Printed by George Faulkner, in Pembroke-Court, Castle Street.

(Location: Trinity College Library, Press A.7.4 No 68; National Library of Scotland, Crawford Miscellaneous broadsides, 1277)

43

SPEECH, CONFESSION AND DYING WORDS OF

James Dealy Constable, John Dobin Butcher, and Edward Dunn

who are to be Executed near St. *Stephen's Green*, this present *Saturday* being the 21*st*. of this Instant *January 1726-7*.

The Speech of James Dealy.

Good *Christians,*

SINCE it has pleased the Almighty God, to put a period to this miserable Life of mine, to whose blessed Will and Power I am ready to Submit, and his *All Seeing Eye* knows my Innocency, makes me the more chearfuler to embrace Death; but many of you would willingly know what I Dye for, therefore I shall in as brief a manner as I can, tell the Truth, the whole Truth, and nothing but the Truth, which is as follows.

I drew my first Breath in the place call'd *Drinom* in *Fingal*, of very honest Parents, who tenderly Nourish'd me and gave me good Education, but growing up to Man's Estate, I was made Constable, in which Station I behav'd myself so well, that I had the Love of all that knew me. Thus I continu'd till *New-Years-Day* last, that I went to *Castle Market*, where I continu'd untillOne the next Morning, then I made the best of my way Homwards, and going thro' *Caple-street*, and turning into *Mary's Abbey*, I hard some People a Quarrelling, I went in order to prevent it, and there I saw my Fellowsufferers and some others whom I separated; then my Fellowsufferers and I went back to *Caple-street* again where we heard a noise, I went to a Watchman and ask'd what was the matter, who said there was a Shop broke open, and asked me what I wanted out so late, I told him if I could get what I wanted, I would give him a good Drink, and so we parted, and making my way Home, the Constable of the Watch call'd to me, so we went into the Watch-House, where we were not long before one *Philip Nealor* a Wine-Cooper's Apprintice came in, and said that we knock'd him down that Night at the Fish-Market, and Robb'd him of his Wigg valu'd 15 Shillings, but if I know anything of it, or had act or part in it, let me never see God, altho', I must Dye for the same, but I forgive him, and God forgive him. Having no more to say, but begs the Prayers of you all for my poor Soul, I dye a *Roman Catholick*, and in the 24*th* Year of my Age, and the Lord have Mercy on my Soul, *Amen.*

The Speech of John Dobin.

Good Christians

I Was Born in St. *Thomas Street*, of very honest Endeavouring Parents, who with a deal of Care and Tenderness brought me up, and gave me good Education untill I was fit to go to a Trade, and then they bound me Aprintice to one in *Ormond Market*, to learn the Butchering Tread, during my aboad there, I behav'd my self true and honest. As for the Fact I dye for, it is needless for me to repeate it over, for Mr. *Dealy* my Fellow Sufferer had declar'd it to the full, and if I know any thing of what is laid to my Charge, may I never see God. Having no more to say but begs the Prayers of all good Christians, I Dye a *Roman Catholick*, in the 19*th* Year of my Age, and the Lord receive my Soul, *Amen.*

The Speech of Edward Dunn.

I Was born in White Lyon Court *in* Strand-Street, *of very honest Parents, who gave me what Education they could, and brought me up in the Fear and Love of God, untill I was able to shift for myself, which I have honestly done from my Birth to my Grave, but I am wrongfully accus'd of knocking down one* Philip Nealor, *and taking his Wigg, which Fact I declare before God and the World that I know nothing of it. Having no more to say but begs the Prayers of all good Christians, I Dye a* Roman Catholick, *and in the 19th Year of my Age, and the Lord have Mercy on my poor Soul,* Amen.

Dublin Printed by *C. Hicks* at the Rein Deer in *Montrath Street.*

(Location: Trinity College Library, Press A.7.4 N0101)

44

THE LAST SPEECHES AND DYING WORDS OF

Tulley Slevin, John Dempsy, and Patrick Murphy

who is to be hanged Drawn and Quartred at St. Stephens Green for Coyning Gold this present Wednesday being the 3d of May 1727.

The Speech of Tully Slevin:

Dear Country-Men,

AS it is usual for all Men in my unhappy Circumstance, to give the World some small Account of their past Lives and Conversations, so I think to give an exact Relation of my self, in as brief a manner as possibly I can, viz. I was bred in the County of Longford, but being minded to live like a Gentleman, I took up the way of Coining Gold, which I have followed some considerable Time, but God, who fetches every thing to Light, would not suffer me to go unpunish'd, for Committing so base and Enormous a Crime, as to Violate his Majesty's Authority, and wrong his Subjects, which I must own I am justly to Dye for the same; and as for my Fellow-Sufferers, I declare they are Innocent of the Fact. I forgive my Prosecutor *Shanogh*, tho' he had as great a hand in it as I. Therefore I beg the Prayers of all good Christians, I Dye a Roman Catholick, and in the 40th Year of my Age, and the Lord have Mercy upon my soul. Amen.

TULLY SLEVIN.

The Speech of John Dempsy

Good Christians

I was born in Munster of very honest Parents who gave me Gentlemans Education, and had serv'd several Credible

Gentlemen in this City, as a servant and Clerk but being unfortunate Met with my Above fellow sufferer, who led me into the Secret of Coining of Gold, tho' J never did Coin any, but J must Confess J have done my Endeavour in passing of it to his Majesty's Subjects; Which I am heartily sorry for, and there is Nothing in the World troubles me more than to Leave my three Small Children behind; As for my Prosecutor shannogh J do forgive him, tho' he was the Only Man that Coined the Gold. J have no more to say but begs the Prayers of all You my Spectators and of those who shall hear of this my untimely End; I dye a Roman Catholick and in the 30th Year of my Age, and the Great God have Mercy upon my Soul. Amen.

JOHN DEMPSY.

The Speech of Patrick Murphy.

Good People,

AS for my part I have not much to say but thar I was born in the County of Killdare of yver Honest Parents and was bred a Sawyer and Got my living by it and after some time I kept a publick House in Pill-Lane as is very Well known in this City in good Credit but the fact which I now am to dye for, I do declare before God and the World, and as I shall answer at the Great and Dreadful Tribunal where the Secrets of all hearts will be Disclosed, I am entirely Innocent, therefore I beg that there may be no reflections thrown either upon my Wife or family upon the Account of my Dying this shameful and Ignominious Death. I desire the Prayers of all Good Christians, I dye a Roman Catholick and in the 32d Year of my Age and the Lord receive my poor Soul, Amen.

PATRICK MURPHY.

Dublin Printed by E. Sadleir on the Blind Key 1727.

(Location: Trinity College Library, Press A.7.4 No 134)

THE LAST
SPEECHES

And Dying Words of Tulley Slevin, John Dempsy, and Patrick Murphy, who is to be hanged Drawn and Quartred at St. Stephens Green for Coyning Gold this present *Wednesday* being the 3d of May 1727.

The Speech of Tully Slevin.

Dear Country-Men,

AS it is usual for all Men in my unhappy Circumstance, to give the World some small Account of their past Lives and Conversations, so I think to give an exact Relation of my self, in as brief a manner as possibly I can, viz. I was bred in the County of Longford, but being minded to live like a Gentleman, I took up the way of Coining Gold, which I have followed some considerable Time, but God, who fetches every thing to Light, would not suffer me to go unpunish'd, for Committing so base and Enormous a Crime, as to Violate his Majesty's Authority, and wrong his Subjects, which I must own I am justly to Dye for the same; and as for my Fellow-Sufferers, I declare they are Innocent of the Fact. I forgive my Prosecutor *Shanogh*, tho' he had as great a hand in it as I. Therefore I beg the Prayers of all good Christians, I Dye a Roman Catholick, and in the 40th Year of my Age, and the Lord have Mercy upon my Soul. Amen. TULLY SLEVIN.

The Speech of John Dempsy

Good Christians

I Was born in Munster of very honest Parents who gave me Gentlemans Education, and has serv'd several Credible Gentlemen in this City, as a servant and Clerk but being unfortunate Met with my Above fellow sufferer, who led me into the Secret of Coining of Gold, tho' I never did Coin any, but I must Confess I have done my Endeavour in passing of it to his Majesty's Subjects; Which I am heartily sorry for, and there is Nothing in the World troubles me more than to Leave my three Small Children behind; As for my Prosecutor shannogh I do forgive him, tho' he was the Only Man that Coined the Gold. I have no more to say but begs the Prayers of all You my Spectators and of those who shall hear of this my untimely End; I dye a Roman Catholick and in the 30th Year of my Age, and the Great God have Mercy upon my Soul. Amen.
JOHN DEMPSY.

The Speech of Patrick Murphy,

Good People,

AS for my part I have not much to say but that I was born in the County of Killdare of yvet Honest Parents and was bred a Sawyer and Got my living by it and after some time I kept a publick House in Pill-Lane as is very Well known in this City in good Credit but the fact which I now am to dye for, I do declare before God and the World, and as I shall answer at the Great and Dreadful Tribunal where the Secrets of all hearts will be Disclosed, I am entirely Innocent, therefore I beg that there may be no reflections thrown either upon my Wife or family upon the Account of my Dying this shameful and Ignominious Death, I desire the Prayers of all Good Christians, I dye a Roman Catholick and in the 32d year of my Age and the Lord receive my poor Soul Amen. PATRICK MURPHY.

Dublin printed by E. Sadleir on the Blind Key 1727.

45

THE LAST AND TRUE SPEECH, CONFESSION
AND DYEING WORDS OF

John Mac-Gurran, alias Cockels, and Michael Tankard

who are both to be Executed this present Wednesday being the 27th of the Instant September, 1727. For feloniously breaking open and Robbing the Dwelling House of Squire Winfield in Caple-street, the beginning of this Instant.

The Speech of *John Mc Gurran* alias *Cockels*

Good People

I Was born in the *North* of *Ireland* of very honest Parents, who brought me to *Dublin* when young, and took what Care they could to bring me up in the Love and fear of God untill I was able to shift for my self, which I Endeavour'd to do very honestly, as many here present knows the same, and had the good-will of all that knew me, and so continued till within these few Years past that I became acquainted with loose Idle Men and Women, in whose Company I took more delight than I did in Work.

Thus I contined till I came acquainted with my prefent Fellow Sufferor and another whose Name I omit, tho' he is the chief Person that brought us to Rob Squire *Winsfield's* Houfe in *Caple-street*, which Robbery I own I am Guilty of, for we took a parcel of Pewer Dishes and Plates, and hid them near the new Manufactory where there was a foundation of a House a digging, but was discover'd next Morning by the Labourers, when they went to Work, found them there; we also took a good quantity of Linnen and Woollen, particularly a Shag Coat, which I had the assurance to wear thinking it would not be known, but it was the only betrayer we had: But this is not all the dishoneſt Dealings I have been Guilty off, which is needless now to repeat by reason my Time is short to be among you; but this Caution I give to all young Men, for their one sakes, if they give any regard to the Words of a dyeing Man, let them shun all bad Company, especially the Company of Harlots, for they are the things the Devil beats his Hooks with, to draw poor unthinking Man to Destruction, all which I find to be true when it is too late.

Having no more to ſay, but begs the Prayers of all good Christians, I die a *Roman Catholick*, and in the 30*th* Year of my Age, and the Lord have Mercy on my poor Soul. *Amen.*
     John M'Gurran

The Speech of Michael Tankard.

Good Christians

I Drew my first Breath in this City of *Dublin*, of very honest credible People, as is well known by many in *Newgate-Market* and elsewhere, and they took what Care they could to bring me up in the fear of God, but alas! all their Endeavours were in vain, for when they thought I was at school, I would be among the Black-guards, among whom I took more delight than in my Book.

My Parents finding all their kind admonishments were of none effect, they sent me to Work *Tobbacco*, in hopes it would keep me from the Streets, at which I continued for a considerable time, but would not Work only when the frolick took me: Thus I continued for several Years, till coming acquainted with my fellow Sufferer and others, some of which (I doubt not) are here present, with whom I have been Guilty of several Robberies, partcularly one *Jane Johnson* a Washer Woman, from whom I took several Holland Shirts and several other things; but as to the Fact I dye for I need not repeate, by reason my unfortunate Companion has declar'd the particulars of it, and I acknowledge my self guilty of the ſame, but I hope my Death may be a warning to all that hears or sees me Dye. Having no more to say but begs the Prayers of all Good Christians, I dye a Roman Catholick, in the 32*d* Year of my Age and the Lord receive my Soul, *Amen.*

Printed by C.P.

(Location: Cambridge University Library, Bradshaw Collection, Hib.0.727.1)

46

THE LAST AND TRUE SPEECH, CONFESSION
AND DYEING WORDS OF

Martin Mackanally and Bryan Lacy

who are to be Executed near Kilmainham, this present Wednesday being the 18th of this Instant October 1727. Martin Mackanally for Ravishment, and Bryan Lacy for Robery.

The Speech of Martin Mackanally.

Good People,

I Drew my first unfortunate Breath in St. *James's Street* of honest Parents; who tenderly nourished me untill I came able to shift for my self, then I thought I was no ways oblidged to them, and so went to drive a Carr, with which, I got honest Bread had I minded it, but alas! I was like a great many, that are going now, (that is) when I got any Pence, I would go and drink till I would get my self Drunk, then go and Quarrel with Friend or Foe, which folly often put me to abundance of trouble.

Thus, I continued these several Years past, but thanks be to God there is not one among you, or elsewhere, can charge me with the vallue of one Penny of dishonesty. I could proceed farther but only my time is so short, therefore I shall only inform you with the particulars of what brought me to this shameful and untimely Death, which is as follows.

Last *St Lawrences Day* I went to the Fair of *Palmerstown* along with some other young Lads, thinking of no harm, where we continued untill it was prity duskish, and coming home, we met with one *Neal* a Clive-Man and his Wife a going home also, with whom we fell into Discourse, and finding that the Man did not desire our Company; my Companions told him they would take away his Wife, upon which the Man began to grumble and make a great noise which did realy vex me, for fear People should think we were Robbing him, therefore I knock'd him down, the rest was about the Wife, but I declare that one of them had not the time to have carnel knowledge of her, (let alone three) tho' she swore her private parts was torn and abused, and if so, it must be with their Hands, but be it as it will, they are fled, and I must loose my precious Life.

Now you have you heard the particulars of this my woful Tragedy, I have no more to say but begs the Prayers of all good Christians, I die a Roman Catholick and in the 25*th* Year of my Age, and the Lord have Mercy on my poor Soul. *Amen.*

Signed by me *Martin Mackanally*

The Speech of *Bryan Lacy.*

Good Christians,

I Am brought here this Day to Die a Death which I have strove to shun ever since I was Born, till within these few Weeks past; but I see it is in vain to resist what the Fates doth decree, therefore I shall in a few Words sum up to you the first cause of this my Woe, which is as follows.

I was born in *Dublin,* of poor Endeavouring Parents, who were not able to give me either Trade or Calling, so that when I was able, I got my Bread by going of Erants, in which station I did not continue long, by reason a Gentleman (whose name I omit) took a liking to me and kept me for his Servant, in which Station (with him and others) I continued since, but last *September* I was going thro' *Meath-street* late at night, where I found some Cloaths of Linin and Woolling, the Watch seeing the bulk with me, pursved me and put me to Newgate, where I was Tryed, found Guilty to the value of Nine Pence, and so Whipt about the City, then I was sent here and Tryed for the same Robbery, (and knew nothing of it, but as I told you before) and now must Dye for the same.

Thus Christians have I declared the whole truth of this my unhappy Death, therefore I need say no more but begg all of you to Pray for me whilst I am among you, for I Dye a Member of the Church of Ireland as by Law established and in the 30th Year of my Age and the Lord have Mercy on my Soul, *Amen.*

(Location: Trinity College Library, Press A.7.4 No 210)

47

THE LAST SPEECH, CONFESSION AND DYING WORDS OF

Surgeon John Odwin

*who is to be Excecuted near St. Stephen's-Green:
On Wednesday being the 5th of June, 1728. For the Murder of
his Servant Maid Margaret Keef.*

GENTLEMAN,

BEING in a few Minutes to appear before the Tribunial of GOD, where, tho' most unworthy, I hope to find Mercy, which I have not found from Men. I have endeavour'd to make my Peace with his Divine Majesty, but most humbly begging Pardon for all the Sins of my Life; and I doubt not of a merciful forgiveness, thro' the Merits of the Passion and Death of my *Saviour Jesus Christ.*

    Custom has made it almost necessary, for Persons in my Circumstances, to say, or leave somewhat by their last Words, declaring their sentiments with Relation to what they Dye for, in Compliance with which, I have thought fit, to make the following Declarations.

    I was born in *George's lane, DUBLIN;* my Father who Professed Physick and Chyrrurgery before me, bestowed upon me Gentlemans Education, and I did my utmost endeavour, to gain the Good Will of all People, which (Thanks be to GOD) I did, and always as far as in my Power lay, did every one Justice in my Calling.

    In the first place, I Declare I Dye a Member of the Church of *Ireland*, as by Law Established, (tho a very unworthy one) and I Desire all those of this Communion to assist my Soul with their fervent and Charitable Prayers, I declare that I am in Charity with all the World, and do from my Soul forgive all my Enemies, and all others who have any ways Injured or done me Wrong; and particularly I forgive all those, who have Promoted my Death, by Malicious Mis-representations, or otherwise, and earnestly beg GOD to forgive them, and Grant them the same Blessing, I desire for my own Soul.

And I Likewise ask Pardon of all such as I have offended or injured, and Lament that it is not in my power to make them Reparation, but as they expect to be forgiven, I hope they will do so to me. But as to the fact for which I am to Dye for, the Murdering my Maid *Margaret Keef*, I solemnly Declare in the presence of God, I am entirely Innocent.

And I declare in the same selemn Manner that I know neither Act, nor part of the said Murder, nor knew who did it, nor neither did I know any thing of the Matter, directly nor Indirectly, till I came and saw her Weltering in her Gore of Blood.

But I do Confess that I have led a most Wicked Life, and has been Guilty of a great deal of folly in my Time, but never did I spill the Blood of any Person whatever, but I put my Trust in my most Omnipotent God, who knows the Secrets of all Hearts, that he will forgive me my manifold Offences, and Shut not his Mercifull Ears against me, but that as soon as my Soul shall depart out of my Body, that he will receive it into his most Glorious place of happiness.

But as my Blessed Saviour and Redeemer suffered an Ignominious and Cruel Death, and the Son of God made Flesh, did not disdain to have his Hands and Feet nailed to the Cross for the Sins of the World; so may I, poor miserable Sinner, as far as Human Nature will allow, patiently bear with the Hands of Violence, that I expect suddenly, to be stretched out against me.

I freely forgive such as ungenerously Report false things of Me, and I hope to be forgiven the Trespasses of my Youth, by the Father of Infinite Mercy, into whose Hands I Commend my Soul.

And as I have upon the Word, and Solemn protestations of a Dying Man, Given you as much Satisfaction as in my power lyeth, Begs, you'le fling no Aspersion upon my friends, for me Dying this shameful and Ignoninous Death; And I bless my God, who has given me the Grace to submit and bear patiently all the Injuries that has been done me; having no more to say, I humbly beg the prayers of all good Christians.

JOHN ODWIN

I Die of the Communion as aforesaid, and in the 30th year of my Age and the Great God receive my Soul. *Amen.*

FINIS.

DUBLIN: Printed by S. Hardding, 1728.

(Location: National Library of Ireland, Thorp Pamphlets, No. 788)

48

THE LAST AND TRUE SPEECH, CONFESSION
AND DYING WORDS OF

Alexander Mac Daniell, and Philip A-Thoush (alias Malone)

who is to be Executed near St Stephen's-Green, this present Saturday being the 24th Day of January, 1728–9.

The Speech of Alexander Mac-Daniell.

Good Christians,

I Was born in the County of *Mayo*, of very Credible Parents, but would by no means be govern'd by them, I Listed in the Right Honourable Collonel *Murray's* Reigment of Foot, when I was about 15 Years of Age, in which said Service, I behaved myself honest to my Colours, till about *October* last; I was Drinking with two of my Fellow-Soldiers, in *Barrack Street*, in the House of one *John Sale*, and some Words happening between the said Sale, and my Company, he Received a Wound on the Head, of which he Dy'd, upon the same, I was committed to *New-Gate*, and Try'd last *Michaelmas* Term, which was my entire ruin, for coming in Company with one *Reily*, a broken Soldier, who was confin'd in the said Geol, we went and Robbed a Gentleman, upon which he made his escape, I was taken, and sent to *Bridewell*, and after turn'd over to the *Civil-Law*, for which Fact I Received one thousand Lashes, and was Drumed from the *Barracks* to *Essex Bridge*, and before my Back was well, I went and Robbed Mr. *Price's* in *Twatling street*, and broke in at the Window, and stole from thence a Bed quilt, and going again the next Night, I was taken by the Watch, and sent to *New-gate*, it was my own Confession that took away my Life; I Dye an unworthy Member of the Church of *England*, and the Lord have mercy on my Soul. *Amen.* I am about 23 Years old.

The Speech of Philip Malone,

Good Christians,
I *Philip a Toush* (alias *Molene*) was born in the County of *Meath*, of Poor but very honest Parents, who put me Aprentice to a Slator by Trade, but that not answering my expectation, went and Stole some Cows, from one Mr. *John Brannan*, in *Church Street*, and was Try'd and Clear'd for the same; and after that I went and Stole a Trunk out of a House in *Smith-field*, wherein was 28 pounds *Sterl.* the latter in the Fact for which I suffer, I Dye a Roman Catholick and am about 26 Years of Age, and the Lord have mercy on my poor Soul. Amen.

Dublin Printed by S. Harding

(Location: Trinity College Library, Press A.7.5 no 16)

The last and True

SPEECH

Confession and Dying Words of *Alexander Mac-Daniell*, and *Philip A-Thoush* (alias *Malone*,) who is to be Executed near St *Stephen's-Green*, this present *Saturday* being the 24th Day of *January*, 1728-9.

The Speech of Alexander Mac-Daniell.

Good Christians,

I Was born in the County of *Mayo*, of very Credible Parents, but would be no means be govern'd by them, I Listed in the Right Honourble Collonel *Murray's* Reigment of Foot, when I was about 15 Years of Age, in which said Service, I behaved my self honest to my Colours, till about *October* last; I was Drinking with two of my Fellow-Soldiers, in *Barrack street*, in the House of one *John Sale*, and some Words happening between the said *Sale*, and my Company, he Received a Wound on the Head, of which he Dy'd, upon the same, I was committed to *New gate*, and Try'd last *Michaelmas* Term, which was my entire ruin, for coming in Company with one *Reily*, a broken Soldier, who was confin'd in the said Geol, we went and Robbed a Gentleman, upon which he made his escape, I was taken, and sent to *Bridewell*, and after turn'd over to the *Civil-Law*, for which Fact I Received one thousand Lashes, and was Drumed from the *Barracks* to *Essex Bridge*, and before my Back was well, I went and Robbed Mr. *Price's*, in *Twatling street*, and broke in at the Window, and stole from thence a Bed quilt, and going again the next Night, I was taken by the Watch, and sent to *New-gate*, it was my own Confession that took away my Life; I Dye an Unworthy Member of the Church of *England*, and the Lord have mercy on my Soul *Amen* I am about 23 Years old.

The Speech of Philip Malone.

Good Christians,

I *Philip a Toush*, (alias *Molene*) was born in the County of *Meath*, of Poor but very honest Parents, who put me Aprentice to a *Slator* by Trade, but that not answering my expectation, went and Stole some Cows, from one Mr. *John Brannan*, in *Church street*, and was Try'd and Clear'd for the same; and after that I went and Stole a Trunk out of a House is *Smith-field*, where in was 28 Pounds Sterl. the latter in the Fact for which I suffer, I Dye a Roman Catholick and am about 26 Years of Age, and the Lord have mercy on my Poor Soul, Amen.

DUBLN Printed by S. Harding

49

THE LAST AND TRUE SPEECH, CONFESSION
AND DYING WORDS OF

Daniel Ross

who is to be Executed near St. Stephen's-Green, this present Saturday, being the 15th of this Instant February 1728–9

Good Peoples

AS It is usual for all Men under this my Dismal Case, to say something in Relation to their past Lives, and Manfold Misfortunes they have undergone; I think it requisite to give some small Relation of my past Life, and Actions, in as Brief a Narrative as possible I can V*iz*: I was Born in *Cook Street*, in the Parish of St. *Audeon's* in the City of *Dublin*, of very honest Parents, but Arriving to the Age of Maturity, and getting into Ill Company, breeding of Riots, and being Committed to Goal, for such evil practices, I as last betook myself to Robbing, which now has brought me to this shameful Death, I must own that I have been Guilty of several Robberies, and hath been several times Try'd for my Life, but now as last am to Dye for the Fact, which was justly Alledged against me; I was one who had a Hand in Robbing the Chancellors Gentleman, and then to save my own Life, I swore it was one *John Mac- Coy, John Smith,* and one *Geoghgan,* that Robbed him, which I Declare I was Head man in the said Fact. The Persons that Swore my Life away were *James Carty*, and *Mary Fletcher*, who was in the Robbery, with me but doing as I have often done, that is turning the King's Evidence against me, took my Life away, though they got more of the Booty than I did.

The said *Mary Fletcher* Swore at my Tryal, several things against me, I Writ to her, to send me one of the Holland Shirts, and a Cambrick Handkerchief, to make a Cap to Dye in, but Received none. This being all I have to say, having but a few Minutes to stay in this Wicked World, I beg the Prayers of all good Christians; I dye an

The Last and True

SPEECH

Confession and Dying Words of *Daniel Ross*, who is to be Executed near St. *Stephen's-Green*, this present *Saturday*, being the 15th of this Instant *February* 1728-9.

Good People,

AS It is usual for all Men under this my Dismal Case, to say something in Relation to their past Lives, and Manifold Misfortunes they have undergone; I think it requisite to give some small Relation of my past Life, and Actions, in as Brief a Narrative as possible I can *Viz*: I was Born in *Cook street*, in the Parish of St. *Audeon's* in the City of *Dublin*, of very honest Parents, but Arriving to the Age of Maturity, and getting into Ill Company, breeding of Riots, and being Committed to Goal, for such evil practises. I at last betook my self to Robbing, which now has brought me to this shameful Death, I must own that I have been Guilty of several Robberies, and hath been several times Tryed for my Life, but now at last am to Dye for the Fact, which was justly Alledged against me; I was one who had a Hand in Robbing the Chancellors Gentleman, and then to save my own Life, I swore it was one *John Mac-Coy*, *John Smith*, and one ----*Geoghgan*, that Robbed him, which I Declare I was Head man in the said Fact. The Persons that Swore my Life away were *James Garty*, and *Mary Fletcher*, who was in the Robbery, with me but doing as I have often done, that is turning the King's Evidence against me, took my Life away, tho' they got more of the Booty than I did.

The said *Mary Fletcher* Swore at my Tryal, several things against me; I Writ to her, to send me one of the Holland Shirts, and a Cambrick Handkerchief, to make a Cap to Dye in, but Received none. This being all I have to say, having but a few Minutes to stay in this Wicked World, I beg the Prayers of all good Christians; I Dye an Unworthy Member of the Established Church, and in the 22d. Year of my Age, and the GREAT GOD Receive my poor Sinful Soul, *Amen.*

N. B. *Last Night I Received a false, lying, scandalous Speech, (which Obliged me to Print this) Done by a Person in* Montrath-street, *which I shall declare at the Place of Execution, to be false, this being my true one, and no other. Taken from my own Mouth, and Delivered to the Printer hereof.*

Daniel Ross.

D U B L I N: Printed by S. *Harding* in *Copper-Alley.*

Unworthy Member of the Established Church, and in the 22d. Year of my Age, and the GREAT GOD Receive my poor Sinful Soul, *Amen.*

    N.B. *Last Night I Received a false, lying scandalous Speech, (which Obliged me to Print this) Done by a person in* Montrath-Street, *which I shall declare at the Place of Execution, to be false, this being my true one, and no other. Taken from my own Mouth, and Delivered to the Printer hereof.*

Daniel Ross.

DUBLIN: Printed by *S. Harding* in *Copper-Alley.*

(Location: Trinity College Library, Press A.7.5. No 26)

50

THE LAST SPEECH, CONFESSION AND DYING WORDS OF

Alexander Graham, and Michael Kearone

who is to be Executed near St. Stephen's Green, this present Saturday, being the 6th of this Inst. Sept. 1729, for several Robberies committed by them.

Good People,

I Was born in Pill-Lane, in the Parish of St. Michans's, of very honest Parents, and Bread in the Parish of St. John's and was at the Parish School for a considerable time, but to my great grief and Misfortune I came acquainted with Mr. M———ters Sons, who was the first Ruination of me, when my Father and Mother found I was growing into wickedness they put me to Sea, and it was the will of the Almighty God for the Vessel to be cast away, and all the Crue lost except me and three others who Swom to Shore, and when I came to shore I made the best of my way to Dublin, where I unfortunately met some of my former Companions who brought me to my former business, the Fact for which I die for was Committed as follows, in August last between the hours of 10 & 11 of the Clockta Night being somewhat in Liquor had the misfortune to come down into Mrs. Whites, Cellor at the corner of Crane Lane, and it being a usual thing for the Boys of Essex-Street to play about the Cellor, and I had the bad Look to pull her by the Apron, and her Pocke and Apron came off, but as I am a dying Man I did not know that there was any Money in it, nor had I any thoughts of taking any thing from her, but when the Pocket came with me and found the Money in it I did not return it and made off, and was soon taken after, and found the Pocket and Money in my Custody, which was 9l. in Cash, and two Gold Rings valu'd 2l 6s. therefore I Confess to be Glilty of the Fact for which I die for.

    Having no more to say but disire all young Boys to take warning by this my Shamefull Death, I Desire all your Prayers while I am a live, I die an unworthey Member of the Church of England as by Law Establish'd, and in the 17th Years of my Age, and the Lord have mercy upon my poor Soul Amen.

This is my true Speech given from my own Mouth to the Printer hereof, and if any other Speech is publish'd but this, it a Counterfeit, as Witness my Hand this 5th of Sept. 1729.

Alexander Graham.

The Speech of Michael Kearons.

Good People,

I *Was born in the County of Roscommon, of poor, but honest Parents, with whom I stay'd untill I was able to travel, and then came to Dublin, and got to live with Mr. Brown the Brewer, with whom I lived for a considerable Time, until there hapned two Horses to be stolen from my said Master, who charged me with the same, but as I am a dying Man I was innocent of what they laid to my Charge; as for what I am to die for is for selling of two Horses in company with my Father, and he that pretended to own the Horses, and upon the same my Father and I was taked and Committed to Goal, and he made off that gave us the Horses, and when we come upon Tryal I found Evedence against us, I took it all on my self to clear my Father, I forgive all the World and I hope the Lord will forgive me. I die a Roman Catholick and in the 26th Year of my Age and the Lord have mercy upon my Soul. Amen.*

Michael Kearons.

Dublin, Printed by Nicholas Hussey on the Blind-Key, 1729.

(Location: Trinity College Library, Press A.7.5 No 132)

51

THE DECLARATION AND DYING WORDS OF

Daniel Kimberly, Gentleman

Who was Executed at St. STEPHEN's GREEN, on Wednesday, May 27th, 1730 at 38 Minutes past three o' Clock in the Afternoon.

Deliver'd to the REVD. MR. DERRY at the Place of Execution.

AS it is Expected, That a Man leaving the World in my Circumstances should make some Confession either of my Guilt or Innocence of the Fact for which I Die, I do therefore in the Manner following Endeavour to satisfy the World herein: FIRST, in regard Mr. *Dan Reading*, Printed a Case against me, upon which occasion I caus'd a Case to be Printed for me and given to some particular Persons, tho' not publicly dispers'd, before my Trial, in Justification of my Character, I now thought proper to mention some parts of the Paragraphs of my said Case which are true in every Respect according to the best of my knowledge, hear-say, and belief; and which I now make mention of to Satisfy the World, That, notwithstanding any Doubt that was heretofore of the Veracity thereof, the World may now believe the following parts of my saidCase (which I affirm to be true) are true; And which, I believe do contradict or shew sd. *Reading's* Case to be false in many Instances, which Paragraphs of my said case are as follow, *viz.*

THAT I the said *Dan. Kimberly* in *January* 1727 (being employ'd by *John Hamilton*, of *London*, Esq., *Int. alis.* to speed a Commission at *Dublin*, to Examine Witnesses to prove the Legitimacy of my other prosecutor *Bridget Reading*, who then claim'd a third part of a Freehold estate of 27ol. *per. Ann.*) went to *Dublin*, and during my stay there receiv'd a letter from said D *Reading*, desiring me to enquire after his Daughter, then and almost from her Infancy with one *Mrs.*

Browne, (who nurs'd her) a small Distance from *Dublin*, and if it were possible to get her out of the Nurses Hands, in order to bring, or send her to *London*, on my return.

THAT I the said *Dan. Kimberly*, told Mrs. *Browne*, said *Reading's* Desire, who answer'd me that there was a considerable Sum of Money due to her, for said *Bridget's* Keeping; she never having receiv'd one Penny from her Father, who she said was an ill man, and sd. she wou'd therefore be first paid her Money before she wou'd part with her, of which Resolution and demand of said Nurse, I soon after wrote to said *Reading*.

THAT I the said *Dan. Kimberly*, soon after, receiv'd other Letters from sd. *Reading* most earnestly pressing me to get his Daughter out of said Mrs. *Browne's* Hands, for that he could not receive any Money to send over till he had her in his Custody, and begged no ways might be left unattempted to get her; Whereupon after I had finished my other Affairs, and my Business requiring my speedy return to *London*, I applied to several of said *Reading's* Friends about his remissness in sending the said Nurses Demand to release his Daughter; And told them that I thought her Father to be an Improper Person to manage his Daughters Fortune; for that I had been told said *Reading*, received some Money out of the Rents or otherwise, on his Daughter's account, altho' he was so Remiss in remitting to me the said Nurses Demand, and I was also inform'd said *Reading* had in Conjunction with said *Bridget's* Aunts, Entered into some Articles for Sale of said Estate for 360ol. and, I knowing said *Reading* to be a person of a loose and dissolute Life, living upwards of Ten Years past in Adultery, with a Woman, by whom he had several Children, in a publick manner as his Wife, I did in Compassion to sd. *Reading*, and in hopes of his abandoning that wicked Course of Life (as he often assured me he wou'd do) keep and maintain his True and Lawful Wife, for some time in *London*, about June, 1727.

THAT I the said *Dan. Kimberly* being so informed, that said *Reading*, had entered into Articles with one Mr. *Dodamy* of *London* for Sale of said Estate of said *Bridget*, in Conjunction with her Aunts for said 360ol. and that said *D. Reading* had receiv'd on the Credit of such Estate, several Sums of Money, through the Interest of sd.

Woman's Friend's with whom he Lives in Adultery as aforesaid, therefore, I did conclude that the several Debts which the said *D. Reading* owed were intended by him to be paid out of his Daughter's Substance, in regard he was in low Circumstances.

   THAT I the said *D. Kimberly* for the foregoing Reasons, thought there could not be a better Method taken to prevent her the said *Bridget's* Ruin, than by proposing to some deserving Person, of good Education, and who as I thought would have a suitable Fortune to her's to Marry her, and that Mr. *Bradock Mead* being known to me to be a Gentleman of great Learning, of sober Life and Conversation, did believe him worthy of a Fortune as good as sd. *Bridget Reading's*: And therefore, I represented to sd. *Brad. Mead*, that sd. *Br. Reading*, as the only surviving Issue of her late Mother *Bridget Reading*, alias *Whitfield*, (who was Sister to *Mary* and *Cath. Whitfield*) was a Coheiress with her said two Aunts, and therefore intitled to a third part of 270l. *per. Ann.* and that as the truth is, in *Trinity Term*, 1727, she Filed her Bill in the *Chancery* of England against her Grandmother *Elinor Whitfield*, and her sd. two Aunts, and prayed to be put in possession thereof, and for other Relief, as by said Bill.

   THAT Said Grandmother and Aunts in their Answers denied said *Bridget Reading*, the Daughter of said *D. Reading*, to be intitled to any share of said Fortune, for that she was (as they swore) the illegitimate Issue of said *Dan. Reading* and *Bridget* her Mother, Who, as they swore, was never Married to sd. *Dan. Reading*, as appears by their Answer.

   THAT After I got said letters from said *Dan Reading*, to bring said *Bridget* to *London*, he never gave me or sent the said Nurses Demand, which was 21l. or any part thereof, so that I procured said *Bradock Mead's* Brother to pay, or secure 11l. part thereof, to Mr. *Hatch*, and said Mr. *Hatch*, thereupon, assumed to pay the remaining 10l. part of said 21l. to said Mrs. *Browne*, the Nurse; Whereupon said Mrs. *Browne*, and her Husband gave me a Receipt in full for sd. 21l. and thereupon Deliver'd said *Bridget* into my Custody, for which Trouble, of so getting her, I had no Consideration promis'd or allowed me by said *Reading*, or any other Person.

   THAT Said *Bradock Mead* soon after, by my consent, and introducement, applyed to said *Bridget* in the way of Courtship, and on the 11*th* of *April*, 1728, said *Mead* Marryed her in *Dublin*, when and where no Force, Threats, or Compulsion was made use of by any Person towards said *Bridget*, to come into said Marriage.

THAT in *May* 1728, said *Mead*, and his wife *Bridget*, and I arrived in *London*, and acquainted said *Dan. Reading*, with said Marriage, and in some Days after, said *D. Reading*, caused said *Mead* and me, the said *Kimberly*, to be Apprehended upon the Statute of *Marrying* a Woman-Child without her Parents Consent, and thereupon said Mead and I the said *Kimberly*, were Committed to Prison on Mr. Justice *Ellis's* Warrant, upon her said Aunts having sworn said *Bridget* to be under the Years of Twelve at said Marriage, which was False, in regard, said *Bridget*, was at the time of said Marriage almost 13 Years, as was prov'd in *Doctors Commons*, by a Certificate from the Registry of St. *Bride's* Church, Dublin, and by Means of such Oath, said *Bridget* was by Order of said Justice *Ellis* ordered to be and was accordingly produced by the said *Mead* to be Examined and she then and there, upon a solemn and serious *Examination*, did declare, *that she was Marry'd with her own freewill, consent and good-liking, and there was no force or illegal means made use of to induce, or compel her to such Marriage*, but it being insisted on *that in regard her Grand Mothers and Aunts or one of them, Swore her to be under 12 years at said Marriage, that she should be put into the Hands of an indifferent Person, till further Inquiry should be made to clear that Point*, and thereupon she was *accordingly put into the Hands of one Mr.* Humpherys *where she remained for some time, until the said* D. Reading *got her into his hands*.

THAT during the said *Mead's* and my Confinement, the said *D. Reading* by himself and Agents proposed to *Mead, That unless he would enter into Bonds, and Releases to Renounce all his Right to said* Bridget *and her Fortune, he the said* D. Reading *would Engage his said Daughter to Swear a Rape against the said* Mead, whereupon soon after, viz, in June 1728, such Bonds and Releases were mutually Enter'd into, and sd. Mead and I sd. *D. Kimberly*, were thereupon Discharged, but said *Reading*, afterwards finding as I heard, and believe, *That such Bonds and Releases were not binding to bar the said*

Mead's *right*, soon after Commenced a *Cause* in D*octors Commons*, to Null the said Marriage if possible.

THAT In the Course of the Proceedings in *Doctors Commons*, the *Examination* and *Confession* of the said *Bridget*, that the said *Marriage was had with her Consent, was proved by Mr. Justice* Ellis, *and also by a Gentlewoman present at such Examination*, and the consent and good liking of the said *Bridget* to the said *Marriage* is also proved in *Doctors Commons*, by several credible Witnesses, *tho' she swore the contrary on my Tryal.*

THAT During the litigation of the said *Marriage in the Commons, the said* D. Reading *and his Agents applied to, and Endeavour'd to prevail on me to give Testimony, to set aside the said Marriage, which base Proposal I rejected, with Threats to Indict them*, whereupon when the said *Reading* could not prevail with me to give such Testimony, *he publicly vowed Revenge against me*, and soon after made his Daughter the said *Bridget Reading* to swear *Examinations of Felony against me, in relation to the said Marriage, on pretence of forcibly Carrying her away and Marrying her against her Consent:* Whereupon I the said *D. Kimberly* was on that Account taken on a Warrant from Sir *William Billars*, and committed to *Wood-street-Compter*, where I remain'd until transmitted to *Newgate* in *Dublin*, the 3d of *January* 1729.

And, As to my Tryal and Proceedings thereon, I must beg Leave to satisfie the World thereof, in the following manner, *vizt.*

THAT My Prosecutor D. Reading *and his Friends were so violent against Me,* That *my another Prosecutor* Bridget Reading, *as I have been credibly informed and believe, was carry'd about and waited on several Gentlemen intended to be on my Jury, to influence and prepossess them of the said* Bridget's *Proceedings against Me.*

AND, Whereas, the said *D. Reading*, hath sworn on my Tryal, *that I first apply'd to him before he applyed to me, to bring his Daughter the said* B. Reading *to him from* Dublin *to* London, *and that, for that purpose the said* D. Readings, *had paid me 10l. I declare the same is false, for that some time in* January 1727, *or thereabouts, the said* D. Reading *knowing that I was then Employ'd by* John Hamilton *of* London, *Esq; to go* to Ireland, *to speed a Commission did then in* London, *desire me to*

Enquire after his Daughter, the said B. Reading *and to bring her over to* London *with me, but I deny that he the said* D. Reading, *or any other Person for his Use,* paid *to me or to any other Person for my Use any Money in* London *to bring the said* Bridget *thither, nor did* I *then, or at any other time come to Dublin* for the *Particular Purpose* to bring the said *Bridget* to *London;* but in *Jan.* 1727, I came to *speed sd Commission* by Direction of sd. Mr. *Hamilton* and also, to do *other business* which I then had to do in *Dublin, and not for the sd. Bridget to bring her to* London, *nor did I at any Time before I came to speed sd Commission, apply* to Mr. Reading *or to any Person in his behalf, to bring his sd. Daughter* to London, *until the sd.* Dan Reading *first apply'd to me in* London *for that purpose,* as aforesaid, and afterwards by his Letters to *Dublin,* Desiring me *to bring her to him*: And whereas, the said *Brid. Reading* on my Tryal swore, that she never was in Company with *Brad. Mead* but once before her said Marriage, and further swore, that when sd Brad. Mead *and I had brought a Clergyman to her Lodgings, that when she was going to be married I had then and there, at three a* Clock at *Noon,* shut *the Windows and* locked *the Doors, and that I then and there told the sd Clergyman, that, I was the sd* Bridget's *Father, and that when she was going to say I was not her Father that I did stop her Mouth with a Handkerchief, and that I shaked her by the Shoulder, and brought her from the Fire-side to a Corner in the Room, and forcibly made her say the Words* I will, *after the Words of Marriage:* And, the sd *Br. Reading* further swore on my Tryal *that she never was let to go abroad, nor even look out at the Window, whilst she Lodged at Mrs.* Peter's *and that she never during that Time went to* Rings End *until she went on Shipboard to go for England*: All which I *solemnly Declare* (as I expect Salvation) is FALSE, In the first Place, for that the said *Brad. Mead* for near eleven Days before the said Marriage, to the best of my Knowledge, came every Day to the said *Brid.* Lodgings, and came thither some times twice a Day, and sat with the said *Brid.* Reading, and Convers'd with her in my presence, several Days before the said Marriage, and I do *further Declare* that on some Day before the said Marriage, the said *Brid. Reading, Brad. Mead*, Mrs. *Peters* and I, went to *Rings-End*, in a Coach, Dined in *Rings-End*, at the sign of the *Highland-Man*, Drank Punch, came on *Rings-end Cars* in the evening from *Rings-End* to *Dublin*, altho' the said *Bridget* on my Tryal swore, that she never went to *Rings-End* before the said Marriage, which I declare is false, and I do further declare the sd. *Clergyman* did not come to the said *Bridget's* Lodgings till between 8 and 9 o' Clock in the Evening, at which time, I believe it was Duskish and for that Reason, the Windows were shut and Candles Lighted, and I Declare, I did not at, before, or after the said Marriage, tell any *Clergyman,* or any other Person, that the said *Brid Reading* was my Daughter, but on the Contrary told him, she was one *Reading's* daughter. And I do further declare, that I did not, at, before, or after the said Marriage stop, or attempt to stop the said *Bridget's* Mouth with a Handkerchief, or with any other thing, for any purpose whatsoever; neither did I, at the said Marriage, or at any other time, carry, or Endeavour to carry the said *Bridget* from the Fire-side to a Corner of the Room, in her Lodgings, or elsewhere, nor did I ever shake her by the Shoulder, nor forcibly make, or Endeavour to make her say the Words (I will) after, the Minister, nor did I at anytime, at, before, or since the said Marriage use any force, threats, uncivil or unkind Treatment towards the said *Bridget* in Order to Oblige Her to Marry the said BRADOCK MEAD or for any other purpose, neither did I ever hear that she made the least Complaint of any such Treatment till after she came into her Fathers Hands, as aforesaid, but on the Contrary, the said *Bridget*, always until she so came into her said Fathers Hands, Expressed a great Regard for the said *Mead,* and for several Months after she came into her Fathers Hands, Declared such Regard for Me. And the said *Bridget*, on the Day and Time of her Marriage behaved herself as Chearfully and as agreeably well pleased with all that was Done; as any Person of her Sense or Understanding might have done on the like Occasion.

AND, WHEREAS, It was reported or imagined, that the Motive that induced me to consent to the said Marriage was a Reward Paid or Secured to me or for my use, and so mentioned in several *Spurious* and *False Speeches,* Printed by *Christopher Golding*, in *Montrath-street*, under the *Feigned Names* of *J. Neal* and *Hugh Doherty*, &c. I Declare the said Report or Imagination is groundless and untrue: And I do Declare that my chief Motive for consenting to the said Marriage proceeded from the Reasons herein before, and after set forth, and no other, viz.

FIRST, Because I knew that said *Dan. Reading*, has been very remiss of said *Bridget*, and that he had two Wives then, and still Living, as I believe, and lives in Adultery with one of them, and has deny'd his Lawful Wife for many years past.

SECONDLY, For that, as I heard and believe, sd *Dan. Reading* in Conjunction with the Grandmother and Aunts of sd *Br. Reading* had entered into Articles of Agreement for Sale of the Interest of said *Bridget*, as well as of the said Aunts in the said Estate; for 3600l. to the said Mr. *Dodamy;* And that said *Dan. Reading* in order to get said *Bridget's* part of said Purchase Money into his own power, in order to pay his Debts, had, as I heard and believe, sent for said *Bridget*, to Confirm said Sale.

THIRDLY, For that I had been Credibly inform'd, that one *Harrington* a Weavers Boy, Intended to run a-way with said *Bridget*, and therefore I did, in regard to the Welfare of said *Bridget*, and to avoid the Mischief which I Apprehended might befall to her either from her Father, or the said *Harrington*, and in regard to the Love and Affection which I bore to the said *Bradock Mead*, and to the good Opinion which I had and still have of him, to be a Learn'd Gentleman of Sober Life, and Conversation, I did consent to Marry the said *Bridget* to said *Bradock Mead,* which I thought was a just and good Act, both before God and Man, to Marry her to said *Mead*, whose Brother on his account secured and pay'd Money towards her said Nurses Demands on her, which her Father neglected to do, without which I could not get her out of her said Nurses Hands in order to prevent her Ruin, which as I believe in all Probability would have happened to her, for all which Reasons and not for any *Gratuity, Fee*, or *Reward,* either paid, secured or promised to me, for consenting to the said Marriage, there being no such *Gratuity, Fee* or *reward*, ever paid, *secur'd* or *Promis'd* to me or to *any* for *my Use*, to my Knowledge, or Belief, on Account of said Marriage, I did introduce the said *Brad. Mead*, to pay his Addresses, by way of Courtship to said *Bridget*, and after he had about 11 Days acquaintance with her, such Marriage with her own *Free-will, Consent, Good-Likeing*, and *Approbation*, was *had;*

Whereat (*at the Earnest request of the said Bradock Mead*) I was prevail'd on to be present, but I *Solemnly Declare,* the said M*arriage,* was so *had* and *Solemnis'd* without any *Force, Violence, Threats,* C*ompulsion,* or *Uncivil Treatment,* given to the said *Bridget,* either by *me* or by any other Person to my *Knowledge* or *Belief* at, or before the time of the said *Marriage* or at any T*ime* whatsoever, and I refer myself to the Testimony of Mr. *Ambrose* and the Persons present at said Marriage, whether I have not to their Knowledge Declar'd the TRUTH Concerning the same; Therefore, I hope the great God will not Impute that Action as a Crime or Charge to me, in regard, I thought the same would rather Contribute to the Happiness and Good of said *Bridget,* than to her Prejudice and if no such Marriage had yet hapened, and that said *Bradock Mead* shou'd be now Marry'd to the sd. *Bridget,* I do believe that such Marriage wou'd Contribute to her Good and Happiness.

And, I do Declare that *any Accounts I have herein given of the said D. and* Bridget Reading, *which may seem as an Invective, were not for that Purpose, or with any Malice or bitterness of my Soul herein mentioned by me, but in order to Introduce the reasons and motives of my* Transacting *the said Marriage, which I did with a good,* but not with a Felonious or Evil intent:

I beg *leave to return my sincere, unfeigned and hearty Thanks to, and pray the Almighty may* pour down his Blessings on *the Worshipful* Gentlemen *of the* Grand Jury, *the* Lord Mayor *and* Aldermen *of the* City of Dublin, *who represented Me* as an Object of Mercy, *the* Minister, Church Wardens, *and* Inhabitants *of the Parish* of St. Michan's, *the* Officers *and* Attorneys of the Court of Common Pleas, *the several* Lords, Gentleman *and* Ladies, *and all* Other Charitable *and* Good Christians *who made any Application to the* Government, *or otherwise for my* Relief, *or* Who *contributed any way in* showing Mercy to me. *And, as for my* Prosecutors, *or* Such as *have* Persecuted Me, *or fought any* Perjurious *or* indirect Ways to take away my Life, I *freely forgive* Them: And, in Order to prevent the Publishing of any *False* or *Spurious* Accounts of Me, which are usual on this Occasion, I do therefore Humbly intreat my very Worthy Friends, the Rev'd. Dean *Percival,* the Rev'd. Mr. *Derry, John Hacket,* Esq; *Edmd. Fenner,* and

James Tetherington, Gentlemen, or any Two or more of Them, to Order the *Printing and Publishing* of this DECLARATION by *Richard Dickson*, of *Silver Court*, in *Castle Street*, Printer, which said Declaration I Publish and Declare, under my Hand, in the presence of Mr. *Mich. Fitz-Gerald, John Darcy* and *John Price*, this 22d Day of May 1730.

Signed, Published and Delared by me the
said *Daniel Kimberly* in the presence of
MICH. FITZGERALD.
JOHN DARCY.
JOHN PRICE.

Daniel Kimberly

ADVERTISEMENT

N.B. There are several other Materials PAPERS and LETTERS Concerning the Proceedings against the above-Mentioned Unfortunate Gentleman, which will be put to the Press and Publish'd as Speedily as Possible by the Printer hereof.

Dublin, Printed by RICH. DICKSON in Silver Court, in Castle-Street where Advertisements are taken in for the Old-Dublin-Intelligence, Irish-Journal or Weekly Gazette, and all other Printing Work done at Reasonable Rates.

(Location: Trinity College Library, Press A.7.5 No. 185)

52

THE LAST SPEECH, CONFESSION
AND DYEING WORDS OF

Cathrine M'Canna

who is to be Executed near St. Stephens Green, this present Wednesday being the 23d of this Instant September 1730. She being Guilty of several Robberies, in and about the City of Dublin.

Good People,

SINCE the just Hand of Almighty God has at length over reach'd me, and that I must be cut off in the midst of my Transgressions, I shall in a few Words give you a short Narrative of my base and vicious Life, which is as follows, *viz.*

I drew my first Breath in this City, and descended of very honest Parents, but I wicked wretch about ten Years ago committed a Robbery, and the said Robbery being found with me, I Swore it was my poor Mother gave it me, upon the same she was Hanged, tho' Innocent of the fact; and had I never been Guilty of no other offence but that, I doubt were I to live a thousand Years, I should not be able to make Restitution for that one Crime; and if so, Oh my God! what shall become of me, who have spent my time in Whoring and Thieving since I came to the Knowledge of committing either, yet my God will I not Despair in thy Mercies, tho' I must Confess thou have been over and above good to me, in saving my Life when I was to be Hang'd at *Killmainham* not long since, that thy saying might be fulfilled, *who desireth not the Death of a Sinner, but that he should live and save his Soul alive*: But it was not so with me, for I no sooner got my Liberty, but (Dog like return'd to his Vomit,) I follow'd my old Trade again, spearing neither Rich nor Poor. Thus I ran on till about the begining of *August* last, I went to the Pyde Bull in St. *Thomas Street*, and Stole thereout the vallue of five Pounds in Linnen and other things, belonging to one Mr. *Murphy* in said House, but I was

CATHRINE M'CANNA

soon taken and committed to Newgate, but when I was Try'd and lawfully convicted for the same, I began to plead my Belly, thinking to save my life but all was in vain, for my Jury of Mattrons would not forswear them selves for me, so I must Dye this Day.

Having no more to say, but beg of all Children to be more Dutiful to their Parents than I have been, I also beg the Prayers of all goood Christian, I dye a Roman Catholick, in the 38th Year of my Age, and the Lord Receive my Soul. Amen.

Dublin. Printed by *J. Neil* near the *Old-Bridge*.

(Location: Trinity College Library, Press A.7.5 No 203)

53

THE TRUE AND GENUINE DECLARATIONS OF

Mr. Richard Johnston and John Porter

Who were Executed near Stevens-Green, on Saturday the 12th day of Dec. 1730. for the MURDER *of* PATRICK MURPHY, *a Salter of Beef and Herrings, at the Union on Temple-Bar, early on Wednesday Morning, the 21st of October last.*

MR RICHARD JOHNSTON'S Declaration.

AS there is Nothing more natural than a Desire of Life, and as all, the Virtuous as well as the Vitious Part of Mankind are moved by Desire, so it is I think no Wonder the latter conscious to themselves of having in Numberless Instances offended that GOD, into whose awful Presence DEATH most certainly carries them, should shew an extraordinary earnestness, to keep at as great a Distance as possible from DEATH.

THESE Apprehensions together with the Worldly Dread of an ignominious DEATH, and not the consciousness of being the Person who gave the fatal STAB to the unfortunate Person deceased, induced me to have all the Witnesses that appeared in Court against Me strictly examined, and to produce as many as I could in my own Favour, that I might put off the evil Day a while longer, before, I Should go hence, and be no more seen.

THIS I hope will Satisfy those who may think Me over-active in my defense at My TRYAL, since few Men are either willing or prepared enough to DIE, and I most unprepared.

BUT whilst I name this very slender Part of my private Innocence, that I cannot recollect I gave the STAB, I would not be understood to call in Question the Justice of the Court, or the Gentlemen who were upon my Jury; for I must acknowledge that both behaved with the greatest Impartiality; and I Charitably think that the Witnesses, who had the Character of poor honest Men, swore nothing but what they apprehended to be right against Me.

I freely and Shamefully own in this Fact, that I was very early engaged in the FRAY, that I drew my Sword, and pursued some Persons while it was in my Hand in that manner, and that I sheathed it, and struck a Man with it in the Scabbord at the Sign of the UNION on Temple-Bar, as I also did with My Hand, but whether the deceased or not I cannot say.

IT would be unnecessary to give a particular Account of all the Transactions of that fatal Night; Let it suffice to add thus much to what I have already said, that when I came up to those Men at Essex-Bridge, of whom I suppose the deceased was one, I had not the least Design of proceeding so far as to take away the Life of any of them; and this I hope will be some extenuation of My Guilt in the Eye of that descerning Judge, before whom I am quickly to appear.

BUT since the Laws have thought fit to look upon all Persons concerned in a Fact of this Nature as PRINCIPALS, I resign myself to their Determination, and confess myself to be very instrumental in the Death of that Person for whom I suffer, and indeed was I conscious of having given the STAB, no Consideration Should now induce me to conceal it, since I am in a little Time to appear in the Presence of that GOD, to whom all Things are Naked and Open, who searcheth the Heart and trieth the Reins and who renders to every Man according to his Deeds; the little Reputation if any, which I might hope to acquire by denying it, would be but a poor Recompence for the Loss of Happiness for ever in a better World.

NOW as I endeavour to hide Nothing with Design that relates to this Fact and as I have been always careful to observe the same Method in My private Addresses to My GOD; so I hope this sincere though short Repentance will be graciously accepted by him; and as he shewed Mercy to the MALEFACTOR mentioned in the Gospel, though in the latest Moments of Life converted to him, I humbly hope that he will also mercifully Receive Me through the Merits and Mediation of My Lord and Saviour JESUS CHRIST.

AND as I offer this Prayer for Myself I earnestly offer my Prayers for those that stand in Need of a worthier PETITIONER to HEAVEN than I am; that they may from the Melancholly EXAM-

PLE which I afford them, leave and forsake those wicked Ways, which often lead to such an End as this in the present World, or if they should not lead to this End, let them think and lay to Heart what they will lead to in the World to come; For the Law of GOD as I am made sensible of it is made against the Lawless and Disobedient, the Ungodly, the Unholy and the Profane, against Murderers and Whore-Mongers, against Liars and perjured Persons, and against every other Thing that is contrary to seund Doctrine.

THIS Law of GOD is reasonable and Just, and cannot change, therefore must the Wicked change or endure the sentence, and who can dwell with everlasting Burning.

OH That I had been so happy to begin to change, to turn from SIN, and to turn to GOD under a milder Correction! I pray, I earnestly pray, that my unthinking and unreformed Acquaintance may take speedy Warning from my Miseries, and prevent their own both here and hereafter.

AND now Gracious GOD I return to thee, who hast promised to receive a returning SINNER I Fly to thy Mercy, Oh Pity and Pardon and Save me for Thy Mercies Sake, through the Merit of my Saviour and Redeemer JESUS CHRIST. *Amen.*

Decem. 12th 1730.

RICHD. JOHNSTON

Mr. JOHN PORTER'S DECLARATION.

AS I hope, I did not appear over solicitous, in attempting Evasions for my Defence on my Tryal for the Fact for which I now die, it will become me at this time to own my Guilt. The Wisdom of our Laws have made all Principals, in the heinious Sin of Murder, The Law is wise and just, as it provides the strongest Guard, against the most heinous and most irreparable Crime. But I hope, without Offence, that before the Tribunal of another World, it may be some Alleviation of my Guilt in this Case, that I did not execute the Fact, had no Sword in my Hand, nor design in my Heart to execute it: I do not use this Observation, to excuse my Guilt in this

World, I acknowledge this Crime, with ten thousand Offences more, in which I have presumptuously trangressed my Duty, my most reasonable Duty, to my most Gracious God, this Apprehension of the gracious Goodness of my God, is at once an Aggravation of my Presumption of offending my good Creator, and yet this Excess of the Goodness of God, of his Mercy and Compassion, thro' the Merits and Mediation of my Saviour is the only Comfort, on which I rely, I believe the Promises of God to the truly Penitent Sinner; but, Alas it is, an indifferent Testimony of Repentance, that a Man can give in my unhappy Circumstances.

God knows the Sincerity of all Hearts, he knows the sincerity of mine, which I cannot judge of under this Distress, but I trust it is sincerely penitent, my daily Prayer to him for some time past has been to make it sincere.

But can this little time redeem the long misspent time, even of my short Life? Oh my Lord, and my God, thy Mercies are infinite through the Mercies of my Saviour and Redeemer, I think, I can sincerely declare this, that tho' it would be desirable to me, to live, yet I would rather chuse to die, that to lead a Life of wretched Sin: I pray, and I hope, that my Death in this Manner will reclaim many a wretched Person, and awaken many a hardned Soul, let those, who will not be reclaimed, and awakened by my sad Example, expect some Judgment, or other to fall upon them in this Life, and above all, let them look forward to the dreadful Punishments of another World.

Pray think on this, ye that forget God the wicked are reserved for the Day of Destruction.

I draw this Paper as a Declaration of my Guilt, and to prevent the Guilt of others.

I say little of the rest of my unworthy Life, because I would desire the Memory would be blotted out; I pray God, make my Death happy to myself and other, Gracious God be merciful to me a Sinner through the Merits of my Redeemer JESUS CHRIST, *Amen* and *Amen.*

This my true Declaration to Confirm the same I Sign.

John Porter.

Sir,

I Desire you will print this as it is hither inserted; and add my grateful Acknowledgement to the City in General for their *Prayers.*

I do hereby certify that these Two Declarations are true Copies of the Original Declarations of Mr. *Richard Johnston* and Mr. *John Porter* which were delivered to me.

GEORGE DERRY.

** Speedily will be published by the Printer hereof a Paraphrase on the 139 Psalm which was found in Mr. *Johnston's* Pocket, supposed to have been wrote by him whilst in Confinement.

Dublin: Printed by JOHN GOWAN at the *Spinning Wheel* in *Backlane.*

(Location: Trinity College Library, Press A.7.5 No. 210)

54

THE LAST SPEECH, CONFESSION AND DYING WORDS OF

Edward Keating, Charles Neil, Terence Riely, James Graham, and Will. Henry

who are to be Executed this present Saturday being the 27th of this Instant February 1730–31. near St Stephens Green.

The Speech of *Edward Keating.*

Good People,

MANY are the Misfortunes that attends poor unthinking Man; especially those who never takes the trouble to beg of God for his Grace, in order to defend him from those Temptations, I shall therefore shew you how I have fallen from that Grace defined for me, and embraced my own Destruction in this Life, and I much fear my utter ruin in the other, as you may see by the following Relation.

I drew my first Breath in the County *Wexford*, of very honest Parents, with whom I liv'd for many Years, but they not allowing me Money to support my Extravagancy, I combin'd with three others to go Rob, accordingly we stole a Horse, for which we were soon Apprehended and committed to Goal, and when the Assizes came I turned the King's Evidence and Hang'd them, and I got orders to be seen there no more; then I came to *Dublin* and turn'd Horse Jockey, and by it got my Bread in City and Country, till at last I Marry'd a Wife in *Clindalkin*, and liv'd there with her Parents for many Years, till about Christmas last I unfortunately met with *Mr. Ryan* a Farmer, as he was going from *Dublin* (where he sold some Corn) to his own House in *Newcastle*, and there I knock'd him off his Horse, and took from him five Pounds in Money; but soon after he had me taken and committed to *Kilmainham*, and from that I was Transmitted to *Newgate* where I lay till last Term, then I was Try'd and lawfully convicted, and now this Day I must Dye for the same.

Having no more to say but begs all you Prayers, I dye an unworthy member of the Church of *Rome*, and in the 40th Year of my Age, and the Lord have Mercy on my Soul, *Amen.*

Ed. Keating.

The Speech of Terence Riely.

Good Christians,

I Drew my first Breath in the County of Cavin, of poor but honest Parents, who took what Care they could to give me a little Learning, and bring me up in the fear of God; thus I continued untill I was able to shift for myself, which I did by getting into a Gentleman's Service, in which station I behaved myself well for many Years, but being lately out of Service, and having no Friend to support me, *O'Neil* and I concluded to go to the Country, and going to the House of one *Quin* at the foot of *Tallow Hill,* we Rob'd the said House of all we could find valuable, and so made our way to *Dublin* again, but they pursued us so close that we were taken next Morning and committed to Goal, and at the sitting of the last Term was Try'd and lawfully convicted, and now this Day must Dye for the Same, although it is the first Crime of this nature that ever I committed.

Having no more to say but beging all your Prayers, I dye a *Roman Catholick*, and in the 20th Year of my Age, sweet *Jesus* receive my poor Soul, *Amen.*

Terence Reily

The Speech of Charles O'Neil.

Good People,

I Was Born and Bread in the *North* of *Ireland*, of poor honest Parents, who tenderly Nurish'd me according to their ability,' till I was able to go to a Trade, then they put me to a Weaver, with whom I liv'd for the space of seven Years, then I came to *Dublin*, in hopes to get Work here, but none could I get, so meeting with Riely, I agreed to go with him, and coming to *Tallow Hill*, we went into the House of one *Quin* and took what Money was in the Till, and among the rest there was a bad six pence which was produc'd again for us at our Tryal, upon the same we were lawfully Convicted, and so this Day we must Dye for the same.

Having no more to say but beg all your Prayers, I dye a *Roman Catholick* in the 23d Year of my Age, and the Lord receive my poor Soul, *Amen.*

Charles O' Neil.

The Speech of James Graham.

Good Christians,

AS for my part I have not much to say, by reason I have already made a Speech some time ago, in which I have declared the particulars of the Fact for which I Dye, and had it been the Will of God that I had Suffered at that time, I believe I was better provided then, than I am at present, for the vain hopes of Life, made me delitary of my Duty, yet will I not despair in the Mercies of my God, for he is able to forgive more than I can commit. Having no more to say but beg all your Prayers, I dye a Member of the Church of *England*, in the 18th Year of my Age, the Lord have mercy on my poor Soul, *Amen.*

James Graham

The Speech of William Henry.

Good People,

LET all disobedient Children draw near and see the fatal down fall of an unrulely Child, who thro' my disobedience have mocked my Father, dispised my Mother, and trampled on the Laws of God and Man tho' young I am, for which you see the vengeance of God has overtaken me, and has cut me of in the midst of my Youth; the Fact I die for is Stealing a Grate, and striveing to make my Escape I broke my Leg. Having no more to Say but to beg all your Prayers, I dye a *Roman Catholick*, in the 14th Year of my Age and the Lord have mercy on my poor Soul, *Amen*.

Will. Henry.

N.B. The above we deliver'd to the Printer hereof, in the presence of our Friends, and if there be any others, they are false.

Dublin: Printed by William Taylor on the Blind Quay

(Location: Trinity College Library, Press A.7.5 No 220)

55

THE WHOLE DECLARATION AND LAST SPEECH, CONFESSION AND DYING WORDS OF

Capt. Daniel M'Guire

who is to be Executed near St. Stephens Green, this present Wednesday being the 28th of this Inst. July 1731. For Robbing of Thomas Bryan in Fingal, and puting him on a hot Griddle to make him Confess his Money, the 18th of November last.

Good Christians,

WHEREAS the World may expect, as tis usual to those in my Condition; to give the Publick some satisfaction, for the many wrongs done to them; so may they now expect the same from me, who have not been, I acknowledge in the presence of God, and as I am a Dying Man, less Criminal then a great many who came to this shameful End; but why shou'd I thus speak, whereas no Death (tho' never so Ignominious) ought to be regarded by me as shameful, for was I to Suffer a thousand times more, its what my Sins justly deserves; but my great hope is that these my Sufferings may in some measure appease the angry Frowns of an injured God, before whom I expect in some few Minutes to appear, and as I am a dying Man unworthy to approach so good a God, I shall give the World a true and brief account of my mis-spent Life, and do beg of the Same God, that these my words may mollify the Hearts of these who have been misled as I have been.

I was Born in the County of *Farmanagh*, where I lived till I came to the Years of Twenty, and acquired honest and credible Bread, by going to Fairs and other publick Places, my Employ was selling Merchandize, (but alas! as the unbridled conduct of Youth when they have not the Love and fear of God before their Eyes, are liable to several Misfortunes, such was my unfortunate state to my great Grief, not so much regarding my present state and Misfortune, as the offence I committed against my God, the severity of whose Judgment makes me tremble, but confiding in his infinite Mercy, I now reassume new Courage,) and thus did I continue in my lawfull Employ, till about two Years ago falling into the Company of one who never feared God lead me astray, and I must acknowledge tho' I've been Guilty of several Enormous Crimes ever since, there is not any one of them gives me so great a concern, or loads my Soul with so much Grief, as the misfortune I had to accuse falsely honest Men, which I believe is a Crime of the blackest dye; (but my God whose Mercy surpasses all other thy Attributes, I hope you'll Pardon all these my offences,) and which ought to be deeply considered by all our Gentlemen, before they wou'd Encourage me or any other of my kind to take away the Lives of honest Men; as I am a dying Man, and as I am to appear before the Tribunal of an unbyassed God, I never wou'd Accuse the undernamed honest Men, was I not encouraged by a certain Gentleman who promised me my Life for the said Discovery, (whose Name for a certain reason I do omit) I own in the sight and presence of God, and as I expect in some few Minutes to surpass the severity of his Judgment, I falsely Accused *Dennis Kelly* of *Garishtown* in the County of *Dublin*, *Adam Ward*, *John Tyers*, and his Wife of the said Town: I also declare as before, *Michael Burk* had no share nor knew nothing of the Robbery of Mr. *Fottrel* near *Killsholachan*, or of Councelor *Smith's* Cloaths. I also falsely Accused *James Murphy* in the County of *Caterlough*, and *Edward Hoy* of the Parish of *Crickstown* in the County of *Meath*. But alas! as I am now going to appear before the Face of my God, I hope they will forgive me, as to the Fact I Dye for, the Evidence as it appeared were Injured, but I Dye in Peace with them and all the World, begging that all my Spectators may Pray for me, I prostrate myself at the Feet of my God, begging Pardon for my Sins, I Dye a *Roman Catholick*, in the 24th Year of my Age.

Daniel M'Guire.

N.B. The above is my true Speech delivered to the Printer hereof, in the Presence of the Reverend Father *Andoe*.

Dublin: Printed, at the *Reindeer* in *Montrath Street*.

(Location: Trinity College Library, Press A.7.5 No250)

56

THE LAST SPEECH AND DYING WORDS OF

Daniel Crossagh O-Mullan, Shaen Crossagh O-Mullan and Rory, alias Roger Roe O-Haran

who were Executed at London-Derry, April the 18th, 1733.

I *DANIEL O-MULLAN* was born in the Parish of *Cumber*, in the County of *London-Derry*, of poor, but honest Parents, who not being able to maintain me, and I being idle and extravagant, began to purchase for myself by stealing of Cows, Sheep and some other trifling things (which I thought no great Sin in those Days) being before the Wars of *Ireland*) and being often Try'd for my Life, I had the good Fortune to be acquitted, which Encouraged me to go on in this way of Living; I Married before the Wars of *Ireland*, and my Children enclin'd too much to follow my way of Living, particularly the two Boys, *viz. Shaen* and *Michael*, which I am affraid was too much occasion'd by my bad Example, for which I confess I am justly brought to this untimely End in my old Age, being a very great Sinner. I die a *Roman Catholick*, desiring the Prayers of all good Christians.

The Last Speech of Shaen O-Mullan.

I *SHAEN O-MULLAN* was born in the Parish of *Cumber* and County of *London-Derry*, I cannot say of honest Parents, for in my Childhood, in stead of being brought up in the Fear of the Lord, I was Educated in the Art of Plundering, and I being hardy as well as bold, soon became an accomplish'd Master in that Art, and in it I spent the most of my Life. *William Mcc-Carter*'s Sons were still ready to joyn with me in any Villanous Attempt. I have been try'd for my

The LAST SPEECH
AND
DYING WORDS
OF

Daniel *Croſſagh O-Mullan*, *Shaen Croſſagh O-Mullan* and *Rory*, alias *Roger Roe O-Haran*, who were Executed at *London-Derry*, *April* the 18th, 1733.

DANIEL O-MULLAN was born in the Pariſh of *Cumber*, in the County of *London-Derry*, of poor, but honeſt Parents, who not being able to maintain me, and I being idle and extravagant, began to purchaſe for myſelf by ſtealing of Cows, Sheep and ſome other trifling things (which I thought no great Sin in thoſe Days) being before the Wars of *Ireland*) and being often Try'd for my Life, I had the good Fortune to be acquitted, which Encouraged me to go on in this way of Living; I Married before the Wars of *Ireland*, and my Children enclin'd too much to follow my way of Living, particularly the two Boys, viz. *Shaen* and *Michael*, which I am affraid was too much occaſion'd by my bad Example, for which I confeſs I am juſtly brought to this untimely End in my old Age, being a very great Sinner. I die a *Roman Catholick*, deſiring the Prayers of all good Chriſtians.

The Laſt Speech of Shaen O-Mullan.

SHAEN O-MULLAN was born in the Pariſh of *Cumber* and County of *London-Derry*, I cannot ſay of honeſt Parents, for in my Childhood, in ſtead of being brought up in the Fear of the Lord, I was Educated in the Art of Plundering, and I being hardy as well as bold, ſoon became an accompliſh'd Maſter in that Art, and in it I ſpent the moſt of my Life. *William Mcc-Carter's* Sons were ſtill ready to joyn with me in any Villanous Attempt. I have been try'd for my Life at *Omagh*, *Lifford* and *London-derry*, and had the Fortune to eſcape, which made me go on in my Wickedneſs. When I arriv'd at the Age of 30 Years, I married the Daughter of *Tumlin O-Mullan* who was Executed in *London-derry*. Settling in the Barrony of *Couiraiu*, was taken from thence to keep Poſſeſſion of a Houſe and Lands at a place call'd the *Vow*, in the County of *Antrim*, and behaving my ſelf ſo Valiantly there, I was taken from thence to hold another Poſſeſſion at *Portglenone* in ſaid County, my Father and Brother were alſo both concern'd there, though we all knew it was contrary to Law. On Account of this Rebellion I was Proclaim'd, but I not Surrendring my ſelf according to the time Limitted in the Proclamation, choſe rather to take up Arms with *Patrick O-Haſſen*, *Arthour Mc Cloſky*, and *Owen Donally*; we all ſwore to Live together and take the ſame Fate, and ſo we took the Road; the firſt Exploit we did was that of General *Napper* and Captain *Pawle* whom we Robbed, we afterwards Robb'ed all thoſe who refuſed to Pay us Contribution Money; we began to ſuſpect each other and ſo we parted, each taking a different Road. I being indulged by ſome Gentlemen Reciv'd his Majeſty's moſt Gracious Pardon, the Gentlemen who procured it me Endeavouring to make me an Honeſt Man, I ſpent ſome time in the Country after Receiving my Pardon, but the *Mc Carters* took upon them to take my Brother *Michael* who is a Proclaim'd Tory, they Complain'd that 'twas Impoſſible while I was at Liberty, ſo I was taken on ſuſpicion of Harbouring my Brother and put into Goal: Since I got my Pardon one *James Awl*, ſwore a Robbery againſt me, and I Declare as I am a Dying Man, his Examinations was falſe, as alſo *John Lumbers* and *Manus Muldcens*. Yet I do confeſs I am juſtly deſerving of Death, for many grievous Sins, particularly for debauching many innocent, & in following lewd women but Innocents of that Crime for which I am to Dye; during my Confinement I gave ſome Examinations in behalf of the Crown, againſt thoſe who were wont to Receive part of my Spoil, which were ſuſpected to be falſe, but I do here before God and the World Averr and Declare that they were true, and that I never receiv'd any Reward or Bribe for the ſwearing the ſaid Examinations. I die a *Roman Catholick* deſiring the Prayers of all good Chriſtians.

The Laſt Speech of Roger O-Haran.

ROGER O-HARAN was Born in the Pariſh of *Cumber*, in the County of *London-Derry*, of honeſt Parents, who were able enough to Maintain and Educate me, but I took up my time when Young with *William Mc Carter's* Sons in ſaid Pariſh, who Entiſed me to ſteal from my Father and ſpend it with them, after I had ruin'd my Father they joyn'd with me in ſtealing ſeveral things from the Neighbours, when I came to the Age of 16 Years I began to think of my paſt Life and quit that way of Living until *Shane* and *Michael Croſſagh O-Mullan*, went out in Arms who being my Relations they with the aforeſaid *Mc Carters* Encouraged me to joyn them, and leſt I ſhould inform againſt the ſaid *Mc Carters*, they took me, and ſwore away my Life. During my Confinement I gave ſome Examinations againſt Perſons who had receiv'd ſome things taken in a Robbery by *Shane Croſſagh O-Mullan*, the ſame Examinations were ſuſpected to have been falſe, but I before God and the World do Averr, and Declare, that the ſame Examinations are true. I dye a *Roman Catholick*, deſiring the Prayers of all good Chriſtians.

Life at *Omagh*, *Lifford* and *London-derry*, and had the Fortune to escape which made me go on in my Wickedness. When I arriv'd at the Age of 30 Years, I married the Daughter of *Tumlin O-Mullen* who was Executed in *London-derry*. I Setling in the Barrony of *Coulrain*, was taken from thence to keep Possession of a House and Lands at a place call'd the *Vow*, in the County of *Antrim*, and behaving myself so Valiantly there, I was taken from thence to hold another Possession at *Portglenone* in said County, my Father and Brother were also both concern'd there, though we all knew it was contrary to Law. On Account of this Rebellion I was Proclaim'd, but I not Surrendring myself according to the time Limitted in the Proclamation, chose rather to take up Arms with *Patrick O-Hassen*, *Arthour McClosky*, and *Owen Donally*; we all swore to Live together and make the same Fate, and so we took the Road; the first Exploit we did was that of General *Napper* and Captain *Pawle* whom we Robbed, we afterwards Robbed all those who refused to Pay us Contribution Money; we began to suspect each other and so we parted, each taking a different Road. I being indulged by some Gentlemen Reciv'd his Majesty's most Gracious Pardon, the Gentlemen who procured it me Endeavouring to make me an Honest Man, I spent some time in the Country after Receiving my Pardon, but the *McCarters* took upon them to take my Brother *Michael* who is a Proclaim'd Tory, they Complain'd that 'twas Impossible while I was at Liberty, so I was taken on suspicion of Harbouring my Brother and put into Goal: Since I got my Pardon one *James Awl*, swore a Robbery against me, and I Declare as I am a Dying Man, his Examinations was false, as also *John Lumbers* and *Manus Muldoens*. Yet I do confess I am justly deserving of Death, for many grievous Sins, particularly for debauching many innocent, & in following lewd women but Innocent of that Crime for which I am to Dye; during my Confinement I gave some Examinations in behalf of the Crown, against those who were wont to Receive part of my Spoil, which were suspected to be false, but I do here before God and the World Averr and Declare that they were true, and that I never receiv'd any Reward or Bribe for the swearing the said Examinations. I die a *Roman Catholick* desiring the Prayers of all good Christians.

The Last Speech of Roger O-Haran.

I *R O G E R O-H A R A N* was Born in the Parish of *Cumber*, in the County of *London-Derry*, of honest Parents, who were able enough to Maintain and Educate me, but I took up my time when Young with *William Mᶜ Carter's* Sons in said Parish, who Entitled me to steal from my Father and spend it with them, after I had ruin'd my Father they joyn'd with me in stealing several things from the Neighbours, when I came to the Age of 26 Years I began to think of my past Life and quit that way of Living until *Shane* and *Michael Crossagh O-Mullan*, went out in Arms who being my Relations they with the aforesaid *Mᶜ Carters* Encouraged me to joyn them, and lest I should inform against the said *Mᶜ Carters*, they took me, and swore away my Life. During my Confinement I gave some Examinations against Persons who had receiv'd some things taken in a Robbery by *Shane Crossagh O-Mullan*, the same Examinations were suspected to have been false, but I before God and the World do Averr, and Declare, that the same Examinations are true. I dye a *Roman Catholick*, desiring the Prayers of all good Christians.

(Location: Yale University, Beinecke Library, BrSides, By6 1733)

57

THE GENUIN DECLARATION,
AND LAST DYING SPEECH OF

Pierce Tobin and Walter Kelly

Sailors, who are to be Hang'd and Quarter'd near St. Stephen's Green, for the Murder of Vastin Tunburgh a Dutch Skipper, this present Saturday being the 27th of this Instant July 1734.

Friends, Brethren and *Country-Men,*

I Am here presented a Spectacle both to Men and Angels! Sinking, not so much under the Terrors of approaching Death, as the deepest Remorse, and upbraidings of Consience! Were I brought hither to meet the Fate of ordinary Crimes, then the Confusion of my Face, if not the Terror of my Consience might be less, but my Crime being out of the usual course of Sin, a Crime not only against the Divine, but human Nature in general, how shall I recommend my self to the Mercy of the one, or the pitty of the other! I will endeavour thus, *With my Lips will I confess, and in my Heart will I be sorry for my sins.*

Here mention need not be made of my Birth and Parentage, it being sufficiently known in this City, But I conjure you (as you are People of Candor and Generosity) despite not the Parents for the Sons Crimes; point not your angry Resentment at their Aged Heads.

Were it any advantage to you my Spectators, or else to my afflicted Soul, to ennumerate the several Sins I have been Guilty of, I should draw each forth in their deepest shade of Guilt; I should tell, and expose each Circumstance, till I'd faint away under that grievous Task. But why should I do, what would rather terrify, than Instruct you; it is enough; (too much) to say, *I Walk'd in the Counsel of the Ungodly.*

It also would be unnecessary to give a particular Account of all the Transactions of that fatal Night; let it suffice to add thus much to what I have said, that when I came up to those *Dutch-Men* at *Aston's*

Quay, of whom I svppose the Deceased was one, I said, *Play away*, and gave some stroaks to the Deceased, but had not the least Design of proceeding so far as to take away the Life of any of them.

But since the Law has thought fit to look upon all Persons concerned in a Fact of this Nature, as Principals, I resign my self to their Determination, and Confess my self very Instrumental in the Death of that Person for whom I Suffer, and indeed was I Consious of having given the mortal Wound to the Deceased, no consideration should now induce me to conceal it.

Thus much from a Dying Object, who humbly begs your Prayers to the Great God for my poor Soul; I Dye an unworthy Member of the Church of *Rome*, and in the 19th Year of my Age.

Newgate, July 26, 1734.   *Pierce Tobin.*

The Speech of *Walter Kelly*.

Dear Christians,

I Am brought here this Day, to Dye a base and Ignomenious Death, for the Murder of *Vastin Tunburgh* a *Dutchman*; nor can I say that I am Innocent, since all Persons that are present at the Transaction of so horrid a Deed, are Guilty alike, according to Law; therefore I can make no excuse at all for my self, yet I will lay before you my Spectators, and that in the briefest and clearest method, the particulars of all the Transactions of that fatal Night, *viz.*

Mr. *Tobin*, my present fellow sufferer, and I being intimates, and but just return'd from a Voyage, we both agreed to go to *Bagnio Slip*, in order to get a Whore; and there being some *Dutchmen* there who had a falling-out among themselves; we alas! very presumptiously went to their Room, and took both their Pipes and Canddel from them, I must confes it was very ill done; but they being reconciled, went their way, but one of them took theBarr of the Door with him, in order (as I suppose) to defend themselves, in case we should follow them, but as God is my Judge we had no such thought, untill one of the cursed Women cry'd out, *One of the Dutchmen has taken the Barr of the Door, pray follow them, and take it from them.* We being in Liquor, and hot-headed withall, pursued them to *Aston's Quay*, among us there arose a Quarrel in which the *Dutch Skipper* receiv'd his Death; but how, or by what means, I know not, for my part I had neither Sword or Knife, nor am I any way sensible that I struck any one. But Oh! My God, I must confess that I deserve this Death, for the many innumerable Offences I have committed otherwise against thy Divine Majesty; yet will I not despair of thy Mercy, and I do firmly hope you will say to my Soul, as you did to the Penitent Thief on the Cross, *This Day shalt thou be with me in Paradise*; Grant this O most Heavenly Father, thro' the Intersecion of our blessed Lord and Saviour *Jesus Christ, Amen.*

Having no more to say, but to beg all your Prayers to God for our poor Souls, I Dye an unworthy member of the Church of *Room*, in the 25th Year of my Age, Good Lord have Mercy on my poor Soul, Amen.

Newgate July 26 1734   *Walter Kelly.*

Dublin: Printed, by Tho. Dudlow, near Dirty Lane.

(Location: National Library of Scotland, Crawford Miscellaneous Broadsides, 1339)

58

THE TRUE DECLARATION, AND LAST SPEECH,
CONFESSION AND DYING WORDS OF

Denis Watch alias Watson and John Dougherty

who are both to be Executed near St. Stephen's Green, this present Saturday being the 31st of the Instant July 1736. For several Robberies committed by them.

The SPEECH of *Daniel Watch*.

Good Christians,

I Am come at last to put a period to my poor sinful and wicked Life, and I know that great numbers will flock to the place of Execution to hear what I shall say, concerning my past Life and Actions; to prevent such Assembly's I have sent for the Printer hereof, to whom I have communicated the whole secrets of my Heart, and that in as brief a manner as possible, therefore take the following Relation for Truth.

I drew my first Breath in *Mass-Lane* in St. *Francis Street*, my Father (so I heard) was a very honest Man, but to my sorrow, I cannot say that of my Mother, for she was counted a great Receiver, by which means my Brother (who suffer'd the like as I do now some Years ago thro' my means, as I shall relate hereafter) and I, seeing her giving Money plenty to Thieves, encourag'd us to follow the same pernicious practice; I being free about the Chappel afforsaid, watched my oppertunity till at last I stole the Chalice, and all the Plate belonging to the Altar; nay, I threw the Consecrated Bread into the Privy, and then brought said Plate to *Elizabeth Williams*, alias *Queen* of the *Sluts*. My Brother hearing the Chapple was Robb'd went in quest of me and found me at said *Williams's* drinking merrily, upon the same he beat me and said *Williams*, she thro' spight return'd said Plate, and swore my Brother brought it her, for which Fact he was Transported, and returning contrary to Law, he was soon after Executed for the same.

I continued in my former Vices, till at length I was Transported also, and the present occasion of my Death is for returning from the same, (but I must confes I have Robb'd Esqr, *Waters* House since my returne) which I was induced to do, thro' a temptation of getting a Legacy in Money which I heard (whilst abroad) was left me by my Mother, and deposited for me in the Hands of a Clergyman in this City. Landing in *Ireland* I went to *Kilkenny* I committed a Robbery there and Confin'd for the same, but I broke the Gaol and came to *Dublin*. I found when I came here that there was some colour for the Report of the Legacy, for on application to him, I obtain'd since small supplys from him at several times, but never cou'd be satisfied of the certainty of the Sum left for me, which I impute to the improbability the Gentleman had of ever seeing me, tho' I am well satisfied of his Usage to me since my condemnation, that I here acknowledge his goodness to me, and hope for his Prayers.

There has been a false and scandalous report at my first coming here, that I gave Mr. *Reives* Deputy Gaoler Money to let me goe, but as I am a dying Man I never gave him one Penny on any such account, and had I offered it to him, he has such an aversion to all that follow my vicious way of Living, that I am sure no Money can byass him.

Thus have I given you a short narative of my sinful Life, hoping both Old and Young will take warning by the same; especially as from that abominable sin of Sacriledge, if not they needs must expect this my untimely Death.

Having no more to say at present, by reason my Time is short, but to begg the Prayers of all good Christians, I dye an unworthy Member of the Church of *Rome*, in the 36th Year of my Age, and the Lord have Mercy on my poor Soul, and I hope all good Christians will say *Amen*.

Newgate July 30. 1736.   *Denis Watch*

The SPEECH of *John Dougherty*.

I Drew my first Breath in the County of Longford of very honest Parent's who took all the care possible they could to bring me up in the fear of God, and I behav'd my self well while I was under their Wings; but when I became able to do for my self I came to *Dublin*, where I soon got a Service, in which I remain'd till I became acquainted with the City, then I left said Service and went to another, still Improving wherever I went, at length I went to Mr *Webster*, a very worthy Gentleman, with whom I liv'd for some time, and might have done to still, had not ambitious Thoughts puft me up with Pride and Impudence, for which reasons I was discharg'd, but while I was there I got an Instrument made whereby I could open any Lock in his House, and took several pieces of Cloath and sold them, by which means I gathered some Money; and after I left him I follow'd the same pernicious practices, but God who would not permit me to reign any longer in my wickedness, detected me in my last attempt, so that I was taken with the Velvet that I now Dye for, and sent to Newgate, and at the last sitting of the Court of *Oyer* and *Termyner* I was Try'd, lawfully found Guilty, and now this Day I must Dye for the same according to Law.

    Having no more to say but to begg all your Prayers to God for my poor Soul, I dying a Member of the Church of *England* in the 26th Year of my Age, good Lord take me into thy protection, *Amen.*

    Newgate July 30. 1736.   *John Dougherty.*

Note, The above Speeches was deliver'd to the Printer hereof, in the presence of Mr. *Doogan*, Mr, *Thomas Martain*, and several others.

Dublin: Printed, by *W. Robinson* in Dirty-lane.

(Location: National Library of Scotland, Crawford Miscellaneous Broadsides, 1346)

59

THE GENUINE DECLARATION OF

Edward Shuel

a degraded Clergyman of the Church of Ireland, who is to be Executed near St. Stephens Green, this present Saturday being the 29th of this Instant November 1740. For celebrating the Clandestine Marriage of one Mr. Walker a Protestant, to Margaret Talbot a suppos'd Catholick, on Sunday the 16th of August last, at the World's End near Dublin.

Good Christians.

I Might reasonably have expected my Life wou'd have been saved, having obtain'd a Reprieve; but there being a Point of —— Policy strongly against me, to fulfill which I must Resign this Life sooner than Nature or Accident might have otherwise taken it. I must confess tho' I strove to bear my Sentence with the utmost Resignation and Christian Patience; yet the imbitter'd Reports of my having two Wives tingeing my Character, affected me in some Measure; and in order to clear such infamous and malicious Aspertions which my Enemies (whom the Origin of Heaven and Earth forgive) which I heartily pray for.

To be Concise, I was Born in the *North* of *Ireland*, and bred up in the University of *Dublin*, where I pursued my Studies, and behav'd as became a Student: Having received Orders, I officiated in the Curacy of *Carlingford*, *St Michans*, *Christ* Church *Dublin*, and several others Places; where I behav'd as a Gentleman, and suitable to my Function; untill most unfortunately a vile Woman prostituted herself, and seduced me to her dire Embraces; upon which she Reported that I Married my self to her, which is utterly false; and in Order to acquit my self of that Calumny, of Marrying her my self, and fully to extirpate the publick Notion of my having two Wives, I went to *Georges*

The Genuine
DECLARATION

Of *Edward Shuel* a degraded Clergyman of the Church of *Ireland,* who is to be Executed near St. *Stephens Green,* this present *Saturday* being the 29th of this Instant *November* 1740. For celebrating the Clandestine Marriage of one Mr. *Walker* a Protestant, to *Margaret Talbot* a suppos'd Catholick, on *Sunday* the 16th of *August* last, at the World's End near *Dublin.*

Good Christians.

I Might reasonably have expected my Life wou'd have been saved, having obtain'd a Reprieve; but there being a Point of —— Policy strongly against me, to fulfill which I must Resign this Life sooner than Nature or Accident might have otherwise taken it. I must confess tho' I strove to bear my Sentence with the utmost Resignation and Christian Patience; yet the imbitter'd Reports of my having two Wives tingeing my Character, affected me in some Measure; and in order to clear such infamous and malicious Aspersions which my Enemies (whom the Origin of Heaven and Earth forgive) which I heartily pray for.

To be Concise, I was Born in the *North of Ireland,* and bred up in the University of *Dublin,* where I pursued my Studies, and behav'd as became a Student: Having received Orders, I officiated in the Curacy of *Carlingford,* St *Michans, Christ* Church *Dublin,* and several others Places; where I behav'd as a Gentleman, and suitable to my Function; untill most unfortunately a vile Woman prostituted herself, and seduced me to her dire Embraces; upon which She Reported that I Married my self to her, which is utterly false; and in Order to acquit my self of that Calumny, of Marrying her my self, and fully to extirpate the publick Notion of my having two Wives, I went to *Georges* Church near *Dublin,* and there received the *Eucharist* that I never was Married or Contracted to any Woman under Heaven, but to the Woman now my unhappy Wife, by whom I have two innocent but unfortunate Babes, of which I got a Certificate from the Minister of said Church; which I gave to his Grace —— which must be acknowledg'd.

The Nature of the Crime for which I am to undergo this most Publick and scandalous Death, is notorious in this Kingdom. The Manner in which I now a poor and unhappy Sufferer was precipitately led into it is, that on the 16th of *August* last, one *Richard Walker* came in Disguise in a poor Habit, under the fictitious Name of *Wilson,* with one *Margaret Talbot* and another Woman in Company, who intreated me to Marry them: After I had examined them, and sweating them on the Book, who swore they were Protestants; and I believing *Richard Wilson* as he called himself, to be a Tradesman of no Fortune or Birth, and in his own Power, and I wanting of Support; my Children having not even Bread to Eat that Night, I unfortunately married them 'tis true, for which I received from *Wilson* Six Shillings and Six Pence.

But had I surmised he had been the Son of the Man he was, or any other Person of Credits Son, I would not for any Consideration have perform'd the Ceremoney, Nay, I would have sent to the Parents or next Relation and detected him, and at the same time given up the Woman, to the just resentment of the injur'd Parents.

'Tis true I was degraded and by that Means render'd incapable of supporting an helpless Family; nor was it in my Power to get a Livelihood by Teaching School, for many attempts I made that way which prov'd Abortive, Work either Mechanical or otherwise I was ignorant of; and by my infirmities render'd if capable not to follow it, to beg publickly I was a sham'd, and very well knew the Amount of Charities to Street Beggars, privately I did beg by Petitions to many Persons whose Grants were small, and that but from a very few; and e'en those few wou'd not a second time assist the Wretched, this was my Case; what I then follow'd to support my Family was the Trade as its so call'd of Marrying; but always took care to examine strictly their Religion, Birth, and parentage, avoiding as much as possible to keep out of Disesteem of Families of Credit, so that it might not lie in their Powers to punish me, or to be griev'd at the undoing of their Children.

Yet all this Precaution has not hinder'd my unhappy Exit, which I hope this Calamity of mine, may be a perpetual Bar to others who are after me, who may be drove to the pressing Wants which I have often struggled with, but may God Support them.

O Lord Strengthen me to bear my *Misfortunes,* bless my Children, and be to them a Father, and give them thy Grace, Comfort my Wife, and be to her a Husband, protect my Friends, and forgive my Enemies, and receive me into thy glorious Abode, and that I may this Day sing Praises and Thanksgiving unto thy holy Name, Ad infinitum, Amen.   *Edward Shuel.*

Note. The above was deliver'd to the Printer hereof, in the Presence of Mr. *Nelson* and several others, in his own Hand Writing, and Word of Mouth.

Dublin: Printed in *Montrath-Street,* by *Chr. Goulding* Book-Seller.

Church near *Dublin*, and there received the *Eucharist* that I never was Married or Contracted to any Woman under Heaven, but to the Woman now my unhappy Wife, by whom I have two innocent but unfortunate Babes, of which I got a Certificate from the Minister of said Church, which I gave to his Grace____ which must be acknowledg'd.

The Nature of the Crime for which I am to undergo this most Publick and scandalous Death, is notorious in this Kingdom. The Manner in which I now a poor and unhappy Sufferer was precipitately led into it is, that on the *16th* of *August* last, one *Richard Walker* came in Disguise in a poor Habit, under the fictitious Name of *Wilson*, with one *Margaret Talbot* and another Woman in Company, who intreated me to Marry them: After I had examined them, and swearing them on the Book, who swore they were Protestants; and I believing *Richard Wilson* as he called himself, to be a Tradesman of no Fortune or Birth, and in his own Power, and I wanting of Support; my Children having not even Bread to Eat that Night, I unfortunately married them 'tis true, for which I received from *Wilson* Six Shillings and Six Pence.

But had I surmised he had been the Son of the Man he was, or any other Person of Credits Son, I would not for any Consideration have perform'd the Ceremoney, Nay, I would have sent to the Parents or next Relation and detected him, and at the same time given up the Woman, to the just resentment of the injur'd Parents.

'Tis true I was degraded and by that Means render'd incapable of supporting an helpless Family; nor was it in my Power to get a Livelihood by Teaching School, for many attempts I made that way which prov'd Abortive, Work either Mechanical or otherwise I was ignorant of; and by my infirmities render'd if capable not to follow it, to beg publickly I was a sham'd, and very well knew the Amount of Charities to Street Beggars, privately I did beg by Petitions to many Persons whose Grants were small, and that but from a very few; and e'en those few wou'd not a second time assist the Wretched, this was my Case; what I then follow'd to support my Family was the Trade as its so call'd of Marrying; but always took care to examine strictly their Religion, Birth, and parentage, avoiding as much as possible to keep out of Disesteem of Families of Credit, so that it might not lie in their Powers to punish me, or to be griev'd at the undoing of their Children.

Yet all this Precaution has not hinder'd my unhappy Exit, which I hope this Calamity of mine, may be a perpetual Bar to others who are after me, who may be drove to the pressing Wants which I have often struggled with, but may God Support them.

O Lord Strengthen me to bear my Misfortunes, bless my Children, and be to them a Father, and give them thy Grace, Comfort my Wife, and be to her a Husband, protect my Friends, and forgive my Enemies, and receive me into thy glorious Abode, and that I may this 'Day sing Praises and Thanksgiving unto thy holy Name, Ad infinitum, Amen.

Edward Shuel.

Note. The above was deliver'd to the Printer hereof, in the Presence of Mr. *Nelson* and several others, in his own Hand Writing, and Word of Mouth.

Dublin: Printed in *Montrath-Street*, by *Chr. Goulding* Book-Seller.

(Location: British Library, 1890.e.5 (192); National Library of Scotland, Crawford Miscellaneous Broadsides, 1390)

60

THE LAST AND TRUE SPEECH OF

Mr. Sewell

a degraded Clergyman, who was executed last Saturday the 29th of November 1740, at St. Stephen's-Green, for a clandestine Marriage delivered by him at the Place of Execution.

Countrymen and Christians,

IT may be thought, perhaps, that the Length of Time given me by the Clemency of the Lords Justices might turn my Thoughts to poor Transitory, Worldly Affairs, I hope thro' the Merits of Christ I have not been affected so foolishly, for I will not boast, but will humbly hope, I have so numbered my Days as to apply my Heart unto Wisdom, for the Love of the Lord is the Beginning of it. I return to the Chief Governors of Ireland, the only Return I can make, my Thanks and Prayers for their Benignity in extending my shortning Length of Days to the present, in this World unhappy, but in the World, thro' Christ, in the future, a Blessed Consummation. – Praise be to God on High Peace and Good Will amongst Men.

I Am brought forth this Day, as a Precedent and Example to the Marriage Act, as a Sacrifice to its Rigor, the first, and I hope through the Almighty, the last of the kind that shall hereafter be read of in the Annals of the Holy Catholick and Reform'd Protestant Church; nor is it the smallest Pang that I feel in this solemn Anguish of my Spirit that my Memory shall reflect some Disgrace upon my Reverend, Learned and Pious surviving and future Brethern of the Ministry. Could Worldly Things now amuse or disturb my Mind, I might also be touch'd with a Sense of the Triumph, my unhappy Catastrophe, must give to the Enemies of the Establish'd Religion; but in this, as in all Things else in Heaven and Earth, the Will of the All Powerful and Eternal Father be done, yet let them consider that the Man, the poor weak Man transgress'd and not the Function; let them think that the Transgressor suffer'd, and with his Blood wash'd away Polution from the Sanctuary. The blessed Twelve should not be blamed for their fallen Member, nor should the Body of the Clergy be reproached for one wretched, sinful, misguided, but thro' Grace repentant Brother.

Speeches and Declarations are a Custom I know observed by People in my wretched Circumstances; but this has no Influence on me, I only promulgate these few Lines to prevent many gross and ignorant Pieces of Print which may be ascribed to me, when I am past the Power of contradicting such Falshoods. I am, bless'd be my Saviour, in universal Charity with the World, and therefore neither Bitterness nor Untruth shall fall from me: I am convinced, as my Condition is particular and my self remarkable, the World will be desirous to know what I may say either in defence of myself, or Attenuation of the Crime for which I die; I will therefore briefly go thorough the Heads of my Accusation and Conviction.

I confess that I did solemnize a Marriage between Walker and Talbot, but at the same Time I declare I did not suspect that he was any other than an ordinary working young Man, and not the Son of one of so much Consequence in the City. I had their Oath of Secrecy and an Assurance of their both being of the Protestant Religion, but he appear'd as an Evidence against me; Heaven forgive him and me, and for this Crime I lay down my Life. Were it worth a Moment of my little remaining Time, I might here controvert Margaret Talbot's Marriage not within the Act, a Point of Law which I did but faintly Urge upon my Tryal: I might have pleaded the Inefficacy of my Degradation, the Indelibility of the Clerical Character, Validity of a Sentence pass'd by a Layman on a Person Canonical, and have spoken to an Appeal which I always apprehended was lodg'd in order to the Subversion of the Sentence of Degredation; but alas! they are Things below my Notice, for my Mind is above, and perhaps were I to illustrate on these Particulars, it may be construed either Indiscretion or Malice in a Dying Clergyman, and in my last Moments, what ever my past Life may be, I would not give Scandal to the Divine Function.

I acknowledge that I have been a frail weak Man, and that my

Transgressions are numberless, and that I have done several unwarrantable and idle Things, inconsistant with the Character of a Gentleman, a Scholar, and a Divine, but let Man deal with me as I hope to be dealt with by my Heavenly Father, who will thro' the Merits of Christ cast a Veil over my Sins, and blot out my Transgressions for ever.

I would Recommend to all Parents, with my dying Breath, a Resolution of never forcing the Dispositions of their Children, or thrusting them into a College with a View of the Pulpit, till they, if they are capable, or some Person of sound Judgment shall thoroughly examine if they have such Qualities, and Propensions as may fit them for such Office. On this Rock many Split, too many, and after some Years of Study, they come forth either contemptible for their Ignorance, or abhorr'd for their Vice. But, suppose them never so well endowed for the Ministry, the miserable Provision made for the Inferior Clergy, still more miserable by their Number, and their generally ill-judg'd Early Marriages throws them upon things which after endanger their Bread, and sometimes their Lives, of which I am a wretched Instance.

I beg that my wretched Family may not be Reproached with the Ignominy of my Death, to which I submit with Meekness, Resignation, and Resolution, hoping my Sufferings shall be Sanctified to me, and thro' this Gulf of Darkness a Passage to Eternal light and Joy thro' the Merits and Mediations of Jesus Christ my Saviour, to whom, with the Father and Holy Ghost be given all Praise and Worship now and ever more. Amen.

EDWARD SEWELL

An HYMN.

Compos'd by the Reverend Mr. Sewell, while under Sentence in Newgate, and sung by him in the Coach as he went to Execution.

Oh Fountain of Eternal Light !
Oh glorious Lord of Host !
With Mercy view my wretched Plight,
Oh spare me or I'm lost.

Grim Death in all it's Horrors dress'd
Is ever in my View,
Where is my Hope, now I'm oppress'd ?
My only Hope is You.

Injutious Man has laid the Snare,
I'm fallen, alas, I'm caught,
Man drink my Blood, but Father spare
The Soul thy Son has bought.

And suffer not my Blood to reign
O'er his Posterity,
Oh God wash out the the Scarlet Stain
And cleanse both him and me.

From Vengeance turn thy gracious Eye,
And see my throbbing Heart,
That melts at thy Divinity,
And feels and heavenly Smart.

And thou, O Son, who didst sustain
A Cross and shameful Death,
Who suffering more than mortal Pain
Groan'd out thy dying Breath.

EDWARD SEWELL

Sustain me in the Hour of Death,
In the disgraceful Cart,
And when the Halter stops my Breath,
Save my Immortal Part.

Thou dost not judge like wretched Man,
For shoudst thou be severe
And all the Faults of Mortals scan,
Who cou'd thy Judgments bear.

Receive me Blessed Trinity,
Receive my Soul in Grace,
And in thy Kingdom let me be
When Times and Worlds shall cease.

DUBLIN, Printed by Edward Jones in Dirty-lane.

(Location: British Library, 1890.e 5 (153))

61

THE LAST SPEECH,
CONFESSION AND DYING DECLARATION OF

Gerald Byrne and James and Patrick Strange

who were executed at Gallows-green, Kilkenny, on Saturday the 2d of December, 1780, for carrying away Catherine and Ann Kennedy, from Graigenamana, in the County of Kilkenny.

Good People,

    As we have for some time past excited the publick attention, it may be expected in our last moments to say a few words regarding the cause for which we suffer. As to out births; we have come from respectable families near Graigenamana, in the counties of Kikenny and Carlow; from an early acquaintance with the Miss Kennedy's, we unfortunately conceived an affection for them, grounded on the most virtuous and honourable terms; they received our addresses and seemed to approve of our passions by the mutual exchange of their love for ours; but alas! how we have been deceived. Thus encouraged with the many repeated assurances that we were not disagreeable, made us imprudently determine to take them away, which resolution we unhappily put in execution, and immediately after, married them, and during the time of their living with us no woman could be happier, as we used them in the most tender, loving and affectionate manner; however, illnatured people have shamefully propagated, that we treated them ungentleman-like; but such ill-natured reports have been founded and circulated by malice, and, we hope, in the humane and honest mind will have no weight. We freely forgive our unnatural wives, beseeching the Searcher of all Hearts, when they appear before his awful tribunal, will mitigate the cruelty they have shown to us, and receive them into the mansions of bliss. We die members of the Church of Rome, in peace with the world, in the 23d and 20th years of our age, and may the Lord have mercy on our Souls

                                            Gerald Byrne, James Strange

The last SPEECH of PATRICK STRANGE, who was executed for aiding and assisting in taking away the Miss Kennedy's

Good Christians,
    As it is usual for persons in my unhappy situation to give some account of their past life, I shall only trespass on the public, to mention, that I was born in the county of Carlow, come from a reputable family, and always preserved an unblemished character, the cause I die for was of assisting Mess Byrne and Strange, in carrying away the Miss Kennedy's. I forgive my prosecutors, requesting the prayers of all good Christians, and depart in peace with mankind, in the 24th year of my age.

Patrick Strange

ENISCORTHY: Printed by R.JONES

(National University of Ireland, Maynooth, Russell Library, Shearman Mss: Collections on historical and various subjects, f. 255).

62

THE FINAL CONFESSION OF

Thomas Neil

I THOMAS NEIL, do at this awful moment, acknowledge the justice of the Sentence now going to be executed on me; and that I was present at the Murder of PATRICK MURPHY; — but I must declare, that it was against my Will, and from Threats of Destruction to myself, my Family, and my Property, that I have been brought to consent to this wicked Conspiracy. I further declare, that I never had any Knowledge respecting the Rev. Mr. O' Neil, of *Ballymacody*, having been a Party in any Conspiracy whatsoever, or in any manner whatsoever; but that all I did say respecting him was merely on the Declarations of others, as I told Lord Loftus; — I think I owe him this candid Declaration, at this dreadful moment.

I beg forgiveness of all Men, and of my Creator.

I warmly conjure my deluded countrymen, to return to the ways of innocence and peace, and to abstain from those wicked associations which lead them insensibly into crimes; and to give the only retribution in their power to their injured country, by making such declaration of their wicked ways as may be the surest pledges of their repentance; and which I have often declared before to many of them. I solemnly call all their attentions to my just though dreadful state.

THOMAS NEIL.

Present,
Thomas O'Connor, *Vicar of St. Mary, Shandon.*
John Bourchier, *Lt. Col. R.I.A.*

Thomas Townshend.
George Hay, *Major E. F. Regt.*

N.B. This ill-advised, unfortunate gentleman, possessed landed property to the amount of £500 a year, and personal property to the amount of £5000.

Select bibliography

Toby Barnard, 'Learning, the learned and literacy in Ireland, c.1660-1760' in Toby Barnard, et als, eds, *'A miracle of learning': studies in manuscripts and Irish learning* (Aldershot, 1998), pp 219–21.
— , 'Reading in eighteenth-century Ireland: public and private pleasures' in Bernadette Cunningham and Maire Kennedy, eds, *The experience of reading: Irish historical perspectives* (Dublin, 1999), pp 60–77.
J.M. Beattie, *Crime and the courts in England, 1660–1800* (Princeton, 1986).
R.A. Bosco, 'Lectures at the pillory: the early American execution sermon', *American Quarterly*, 30 (1978), pp 156–76.
Catalogue of the Bradshaw collection of Irish books in the University Library, Cambridge (3 vols, Cambridge, 1916).
Roger Chartier, ed., *The culture of print: power and the uses of print in early modern Europe* (Oxford, 1989).
Roger Chartier, 'Texts, printings, readings' in Lynn Hunt, ed., *The new cultural history* (Berkeley, 1989), pp 154–75.
Aidan Clarke, 'The Atherton file', *Decies*, 11 (1979), pp 45-54.
D.A. Cohen, *Pillars of salt, monuments of grace: New England crime literature and the origins of American popular culture, 1674–1860* (Oxford, 1993).
R. Cargill Cole, *English books and Irish readers, 1700–1800* (London, 1986).
S.J. Connolly, *Religion, law and power: the making of Protestant Ireland, 1660–1760* (Oxford, 1992).
Robert Darnton, 'An early information society: news and media in

eighteenth-century Paris', *American Historical Review*, 105 (2000), pp 1–35.

Stephen Dunford, *The Irish highwayman* (Dublin, 2000).

Hugh Fenning, 'The last speech and prayer of Blessed Terence Albert O'Brien, Bishop of Emly, 1651', *Collectanea Hibernica*, 38 (1996), pp 52-8.

Michel Foucault, *Discipline and punish: the birth of the prison* (London, 1979).

Neal Garnham, *The courts, crime and the criminal law in Ireland, 1692-1760* (Dublin, 1996).

Malcolm Gaskill, 'Reporting murder: fiction in the archives in early modern England', *Social History*, 23 (1998), pp 1–30.

Raymond Gillespie, 'The circulation of print in seventeenth-century Ireland', *Studia Hibernica*, 29 (1995-7), pp 31–58.

Michael Harris, 'Trials and criminal biographies: a case study in distribution' in Robin Myers and Michael Harris, eds, *Sale and distribution of books from 1700* (Oxford, 1972), pp 16–26.

Brian Henry, *Dublin hanged: crime, law enforcement and punishment in late eighteenth-century Dublin* (Dublin, 1994).

Christian Jouhaud, 'Readability and persuasion: political handbills' in Chartier, ed., *The culture of print: power and the uses of print in early modern Europe* (Oxford, 1989), pp 235–60.

James Kelly, '"A most inhuman and barbarous piece of villainy" an exploration of the crime of rape in eighteenth-century Ireland', *Eighteenth-Century Ireland*, 10 (1995), pp 78–107).

—, 'The abduction of women of fortune in eighteenth-century Ireland', *Eighteenth-Century Ireland*, 9 (1994), pp 7–43.

—, 'Capital punishment in early eighteenth-century Ireland' in Serge Soupel, ed., *Crime et chatiment/Crime and punishment* (Paris, forthcoming).

T.W. Laqeuer, 'Crowds, carnival and the state in English executions, 1604-1868' in A.L Beier, David Cannadine and J.M.Rosenheim, eds, *The first modern society: essays in English history in honour of Lawrence Stone* (Cambridge, 1989), pp 305–55.

James Lindsay, Earl of Crawford, *Bibliotheca Lindesiana: catalogue of English broadsides, 1505–1897* (privately published, Aberdeen, 1898).

Peter Linebaugh, 'The Ordinary of Newgate and his Account' in J.S. Cockburn, ed., *Crime in England, 1550–1800* (London, 1977), pp 246-69.

Frank McLynn, *Crime and punishment in eighteenth-century England* (London, 1989).

G. Morgan and Peter Rushton, *Rogues, thieves and the rule of law: the problem of law enforcement in north-east England, 1718–1800* (London, 1998).

R.L. Munter, *A hand-list of Irish newspapers, 1685–1750* (Cambridge, 1960).

Robert Munter, *The history of the Irish newspaper, 1685–1760* (Cambridge, 1967).

Niall Ó Ciosáin, *Print and popular culture in Ireland, 1750–1850* (Basingstoke, 1997).

Paul O'Higgins, *A bibliography of Irish trials and other legal proceedings* (Abingdon, 1986).

James O'Toole, *Newsplan Ireland* (Dublin, 1998).

M. Pollard, 'Control of the press in Ireland through the King's printer patent, 1600–1800', *Irish Booklore*, 4 (1980), pp 79–95.

Paul Pollard, *Dublin's trade in books, 1500–1800* (Oxford, 1993).

James Raven, 'New reading histories, print culture and the identification of change: the case of eighteenth-century England', *Social History*, 23 (1998), pp 268–87.

Philip Rawlings, *Drunks, whores and idle apprentices: criminal biographies of the eighteenth century* (London, 1992).

J.A. Sharpe, '"Last dying speeches": religion, ideology and public execution in seventeenth-century England', *Past and Present*, 107 (1985), pp 144–68.

Pieter Spierenburg, 'The body and the state: early modern Europe' in N. Morris and D.J. Rothinan, eds, *The Oxford history of the prison: the practice of punishment in western society* (Oxford, 1995), pp 50–61.

Margery Weiner, *Matters of felony: a reconstruction* (London, 1967).

Robert Winnett, 'The strange case of Bishop John Atherton', *Decies*, 39 (1988), pp 55-7.

Index

alcohol, 89, 90, 91, 102, 104, 105, 111, 167, 193, 212, 221, 227
Anderson, William, 198
Antrim, County, 149: Ballymena, 100; Belfast, 181; Carrickfergus, 176; Grogan, 176; Portlanone, 118, 260
apprenticeship, 49, 88, 93, 100, 107, 144, 147, 148, 153, 173, 186, 187, 190, 203, 204, 213, 219, 228, 253
Armagh, County, 112, 116, 164: Cregan, 95; Fews, 145; Kilalee, 164; Loghross, 144; Lurgan, 93, 120; Loughgall, 130
army, 86, 88, 94, 96, 97, 117, 133, 137, 143, 152, 177, 186, 193, 208-10, 227
Atherton, Bishop John, 19-20, 21
Audouin (Odwin), John, 32, 61, 224-6

Balfe, John, 85-7
Barnard, Toby, 8, 22, 58-9
Barnet, Thomas, 47, 187, 190
Barnwell, Patrick, 47, 204-5, 207
Bernard, Nicholas, 19-20
Binks, Katherine, 16
Blood's plot, 21
Bosco, R.A., 50
Bourk, Alexander, 116
Bradshaw Collection, 7
British Library, 7
broadside, 24, 27-8, 30, 34, 60; audience, 37-8; description, 8
Budd, Edmund, 61, 98-9
Burn, Charles, 134
Burn, Francis, 134
Byrne, Garret, 40, 61

Byrne, Gerald, 277

Caffery, Hugh, 92
Carlow, County, 120, 133, 187, 200, 203, 210, 278: Graigenamana, 277
Carnay, John, 85
Carragher (Calaher), Charles, 41, 61, 142-3, 144, 145
Carragher, Patrick, 144
Carrol, Charles, 119
Carrol, Martin, 116
Casady, James, 159-60
Cavan County, 158, 167, 199, 253
chapmen, 57, 59
Chartier, Roger, 7, 37, 57, 59, 60, 62, 66
Chesterfield, Lord, 59
children, 50
Clare, County, 191
Clark, Sandra, 15
Cleary, Michael, 118-19
clergy, 17, 29, 43, 44, 48, 54, 152, 243, 257, 268
Cohen, Daniel, 12, 58
Collins, Captain, 29, 154-5
Comber (Coamber), John, 31, 47, 170-2, 173-5
Commins, James, 117
Connor, diocese of, 101
conversion sermons, 42
Cork, County, 97, 124, 150, 201: Cork, 88, 107, 208
Craven, Thomas, 198
Crawford Collection, 7
criminal autobiography, 37-8

INDEX

crime: abduction, 277-8; arson, 117; assault, 86, 87, 156; bigamy, 91, 93, 109, 268; burglary, 16-17; clandestine marriage, 235-44, 268-74; counterfeiting, 164, 177, 215-16; horse stealing, 137, 138, 139-40, 148, 149, 158, 234, 252; infanticide, 183-4; jacobitism, 55, 208; murder, 17, 98, 101, 111, 117, 118, 121,142, 167, 170-71, 206, 224-5, 227, 247, 263, 279; pickpocketing, 158, 201, 206; rape, 221; robbery, 47, 84, 85-6, 88-9, 90, 94, 95, 96, 97, 105, 109, 110, 113, 119, 121, 122, 123, 124, 128, 134, 136, 142, 145, 149, 151, 156, 158, 159, 162, 170, 186, 190, 192, 193, 195, 196, 197, 200-1, 206, 213, 218, 219, 221, 223, 227, 228, 230, 245, 253, 254, 255, 256, 258, 267
Crookshank, Judge Alexander, 42
Cunneen, William, 200-1

Dalton, Peter, 104-6
Darnton, Robert, 67
Davis, John, 107-9
Dealy, James, 212
Demsye, James, 109-10
Demsye, John, 215-16
de Rojas, Fernando, 61-2
Derry/Londonderry, County, 165, 186, 189: Comber, 258, 260
Derry, Rev. George, 235, 243, 251
Dickson, William, 164-6
Dobin, John, 213
Donegal, County, 200: Lifford, 260
Donnell, Charles, 61, 100-2
Donnell, Rev. Robert, 102
Dougherty, John, 267
Down, County, 114: Downpatrick, 111; Kilmore, 111; Newry, 114; Newtownstuart, 177
Dublin, County, 207: Cabra, 90; Cavan's Fields, 89; Clondalkin, 240-1; Donnybrook, 158; Drimon, 153, 212; Drumcondra-Lane, 131; Glasnevin, 140; Greenhills, 89; Kilmainham, 96, 158, 159, 193, 198, 221, 245; Lucan, 191; Newcastle, 252; Palmerstown, 195, 221; Ringsend, 240-1; Smithfield, 92, 199, 228; Swords, 198
Dublin, 20, 21, 22, 25, 29, 48, 49, 56, 83, 88, 104, 122, 124, 130, 137, 148, 150, 152, 156, 161, 163, 187, 189, 191, 198, 200, 201, 206, 218, 219, 223, 233, 235-44, 253, 266, 267; book trade, 57; literacy, 59;
streets: Arundal Court, 131; Back Lane, 120; Bride's Alley, 130; Capel St, 102, 212, 218; Channel Row, 109; Church St, 126; Cork Hill, 173; Cork St, 99, 230; Essex St, 162-3; Fishamble St, 183, 186; Fishmarket, 194; George's Lane, 226; Grafton St, 31, 186; Henry St, 172, 173, 174; High St, 118, 130; Mary's Lane, 172; Montrath St, 161, 201, 202; New Row, 120; New St, 88, 170; Pill Lane, 194, 216, 233; St Audeon's parish, 230; St Bride's St, 131; St Francis St, 156, 201, 265; St James' St, 130, 194, 221; St John's parish, 233; St Michan's parish, 91, 126, 233, 243, 268; St Patrick's St, 130, 131, 199; School House Lane, 98; Strand St, 213; Stephens' Green, 53, 85, 88, 90, 100, 104, 107, 120, 124, 126, 130, 136, 139, 147, 156, 161, 170, 186, 196, 200, 202, 206, 208, 212, 215, 226, 227, 230, 233, 235, 245, 247, 252, 256, 262, 265, 268, 272; Swift's Alley, 89; Tallow Hill, 194; Thomas St, 120, 213; York St, 196
Dunbar, James, 52-3, 58, 164, 176-82
Dunn, Edward, 213-14
Dunton, John, 25

editorial principle, 67
elegies, 33
England, 11, 12, 13, 14, 25, 28, 35, 102, 114, 128, 152, 156, 187
English, Edward, 88-9
execution: attitude to, 38-9; audience, 53-4: ballads, 12; day, 53; procession, 53; reporting of, 36-7; ritual, 41-3; sermon, 12-3, 50
Evans, Rice, 17

INDEX

Farrel, Jeremiah, 122
Fenning, Hugh, 8
Ferly, Hugh, 147-8
Fermanagh, County, 167, 256
Fitzgerald, Captain Maurice, 133
Fitz-Symmons, John, 129
Flanders, 86, 177
Flood, Edward, 90-1
Foucault, Michel, 11
Fox, Edward, 158
France, 133, 174, 206, 209; Paris, 67
Freney, James, 38

Galway, County, 94: Ballymore, 150; Eyrescourt, 109; Loughrea, 203; Portumna, 116
Garnham, Neal, 8
Gaskill, Malcolm, 11
Geoghegan, James, 25-6, 52, 58, 83-4
Geoghegan, Owen, 47, 187-8, 191, 230
Gillespie, Raymond, 66
Glasgow, 115
Glorious Revolution (1688), 22
Goodcole, Henry, 14
Gothar, John, 43
Graham, Alexander, 48, 233-4
Graham, James, 254
Grew, Sarah, 51, 63, 130-32
Gramsci, Antonio, 60

Halpeny, Lawrence, 94
Hamilton, James, 8, 52, 58, 111-15
hawkers, 56-7
Hayes, Catherine, 29
Henry, William, 254
highwaymen, 134
Hoar, Councellor, 31, 170-2, 173-4
Hume, Lieutenant John, 42

Ireland, 12, 13, 14, 21, 177, 187
Illan, Patrick, 93-4

Jayne, Captain John, 29
Jacobitism, 55, 61, 152, 167, 193-4, 208-10
Johnson, Richard, 33, 53, 67, 247-9
Jones, Edward, 276

Kealy, Valentine, 161-2
Kearons, Michael, 234
Keating, Edward, 252-3
Keef, Margaret, 32, 224-6
Kelly, Walter, 263-4
Kennedy, Ann, 40, 277-8
Kennedy, Catherine, 40, 277-8
Kennington Common, 17
Kerry, County, 162:
    Lisnaw, 183
Kildare, County, 117, 122, 133, 161, 216
Kilkenny, County, 40, 122, 277:
    Kilkenny, 266
King's County, Phillipstown, 116
king's printer patent, 18, 21
Kingston-in-Surrey, 154
Kimberly, Daniel, 33, 49, 54, 56, 61, 64, 235-44

Lacy, Bryan, 222-3
Lacy, Neal, 118
Landergan, Garret, 124
Last speeches: age of authors, 46-7; condition, 68; contrition in, 16-7;
Last speeches (*contd*)
    36, 42-3, 52-3, 55; delivery, 54-5; denomination of authors, 45-6; development, 13-14; English, 12, 13-18, 29, 50; gender of authors, 46-7; Irish, 18-41; forgery, 45, 46-7; layout, 65-6; length, 45, 48-9, 64; North America, 12; presentation, 62-3; printing, 56 (*see also* printers); publication (Ireland), 8, 13; readership, 58-9; reading, 59-67; religious character, 52-3, 64; sale, 56-7; structure, 48-53; syntax, 47, 68
Lawler, Richard, 120-1
Leadwell, John, 41-2
Ledwidge, William, 110
Limerick, County, 107: Limerick, 107
Linebaugh, Peter, 8
literacy, 22-4, 58-9
London, 20, 21, 25, 56, 150, 152, 190, 196, 203, 206, 235, 239, 241
Longford, County, 190, 215, 267
Louth, County, 147:
    Carlingford, 268, Drogheda, 129,

INDEX

139; Dundalk, 41, 142-3, 144

Malone (A-Toush) Philip, 228
Malone, Robert, 29, 61, 152-3
McCabe, Francis, 200
McCanna, Catherine, 63, 245-6
McCormock, Darby, 147
McCoy, John, 47, 186, 189-90, 230
MacDaniell, Alexander, 227
MacDermott, Captain, 55, 61, 167-9
McDonnald, John, Laird of Largy, 85-6
McDonnald, Grisell, 86
McGann, Jerome, 62
McGuire, Daniel, 256
McGuire, Edmond, 137
MacGurran, John, 218-19
Mackanally, Martin, 221-2
McLynn, Frank, 41
McMahon, Bryan, 148
McMahon, Bishop Heber, 20
McManus, James, 148
MacShane, Patrick, 95
Mayo, County, 227
Mead, Bradock, 237-44
Meath, County, 129, 147, 228: Balgee, 198; Navan, 96, 104, Trim, 109, Tara Hill, 110
Mooney, Nicholas, 38
Monaghan, County, 139, 148
Munter, Robert, 8
Murphy, Patrick, 33, 216

Neal, Thomas, 117
Neil, Thomas, 40, 49, 279-80
New England, 12, 13, 42, 50, 58, 177
newspapers, 23-4, 27, 35-7
Northamptonshire, 98
Northumberland, 56
Nowlan, James, 126-8
Nowland, Moses, 32, 45, 55, 61, 208-11

O'Brien, Bishop Terence, 20-21
Ó Ciosáin, Niall, 37
Odwin, John, *see* Audouin, John
O'Devany, Bishop Conor, 19, 20
O'Haran, Roger Roe, 261

O'Hurley, Archbishop Darby, 19, 20
O'Mullan, Daniel Crossagh, 61, 258, 261
O'Mullan, Shaen Crossagh, 258-60, 261
O Neal, Daniel, 136
O'Neil, Charles, 253-4
Ordinary of Newgate, 14, 18, 56; his Account, 18
Ormonde, Duke of, 21
Orr, William, 40

Page, Alderman, 106
pamphlets, 37
Perry, Richard (alias Barry), 97
Placard, 7, 62, 64
Plunkett, Archbishop Oliver, 16, 84
Poe, Joseph, 61, 193-4
Pollard, M., 8
Popish Plot, 16, 21, 22
Porter, John, 33, 53, 67, 249-50
print technology, 18, 22
printers, 47-8: Brocas, John, 25, 26, 27, 47, 87; Broun, Hugh, 115; Carter, Cornelius, 24, 31, 32, 47, 119, 125, 143, 146, 151, 160, 166, 169, 173-5, 182, 183, 197; Crawley, Patrick, 172, 220; Dickson, Francis, 24n, 47, 99, 103, 174; Dickson, Richard, 24n, 33, 47, 99, 202, 205, 207, 244; Dudlow, Thomas, 25, 264; Faulkner, George, 24, 29, 32, 45, 47, 201, 202, 207, 211; Goulding, Charles, 24n, 34, 47, 271; Goulding, Christopher, 241; Gowan, John, 25, 251; Harding, John, 24, 155; Harding, Sarah, 24n, 32, 226, 228, 232; Hoey, James, 202, 204; Hussey, Nicholas, 24n, 25, 234; Jones, Edward, 25, 34; Kelly, Patrick, 153; Lee, Samuel, 25-6, 84; Needham, Elizabeth, 31, 32, 174; Needham, Gwyn, 24, 140, 205, 207; Neil, J., 25, 246; Overton, John, 32; Robinson, W., 25, 267; Sadleir, Elizabeth, 24n, 25, 129; Sadleir, Sarah, 24 n, 110; Sweeney, Brian, 201; Taylor, William, 25, 255; Waters, Edward, 24, 47, 89, 92;

printers (*contd*),
  Walsh, Thomas, 32; Whalley, John, 24
Prisons: Blackdog, 194; Kilmainham, 139, 152, 199, 252; Newgate, 53, 54, 92, 140, 162, 194, 201, 239, 246, 252; New Gaol, 53-4; Marshalsea, 194; Wood Street compter, 239
prostitution, 130-2, 201, 245
publishers, 43-4
Pullman, Thomas, 102-3

Quin, James, 94
Quinn, Alderman, 104
Quinn, Arthur, 145

Rapparees, 130, 133, 134
Raven, James, 62
Rawlings, Philip, 28, 58
Reading, Bridget, 33, 235-44
Reading, Daniel, 235-44
readers, 37-8
reading, 58-67
Renals, Thomas, 96-7
Riely, Terence, 253
Rightboys, 53
Riley, John, 116
Roscommon, County, 234
Ross, Daniel, 48, 230-2
Rye House Plot, 21

Scotland, 85-6, 123
scripture, 176-82
Scrivener, George, 31, 186-8, 189-91
service, 49, 104, 107, 133, 149, 150, 183, 196, 253, 267
Sewell (Shuel), Rev. Edward, 34, 47, 52, 53, 61, 268-71, 272-6
sexuality, female, 50
Sharpe, J.A., 8, 15, 58
Sherloge, William, 27
Sils, Ellinor, 183-5

Slevin, Tully, 215
Smith, John, 47, 187, 191-2, 230
Spain, 209
Spierenburg, Peter, 11
Stephens, James, 206
Stevens, James, 47, 202-4
Stuarts, 20
Stuart, Charles Edward (the Pretender), 45, 61, 152-3, 167, 208-10
Strange, James, 40, 61, 277
Strange, Patrick, 40, 61, 278
Sulevan, Cornelius, 161
Swift, Jonathan, 24

Thorp Collection, 7
Tipperary, County, 150, 193:
  Ardmale, 117; Clonmel, 44; Fethard, 53; Lorha, 118; Roscrea, 41; Thurles, 173
Tobin, Pierce, 262-3
Tories, 61, 144, 207, 260
transportation, 156, 266
trial reports, 12, 35-6
Trinity College, Dublin, 7, 268
Tyburn, 16, 21, 29, 152
Tyrone, County, 165

Virginia, 100

Watch (Watson), Denis, 265-6
Waterford, 59
Watts, Henery, 156-8
West, Richard, 31
Westmeath, County, 91, 94, 104, 122, 195
Wexford, County, 109, 118, 252
Wicklow, County, 85, 134:
  Blessington, 133, 135
Wilde, Jonathan, 29, 206
William, Elizabeth (Betty), 156, 201, 265
women, attitude to, 50